Security Monitoring

Other computer security resources from O'Reilly

Related titles Managing Security with Snort
and IDS Tools
Network Security Assessment
Practical UNIX and Internet
Security

Security Power Tools
Snort Cookbook
Web Security Testing
Cookbook

Security Books Resource Center *security.oreilly.com* is a complete catalog of O'Reilly's books on security and related technologies, including sample chapters and code examples.

oreillynet.com is the essential portal for developers interested in open and emerging technologies, including new platforms, programming languages, and operating systems.

Conferences O'Reilly brings diverse innovators together to nurture the ideas that spark revolutionary industries. We specialize in documenting the latest tools and systems, translating the innovator's knowledge into useful skills for those in the trenches. Visit *conferences.oreilly.com* for our upcoming events.

Safari Bookshelf (*safari.oreilly.com*) is the premier online reference library for programmers and IT professionals. Conduct searches across more than 1,000 books. Subscribers can zero in on answers to time-critical questions in a matter of seconds. Read the books on your Bookshelf from cover to cover or simply flip to the page you need. Try it today for free.

Security Monitoring

Chris Fry and Martin Nystrom

O'REILLY®

Beijing · Cambridge · Farnham · Köln · Sebastopol · Taipei · Tokyo

Security Monitoring
by Chris Fry and Martin Nystrom

Published by O'Reilly Media, Inc., 1005 Gravenstein Highway North, Sebastopol, CA 95472.

O'Reilly books may be purchased for educational, business, or sales promotional use. Online editions are also available for most titles (*http://safari.oreilly.com*). For more information, contact our corporate/institutional sales department: (800) 998-9938 or *corporate@oreilly.com*.

Editor: Mike Loukides	**Indexer:** Ellen Troutman
Production Editor: Sumita Mukherji	**Cover Designer:** Karen Montgomery
Copyeditor: Audrey Doyle	**Interior Designer:** David Futato
Proofreader: Sumita Mukherji	**Illustrator:** Robert Romano

Printing History:
February 2009: First Edition.

RepKover. This book uses RepKover™, a durable and flexible lay-flat binding.

ISBN: 978-0-596-51816-5

[M]

1233771562

Table of Contents

Preface

Our security team found a new way to make money. In 2006, after perfecting our enterprise malware monitoring, we began to deploy tools for monitoring Cisco's infrastructure more deeply. In doing so, we found our team positioned to monitor applications in new ways. Weary of ignoring the risk presented by new ventures, we offered a solution: fund staff to monitor targeted risk areas, and handle the infrastructure ourselves. The solution paid off—our monitoring team has grown, and we've developed new techniques for finding and addressing the necessary risks of a growing enterprise.

In 2007, we shared this experience with our Forum for Incident Response and Security Teams (FIRST) buddies at the annual conference. Some say we chose that conference because it was being held in Seville, Spain, but we were just doing our part for the security community. We wanted a crowd, so we titled our presentation "Inside the Perimeter: 6 Steps to Improve Your Security Monitoring." We received enough encouragement to repeat the presentation at the annual Cisco Networkers conference later that year, where we expanded the talk to two hours and packed the house with an enthusiastic audience. Feedback was positive, and we were asked to repeat it in Brisbane, Australia; Orlando, Florida; and Barcelona, Spain over the next several months. In the meantime, we felt we had enough ideas to fill a book, and the editors at O'Reilly agreed.

Our audiences told us they liked the presentations because they craved honest experience from security practitioners. We share the challenges you face; we're on the hook for security, and have to prioritize resources to make it happen. We like reading authentic books—the ones that don't try to sell us gear or consulting services—and we've endeavored to write this book with that angle. This book aims to share our experience, successes, and failures to improve security monitoring with targeted techniques.

What This Book Is Not

This book is not an introduction to network, server, or database administration. It's not an introduction to security tools or techniques, either. We assume that you have a foundational understanding of these areas and seek to build on them via specialized application of them. If we lose you along the way, put a bookmark where you left off, and reference the following excellent books:

- *The Tao of Network Security Monitoring*, by Richard Bejtlich (Addison-Wesley Professional)
- *Essential System Administration*, by Æleen Frisch (O'Reilly)
- *Counter Hack Reloaded*, by Ed Skoudis and Tom Liston (Prentice Hall PTR)
- *Computer Viruses and Malware*, by John Aycock (Springer)
- *Writing Secure Code*, by Michael Howard and David LeBlanc (Microsoft Press)

What This Book Is

Hopefully, you've already read books on security. This one aims to take you deeper into your network, guiding you to carve out the more sensitive, important parts of the network for focused monitoring. We haven't coined a term for this, but if we did, it would be *targeted monitoring* or *policy-based monitoring* or *targeted reality-based policy monitoring for detecting extrusions*.

Here is a short summary of the chapters in this book and what you'll find inside:

Chapter 1, *Getting Started*
> Provides rationale for monitoring and challenges, and introduces our monitoring philosophy

Following Chapter 1 are the six core chapters of the book, each successively building on topics discussed in previous chapters:

Chapter 2, *Implement Policies for Monitoring*
> Defines rules, regulations, and criteria to monitor

Chapter 3, *Know Your Network*
> Builds knowledge of your infrastructure with network telemetry

Chapter 4, *Select Targets for Monitoring*
> Defines the subset of infrastructure to monitor

Chapter 5, *Choose Event Sources*
> Identifies the event types needed to discover policy violations

Chapter 6, *Feed and Tune*
> Collects data and generates alerts, and tunes systems using context

Chapter 7, *Maintain Dependable Event Sources*
> Prevents critical gaps in your event collection and monitoring

Following the core chapters are the closing chapter and a trio of appendixes:

Chapter 8, *Conclusion: Keeping It Real*
> Provides case studies and real examples to illustrate the concepts presented in the six core chapters

Appendix A, *Detailed OSU flow-tools Collector Setup*
> Provides detailed instructions for implementing NetFlow collection based on Cisco's deployment

Appendix B, *SLA Template*
> Provides a sample service level agreement (SLA) for maintaining security event feeds from network devices

Appendix C, *Calculating Availability*
> Offers statistical proofs for calculating and calibrating uptime for security monitoring configurations

Conventions Used in This Book

The following typographical conventions are used in this book:

Italic
> Indicates new terms, URLs, email addresses, filenames, file extensions, pathnames, directories, and Unix utilities

`Constant width`
> Indicates commands, options, switches, variables, attributes, keys, functions, types, classes, namespaces, methods, modules, properties, parameters, values, objects, events, event handlers, XML tags, HTML tags, macros, the contents of files, and the output from commands

`Constant width bold`
> Shows commands and other text that should be typed literally by the user

`Constant width italic`
> Shows text that should be replaced with user-supplied values

 This icon signifies a tip, suggestion, or general note.

 This icon indicates a warning or caution.

Using Code Examples

This book is here to help you get your job done. In general, you may use the code in this book in your programs and documentation. You do not need to contact us for permission unless you're reproducing a significant portion of the code. For example, writing a program that uses several chunks of code from this book does not require permission. Selling or distributing a CD-ROM of examples from O'Reilly books *does* require permission. Answering a question by citing this book and quoting example code does not require permission. Incorporating a significant amount of example code from this book into your product's documentation *does* require permission.

We appreciate, but do not require, attribution. An attribution usually includes the title, author, publisher, and ISBN. For example: "*Security Monitoring*, by Chris Fry and Martin Nystrom. Copyright 2009 Chris Fry and Martin Nystrom, 978-0-596-51816-5."

If you feel your use of code examples falls outside fair use or the permission given here, feel free to contact us at *permissions@oreilly.com*.

Safari® Books Online

Safari When you see a Safari® Enabled icon on the cover of your favorite technology book, that means the book is available online through the O'Reilly Network Safari Bookshelf.

Safari offers a solution that's better than e-books. It's a virtual library that lets you easily search thousands of top tech books, cut and paste code samples, download chapters, and find quick answers when you need the most accurate, current information. Try it for free at *http://safari.oreilly.com*.

Comments and Questions

Please address comments and questions concerning this book to the publisher:

> O'Reilly Media, Inc.
> 1005 Gravenstein Highway North
> Sebastopol, CA 95472
> 800-998-9938 (in the United States or Canada)
> 707-829-0515 (international or local)
> 707-829-0104 (fax)

We have a web page for this book, where we list errata, examples, and any additional information. You can access this page at:

> *http://www.oreilly.com/catalog/9780596518165/*

To comment or ask technical questions about this book, send email to:

bookquestions@oreilly.com

For more information about our books, conferences, Resource Centers, and the O'Reilly Network, see our website at:

http://www.oreilly.com/

Acknowledgments

We're kind of shy about putting our names on this book. Chris and I did all the writing, but the ideas we're describing didn't originate with us. They represent the work started by Gavin Reid, Cisco CSIRT's boss and FIRST rep, back in 2003. Gavin built the CSIRT team, assembled from proven network engineers, system administrators, and application developers. You'll find examples of scripts written by Dustin, Mike, and Dave, tuning developed by Jeff, Jayson, and Nitin, investigations led by Chip and Kevin, and procedures written by Lawrence. In many ways, the whole team wrote this book. They're the ones who deployed the gear, wrote the tools, hired the staff, built the processes, and investigated the incidents that form the basis for the ideas presented here.

The book seemed fine until Jeff Bollinger looked at it. He discovered all kinds of inconsistencies and technical gaps, and was kind enough to tell us about them before we published the book. Jeff gave room for Devin Hilldale to school us on style and grammar. Devin pointed out the inconsistencies that derive from multiple authors, and helped smooth out the writing style. He told me to stop leaving two spaces after periods, but my eighth grade typing teacher still controls my fingers. Mark Lucking gave input throughout the book, drawing from his experience in information security for banking.

Good security requires good community. Cisco CSIRT participates in security organizations of our peers in industry and government. We share intelligence, track emerging threats, and assist one another with incident response and investigations. Membership in trusted security organizations such as FIRST and NSTAC NSIE provides access to information in a currency of trust. FIRST requires all prospective members be nominated by at least two existing members. Candidates must host an investigative site visit by a FIRST member, and be approved by a two-thirds steering committee vote.

In Chapter 8, we shared valuable insights from two case studies. Thanks to Scott McIntyre of KPN-CERT, and to the security management at Northrop Grumman: Georgia Newhall, George Bakos, Grant Jewell, and Rob Renew. (Rob and Scott: hope to see you in Kyoto for FIRST 2009!)

This book will help you justify money to spend on security monitoring. Read the whole thing, and apply all six steps from the core chapters to use those resources efficiently.

## CHAPTER 1

Getting Started

It was mid-January 2003. Things were going well in my role as a network engineer supporting data center networks at Cisco. My team celebrated on January 21 when our site vice president powered off the last Avaya PBX; the Research Triangle Park (RTP) campus telephony was now 100% VoIP. We had just completed several WAN circuit and hardware upgrades and were beginning to see the highest availability numbers ever for our remote sites. Then, on January 25 (a Saturday at the RTP campus), the SQL Slammer worm wreaked havoc on networks around the world. Slammer, also known as Sapphire, targeted vulnerable MS-SQL servers using self-propagating malicious code. Security professionals surely remember the event well. The worm's propagation technique created a potent denial-of-service (DoS) effect, bringing down many networks as it spread.

The only attribute distinguishing the Slammer worm from normal SQL traffic was a large number of 376-byte UDP packets destined for port 1434.[*]

ISPs used ingress/egress filtering to block traffic, but by then it was too late to prevent system compromise; rather, it was a mitigation measure to protect the Internet backbone:

> The Sapphire Worm was the fastest computer worm in history. As it began spreading throughout the Internet, it doubled in size every 8.5 seconds. It infected more than 90 percent of vulnerable hosts within 10 minutes.[†]

The rate of replication and multitude of compromised systems on company networks began to saturate network links with propagation attempts. Network administrators saw this issue on some of the WAN links in the United States when their pagers began to light up like Christmas trees with utilization alerts, followed by *link down* Simple Network Management Protocol (SNMP) traps. Initially, the problem was thought to be related to a DS3 network card we had just replaced in one of our Southeast region

---

[*] *http://www.cert.org/advisories/CA-2003-04.html*

[†] *http://www.caida.org/publications/papers/2003/sapphire/sapphire.html*

WAN routers; however, as the issue appeared in other regional office WAN links, it became clear that this was not an isolated incident.

We had experienced the network problems caused by virus outbreaks such as Code Red (which attacked vulnerable Microsoft IIS web servers), but none approached the severity of network impact that Slammer did. A few Slammer hosts were able to generate enough traffic to take down WAN links, causing intermittent connectivity problems in our remote sites globally. Ultimately, a majority of the compromised systems were traced to unpatched lab servers. Identifying and mitigating these hosts was no easy task:

- Too few network intrusion detection systems (NIDSs) were deployed, and no one was responsible to view or follow up on alerts for infected systems.
- Network telemetry (such as NetFlow) and anomaly detection were insufficient to identify infected systems.
- There was no way to prioritize the response; the only data we had were IP addresses and DNS names of affected machines. We didn't have contextual information such as "data center host" versus "user LAN host" versus "lab host."

Over the next 48 hours, global networking teams identified infected systems using a manual process that involved deploying the recommended access control lists (ACLs) on remote WAN routers‡ to block packets. Matches on the deny access control entries (ACEs) for UDP 1434 indicated an infected host at the site. We could not identify the source IP address that was creating the deny entries, as adding the "log" clause to the end of the deny ACE spiked the router's CPU and drastically degraded network performance. The next step required network engineers to analyze switch port utilization in real time, searching for the infected host to disable its port. This manual process required substantial man-hours to address.

If we had implemented a few of the recommendations detailed in this book, our networking team could have contained the threat much more rapidly. A tuned NIDS deployment would have enabled us to locate the infected IP addresses immediately, prioritizing response based on their named network association (data center servers, lab hosts, or desktop systems, as you'll see in Chapter 6). Even prior to the availability of the NIDS signature, we could have used NetFlow to identify infected hosts based on recognized traffic patterns, as we'll discuss in Chapter 3. A prioritized, planned response would have occurred based on this information, with appropriate mitigation measures applied to the impacted systems. The IP information from NetFlow alone could have allowed for quick manual inspection of the router ARP tables and associated MAC-to-IP address mapping. Armed with that mapping, the network engineers could have quickly disabled ports on the access switches, shutting down worm propagation.

‡ *http://www.cisco.com/warp/public/707/cisco-sn-20030125-worm.shtml*

This book details infrastructure and frameworks that would have further helped when Nachi broke out several months later. Since we couldn't see the future, however, Nachi created the same effect and was addressed with the same manual process as Slammer.

A Rapidly Changing Threat Landscape

We've heard it before: "gone are the days of script kiddies and teenagers out to wreak havoc just to show off." The late 1990s and early 2000s produced a staggering number of DoS attacks. Malware, the engine for the DoS attack, has progressed from simple programs that attack a single vulnerability to complex software that attacks multiple OS and application vulnerabilities.

Let's look at the description of the Nachi worm's method of infection (circa 2003):

> This worm spreads by exploiting a vulnerability in Microsoft Windows. (MS03-026)
>
> Web servers (IIS 5) that are vulnerable to an MS03-007 attack (port 80), via WebDav, are also vulnerable to the virus propagating through this exploit.[§]

Here's information on a very popular virus from 2006 called SDBot:

> The worm propagates via accessible or poorly-secured network shares, and some variants are intended to take advantage of high profile exploits:
>
> > WEBDAV vulnerability (MS03-007)
> >
> > LSASS vulnerability (MS04-011)
> >
> > ASN.1 vulnerability (MS04-007)
> >
> > Workstation Service vulnerability (MS03-049)
> >
> > PNP vulnerability (MS05-039)
> >
> > Imail IMAPD LOGIN username vulnerability
> >
> > Cisco IOS HTTP Authorization vulnerability
> >
> > Server service vulnerability (MS06-040)
>
> When it attempts to spread through default administrative shares, for example:
>
> > PRINT$
> >
> > E$
> >
> > D$
> >
> > C$
> >
> > ADMIN$
> >
> > IPC$
>
> Some variants also carry a list of poor username/password combinations to gain access to these shares.

[§] *http://vil.nai.com/vil/content/v_100559.htm*

Weak Passwords and Configurations

Several variants are known to probe MS SQL servers for weak administrator passwords and configurations. When successful, the virus could execute remote system commands via the SQL server access.‖

This more complex form of malware has components to make it persistent between reboots and to cloak itself from detection by antivirus programs. It even includes obfuscation techniques to prevent offline analysis! Many malware programs include a component to steal information from the infected system and relay it back to its creator, leveraging a remote control component (commonly called a *botnet*), which provides a vast array of capabilities to command the compromised system. Group all of these traits together—decentralized command and control structures (such as web-based or peer-to-peer [P2P] structures), and encryption and polymorphism (so that the malware can modify itself upon propagation to another system, evading detection by antivirus software)—and you can easily see why antivirus technology rarely lives up to its promise.

Failure of Antivirus Software

Hopefully, you no longer rely solely on antivirus software to detect and protect your end-user systems. Rather, a defense-in-depth strategy includes antivirus software, adding OS and application patch management, host-based intrusion detection, and appropriate access controls (we said "hopefully" ☺). If you are still relying exclusively on antivirus software for protection, you will be very disappointed. For example, in summer 2008, many of our employees received a well-crafted phishing campaign that contained a realistic-looking email regarding a missed shipment delivery from UPS:

```
-----Original Message-----
From: United Parcel Service [mailto:teeq@agbuttonworld.com]
Sent: Tuesday, August 12, 2008 10:55 AM
To: xxxxx@xxxxxxxx.com
Subject: Tracking N_ 6741030653

Unfortunately we were not able to deliver postal package you sent on July the 21st
in time because the recipient's address is not correct.
Please print out the invoice copy attached and collect the package at our office

Your UPS
```

Attached to this email was a trojan that more than 90% of the 37 antivirus software programs were unable to detect. Table 1-1 shows the test results yielded by analysis of the trojan binary.

‖ *http://vil.nai.com/vil/content/v_139565.htm*

Table 1-1. Trojan binary analysis test results

Antivirus	Result	Antivirus	Result
AhnLab-V3	-	Kaspersky	-
AntiVir	-	McAfee	-
Authentium	W32/Downldr2.DIFZ	Microsoft	-
Avast	-	NOD32v2	-
AVG	-	Norman	-
BitDefender	-	Panda	-
CAT-QuickHeal	-	PCTools	-
ClamAV	-	Prevx1	-
DrWeb	-	Rising	-
eSafe	-	Sophos	-
eTrust-Vet	-	Sunbelt	Trojan-Spy.Win32.Zbot.gen (v)
Ewido	-	Symantec	-
F-Prot	-	TheHacker	-
F-Secure	-	TrendMicro	-
Fortinet	-	VBA32	-
GData	-	ViRobot	-
Ikarus	Win32.Outbreak.UPSRechnung	VirusBuster	-
K7AntiVirus	-	Webwasher-Gateway	-

As you can see from the test results, these antivirus products, which detect malware via "known bad" signatures, failed to identify the trojan. Such technology fails primarily because an insignificant change to the virus will make it undetectable by existing signatures. Vendors are improving their techniques—by including heuristic/behavioral-based detection, for example—but they still fall far short of providing "complete" system security. An excellent source for more information regarding viruses, their capabilities, and why they are able to hide from detection is John Aycock's book, *Computer Viruses and Malware* (Springer).

The prevalence and advanced capabilities of modern malware should be reason enough to closely monitor for its existence in your network. If it isn't, perhaps its use by Mafia-like organizations of criminals for profit via identity theft, extortion, and espionage is more convincing.

Why Monitor?

Organized crime and insider threats are changing the security landscape, and provide ample rationale for proactive security monitoring.

The Miscreant Economy and Organized Crime

An enormous amount of money is being stolen every day—enough, in fact, to drive coordination and cooperation within groups of criminals. This illicit partnership has accelerated the development of sophisticated malware (used for this purpose, it's often called *crimeware*). Most information security organizations, both government and private, are ill-equipped to handle such threats with their existing technology and processes.

A 2008 study by F-Secure Corporation predicted that the use of malware for criminal activity would increase in countries such as Brazil, China, the former Soviet Union, India, Africa, and Central America. This is due to an abundance of highly skilled people who lack opportunities to use those skills in a legal manner.[#]

Although most of this activity is not directed at corporations, we have seen incidents that exploit knowledge of names or team/management relationships, allowing the creation of very believable phishing emails. This technique is often referred to as *spearphishing*.

In contrast, the actions of malicious insiders with access to critical information and intellectual property make up what is referred to as an *insider threat*.

Insider Threats

Studies from the U.S. Secret Service and the U.S. Computer Emergency Response Team Coordination Center (CERT/CC) validate the existence of insider threats. Although many still debate the exact percentage, it appears that between 40% and 70% of all incidents are related to insider threats. This sizable amount, coupled with the insider's access and knowledge, must be met with a proportionate amount of monitoring efforts toward insider activity. A few high-profile incidents should help to drive the insider threat message home:[*]

Horizon Blue Cross Blue Shield
> In January 2008, more than 300,000 names and Social Security numbers were exposed when a laptop was stolen. An employee who regularly works with member data was taking the laptop home.

Hannaford Bros. Co.
> In May 2008, 4.2 million credit and debit card numbers were compromised. Close to 1,800 cases of fraud were reported related to this security breach. It was found that the card numbers were harvested during the transaction process.

[#] *http://www.f-secure.com/f-secure/pressroom/news/fsnews_20080117_1_eng.html*

[*] Source: *http://www.privacyrights.org/ar/ChronDataBreaches.htm#2008*

Compass Bank

In March 2008, a database containing names, account numbers, and customer passwords was breached. A former employee stole a hard drive containing 1 million customer records and used that information to commit fraud. He used a credit card encoder and blank cards to create several new cards and withdraw money from multiple customer accounts.

Countrywide Financial Corp.

In August 2008, the FBI arrested a former Countrywide Financial Corp. employee for stealing personal information, including Social Security numbers. The insider was a senior financial analyst at a subprime lending division. The alleged perpetrator of the theft sold account information weekly in groups of 20,000 for $500.

Not all of the aforementioned incidents were malicious in nature, but all of them began with a violation of security policy. Chapters 2 and 6 provide a framework for you to detect malware and insider threats. Chapters 4 and 5 will help you prioritize your limited monitoring resources and choose the event data that provides the "biggest bang for the buck."

Challenges to Monitoring

Product limitations, the realities of operational monitoring, event volumes, and the necessity of privacy protection are challenges faced by security professionals when constructing a monitoring approach.

Vendor Promises

"Just plug it in; it will sort out everything for you!" This advice on setting up vendor XYZ's Security Information Manager (SIM) system to "automagically" correlate security events may work in small, strict, well-maintained environments. However, utopian environments such as these are rare in our experience and in talking with our customers. Security monitoring is not like a Ron Popeil Showtime Rotisserie; you can't "set it and forget it."

Security technology cannot automatically provide the contextual information necessary for you to prioritize and focus your security monitoring. Every environment is unique, but the methods we discuss in Chapter 3 will enable you to build this critical contextual information into all of your security tools. "But wait, there's more!"

Operational Realities

"Turn on auditing for all your database tables." Database operations in a busy enterprise environment prioritize performance and stability, which gave us pause when considering such advice. What are the potential performance impacts? What risks does this introduce to business operations, change controls, stability, and uptime? We began to discuss these concepts through email with an IT database administrator. He stopped replying to our emails after we relayed the "turn on auditing for all your tables" advice! Indeed, such intensive database auditing in any but the most rarely used environment would reduce system performance to unacceptable levels. Our recommendations in this book are tested and proven by our own operational experience in IT, where we have both supported enterprise infrastructures. We won't suggest methods that will negatively impact availability, thus harming your relationship with the support staff.

Volume

In the context of monitoring, logging data quickly degrades from essential lifeblood to useless swamp water when the volume is too high. An improperly tuned NIDS or syslog daemon can create so many messages that it literally crashes your collection systems. Even if your collector or SIM can handle the flood of event data, a huge volume of unsorted events will overwhelm your monitoring staff and drive them to ignore the data source. The guidelines in Chapters 5 and 6 will give you the right direction for making event volume manageable even in the most complex environments.

Privacy Concerns

You must take care to comply with local privacy laws and regulations, as they vary widely by country. The best advice we can give is to ensure that your human resources department and legal counsel are aware of your monitoring activities, formally documenting their approval for future reference. This is typically done in a monitoring statement, which should be included in your company's acceptable use policy.

Outsourcing Your Security Monitoring

In many companies, security is little more than a checkbox on a compliance document. "Employees, check! IT Services, check! Security, check!" And so on....

If you've already outsourced the whole of your security monitoring to a managed security services vendor so that you can check your compliance boxes, stop reading and sell this copy on eBay. You probably haven't even cracked the binding, so you can list it "like new." In our experience and with talking to customers, it is extremely rare to find an outsourced security services vendor who really understands the network and security context of its clients, and as such restricts its effectiveness to the simplest of security problems. Imagine the following proposal: you want to know when someone copies customer data from your database systems to his desktop. How would an outsourced security provider do this? Rather, how much would such a provider charge to do this? The service supplied by most providers is limited to regular reports of selected NIDS alerts—the same NIDS alerts selected for every client—and affected IP addresses—not all that useful, in our opinion.

Monitoring to Minimize Risk

B2B, *partner*, *outsource*, *extranet*; words that make security professionals cringe with disdain. Sometimes directors must accept high risk, such as connecting a partner network before proper risk assessment can be completed, due to urgent business drivers. Often, however, such decisions are made by those without authority to assume such a high level of risk. Such decisions affect an entire corporation, and are often made with flawed or incomplete information. In response, those charged with information security are tempted to get frustrated and surrender to chance. Such capitulation is not necessary. If you follow the approach laid out in this book, you can tailor a monitoring strategy based on the "special" business situation, minimizing or even mitigating the additional risk. Require targeted security monitoring, funded by the risk-taking sponsors, by saying, "If you want to venture into this risky project, you will need to fund additional monitoring resources for hardware and headcount."

Policy-Based Monitoring

We want to differentiate our framework for policy-based monitoring (sometimes we call it *targeted monitoring*) from malware monitoring, intrusion detection, extrusion detection, and popular monitoring frameworks. Policy-based monitoring prioritizes monitoring by enumerating and selecting critical systems, detecting policy deviations via their appropriate event logs. It requires analysis of generated events against defined security policies within the context of the environment. The methods we describe will help you to shift the focus of your monitoring resources to the most business-critical systems, bounding your alerts within the defined security policies for those systems.

Why Should This Work for You?

We strongly believe that the frameworks and methods presented here are effective and sound, based on our experience within one of the most complex and fluid enterprise networks in the world. We both have supported critical systems whose uptime directly impacted business revenue and employee productivity (and ultimately, our careers). This guidance is the result of iterative improvements, and should apply across all technologies in your existing security portfolio. The bottom line: if you implement just some of the recommendations made in this book, you should improve your monitoring and incident response capabilities greatly. If you implement all of the recommendations, you will create a world-class security monitoring capability.

Open Source Versus Commercial Products

Both of us are employees of Cisco Systems, and we use their security products. Because we are giving you advice based on our experience, you will find many references to

Cisco products. We use open source tools when they meet a specific need, and reference them enthusiastically when they work well. Open source products are featured in Richard Bejtlich's book, *The Tao of Network Security Monitoring* (Addison-Wesley Professional), which covers the use of security monitoring tools such as Snort, Bro, Argus, Sguil, and dozens of others. It is a great reference for those who have not already built, or are looking to enhance, their monitoring infrastructure. This book intends to help readers get the most out of their security monitoring tools, whichever products they choose.

Introducing Blanco Wireless

To illustrate our recommendations, we show their implementation within a *fictitious* company named Blanco Wireless. Blanco is a mobile telephony provider based in the United States. As a means of account management, Blanco collects and stores personal information, including names, addresses, phone numbers, Social Security numbers, credit ratings, and other important customer data. At the end of each chapter, we discuss how Blanco Wireless implements the frameworks and methods suggested in the chapter. Examples include diagrams and explanations of how Blanco will use the chapter's guidance to develop security monitoring.

## CHAPTER 2

Implement Policies for Monitoring

My first college apartment had a terrible cockroach problem. Upon returning from a date one evening, I was shocked to see dozens of them scatter away from an empty pizza box when I turned on the lights. After that, it was tough to push away the idea that cockroaches were everywhere—I expected to see them in every corner of the apartment. The first time I fired up Snort I was reminded of that experience; suddenly I could see what was crawling through the network, and I wanted to fix it all at once.

It's easy to get sucked into bug stomping: once you see what's on the network, you have the urge to fix and explain every security event you discover. Here's where the analogy ends, though, for not everything on the wire is a cockroach. Much of the traffic is perfectly fine, if ugly. Once you understand that its ugliness is not a security threat, you can safely let it through. By narrowing your focus to the truly threatening traffic, you can turn your full attention to stomping it out.

Historically, security monitoring tools have demonstrated their worth by showing the cockroaches: they illuminate the dark corners to show you how well they're performing their task. Once you're convinced of a cockroach problem, you need a plan for dealing with the problem, and that plan will likely involve prevention and detection.

A security guard could easily be fooled if his practice was to investigate every movement detected by security cameras. He must work from a plan—when to investigate, when to log activity for further analysis, and when to ignore something as normal or insignificant. To organize his response, he must choose from a combination of the following approaches:

Blacklisting

> Enumerate threatening events and document preparations to detect and address them. For example, the plan might enumerate threatening actors (such as people with weapons and ski masks) and prevent them from entering the premises. Signs forbidding specific items or activities, such as the one in Figure 2-1, are implementing a blacklist.

Figure 2-1. Example of blacklist monitoring

Anomaly monitoring

Enumerate events considered normal, such as the general work schedule and how employees are expected to dress. Watch for events that fall outside of what's normal. Signs such as the *suspicious mail alert* highlighted in Figure 2-2 implement examples of anomaly monitoring.

 This is often called *whitelist monitoring*, as it highlights what is acceptable and considers anything not listed to be unacceptable.

Policy monitoring

Enumerate a set of discernible criteria from which you can evaluate each person or vehicle approaching the premises to determine the response. Signs forbidding entry by all but *authorized personnel*, as shown in Figure 2-3, are examples of such monitoring in action.

Blacklist Monitoring

Creating a list of prohibited events or items (commonly called a *blacklist*) is the most straightforward method of security monitoring. With the blacklist in hand, you can deploy tools to detect prohibited items, and build procedures for remediating them. This technique is most effective under the following conditions:

You can reliably and accurately identify signs of dangerous or malicious behavior

Some signs are accurate indications that something is wrong: an airport security checkpoint screens for the presence of banned items such as weapons and bomb chemicals. If the items you're screening for, however, are not accurate signs of

Figure 2-2. Example of anomaly monitoring

trouble, it will bog down the monitoring process as your staff must take the time to weed out the false positives. For example, because the Transportation Safety Administration (TSA) was unable to identify only dangerous liquids at security checkpoints, it chose to ban all liquids (see Figure 2-4). This presented a problem because many liquids were perfectly safe and necessary, such as baby formula.

Figure 2-3. Example of policy monitoring

The blacklist must also be limited to items that can be reliably identified. Software firewalls running on desktops have historically been very poor at this; they block traffic or prompt the user for harmless connections in an effort to demonstrate that they're still on the job (see Figure 2-5). Unfortunately, this conditions Aunt Mary into answering *OK* or *Allow* to every prompt without considering the danger of doing so, negating the firewall's purpose. If a blacklisted item can be obscured in some fashion, it cannot be reliably identified and will sail past detection and prevention tools.

You have a relatively small list

If you have only a few items to watch for, it's reasonable to keep the list up-to-date with filters that are properly tuned to find the right triggers. If the list is too long, however, it becomes impossible to keep it up-to-date and reliable. For example, the "do not fly" list is reasonably effective only because it represents a tiny percentage of the flying population. If the list doubles or triples in size, it may create chaos at security checkpoints. Antivirus tools have been successful because they can identify a small list of bad files from an infinite list of harmless files.

Most of today's web content filters, often used by libraries and families to keep out unsavory content, police browsing by checking against a list of "known bad" domain names. This works only because there are only a few thousand sites to filter out, compared to the millions of available websites on the Internet.

You cannot constrain events to a narrow set of acceptable criteria

If the TSA could restrict baggage to a narrow list of preapproved items, air travel might be much safer, but at an unacceptable cost. To effectively enforce the rule, the agency would have to draft a list of reliably safe items. Passengers would be permitted to wear and carry items from only a small list of choices. Because that is not practical, the agency screens for blacklisted items.

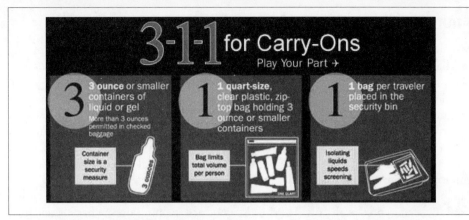

Figure 2-4. TSA rules for liquids and gels

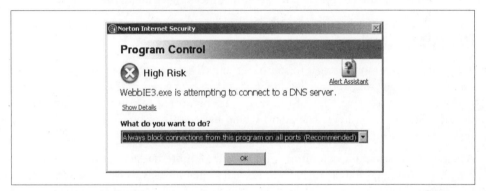

Figure 2-5. Example of confusing firewall message

In an enterprise, however, it is possible to catalog all authorized applications and devices on your network. Though it's a vast task, controlled environments such as data centers allow reasonable limits regarding which items are allowed and expected on the network. On the network perimeter, this doesn't hold true. You must sort through the traffic flowing through your Internet gateways to determine how best to secure yourself in the thick of it.

Therefore, blacklist monitoring has been traditionally applied to the perimeter due to the large volume of data. Monitoring tools must select a small percentage of traffic upon which to alarm. This type of monitoring can be effective against threats that are reliably identified, detecting them with signature patterns on the wire. It's becoming increasingly easy for malware authors to evade simple signature-based detection. A single, inconsequential change to a malware binary can throw off the signature pattern, and encoding or placing null bytes in the payload can further obfuscate the malicious traffic.

Anomaly Monitoring

Monitoring for meaningful deviations from normal traffic and events is a promising technique. It's an emerging area of intrusion detection, and monitoring that uses artificial intelligence and statistical deviations to detect traffic abnormalities. When anomaly detection is initially deployed, the tools must first create a watermark against the traffic that will be measured. Sustained statistical deviations above or below that watermark are triggers for the tool to analyze the traffic further and produce an alert for a network security analyst. Products such as Arbor Peakflow, which provides an early warning of denial-of-service (DoS) traffic and other anomalous patterns, have employed this technique effectively. Intrusion detection systems have a growing set of capabilities to detect anomalies in protocol usage, such as tunneling and nonencrypted traffic over encrypted protocols. They're also good at detecting volume-based incidents, such as port scans. Still, this technique can elicit a high rate of false positives, and it doesn't often capture enough detail to conduct meaningful incident response.

Policy Monitoring

The goal of policy monitoring is to compare events discovered on the network to ensure that they are approved and acceptable. For example, in a sensitive environment, a security guard would have a list of those who are permitted to enter the building after business hours (the policy). The guard would have cause to question and detain any nonlisted person entering the building after hours.

A better example of policy monitoring is applied to counterfeit protection. It's common for retailers to require their cashiers to inspect large bills (say, bills larger than $20 in the United States) before accepting them. Policy-based monitoring is being applied, as the cashier inspects the currency for reliable indications that it is bona fide before accepting it. The only bills legal to create or pass for sale are those minted by the U.S. Treasury. The Treasury designs security features into the currency to help cashiers and others evaluate the bill's integrity. To prove authenticity, the cashier can evaluate certain hard-to-falsify traits of the bill, such as watermarks, holographic images, color-shifting ink, and security threads. This requires the cashier to know and be able to accurately identify such traits. Success depends on both the currency's reliable, unique, and falsification-proof security features, and the cashier's ability to acknowledge these signs.

Policy-based network monitoring is practical where acceptable conditions can be documented as policies. For example, a security colleague once discovered a Windows server in the data center making dozens of connections to sites outside his company's address space, and determined that those sites were botnet controllers. If his company had applied policy monitoring, the server would have been allowed to initiate connections to only a handful of sites. You can enforce this type of control in a firewall, though some network engineers are reticent to impact network operations or performance by deploying them. When firewalls can't be applied, the need for policy-based network monitoring is amplified, and would have called out this compromise immediately.

A network is a good candidate for policy monitoring if it meets the following two conditions:

You have reasonable control over deployed systems and services
Most enterprises have standards that restrict the servers and services allowed into data centers. This allows the network monitoring staff to document a relatively small set of expected protocols on the wire. It also allows administrators to restrict allowable protocols so that policy monitoring can succeed. An environment is ready for policy monitoring if administrators can articulate acceptable traffic patterns.

A malicious payload can be easily disguised
If malevolent traffic can be easily obfuscated so that it slips past your intrusion detection sensors and virus scanners, policy monitoring will allow you to see that traffic in new ways. This can improve the fidelity, accuracy, and timeliness of your blacklist via a hybrid approach.

Monitoring Against Defined Policies

To effectively monitor the enterprise, you must codify acceptable behavior as policies, providing a reference point against which to survey. These policies must be precise and concrete to be successful. When my daughter received her stage one driver's license, she was allowed to drive only between the hours of 6 a.m. and 9 p.m. To monitor for compliance of such a policy, an officer need only check the license status of a young adult against the time of day when evaluating compliance. The policy was clear and concise, and she knew exactly what was expected of her. Of course, in monitoring for determined threats, you should keep your policy details a closely guarded secret, as a true criminal will disguise traffic to evade detection.

In developing policies against which you can build monitoring procedures, it's helpful to reference external standards such as those published by the ISO. The *Site Security Handbook* (RFC 2196) suggests that a solid security policy must have the following characteristics:

- It must be capable of being implemented through system administration procedures, publishing of acceptable use guidelines, or other appropriate methods.

- It must be enforceable with security tools, where appropriate and with sanctions, where actual prevention is not technically feasible.

- It must clearly define the areas of responsibility for the users, administrators, and management.

Management Enforcement

To make policies enforceable, you should base them on a documented "code of conduct" to which all employees are held accountable. Policies may need to be referenced for disciplinary action, so linking them to the code of conduct is a transitive means of enforcing behavior.

The guidelines and rules developed from these policies must be detailed enough to yield rules that can be monitored. For example, a policy requiring employees to use encrypted channels to discuss confidential matters is impossible to monitor and enforce because human context is necessary to determine confidentiality. Context cannot be discovered automatically; it requires detailed analysis. As an alternative, a policy that requires employees to use encryption when sending mail to specific domains is enforceable, as it's possible to determine encrypted channels for mail protocols and to discover the destination of the traffic.

When selecting policies for monitoring, don't bother with policies that you know management won't enforce. For example, your monitoring system may be very adept at uncovering use of peer-to-peer (P2P) applications on the network; it's well understood that P2P networking is often used to violate copyright law and download illegal material. You may even have a policy, as many companies do, against use of such software on the office network. Management, however, may not be willing to restrict employee freedom by enforcing such rules. Lacking enforcement, detection of P2P networking and other recreational traffic can become a distraction from policy monitoring. Focus instead on detecting policy violations you can assign for action. Once you detect an event, you'll likely have an information-gathering step that allows you to validate the information and determine further details about the source and destination of the activity. Once that's complete, you'll route the case to a support team that can fix the problem.

Employees must be aware of policies, especially those for which you will be taking action. This is best done with an awareness campaign that explains what is expected and how best to comply with the policies. One of the best ways to "bake in" policy is to build tools and configuration guides that implement policy details. When an employee changes a password or configures a web server, the tools and configuration guidance you've provided will be readily available to lower resistance to compliance.

Types of Policies

Two types of policies are used for monitoring: *regulatory compliance*, which involves adherence to externally enforced controls, and *employee policies*, which govern the security compliance of employees.

Regulatory Compliance Policies

All companies are bound by some form of IT legislation in the countries where they conduct business. This legislation places obligations and restrictions on the company, and compliance with these rules often requires active monitoring. Examples of such laws include the Sarbanes-Oxley Act of 2002 (SOX), which requires demonstration of integrity in accounting; the Health Insurance Portability and Accountability Act of 1996 (HIPAA), which protects the privacy of personal health information; and California's Senate Bill 1386 (SB1386), which protects the privacy of personal information.

In addition to regulatory compliance, adherence to industry standards is a further necessity, which requires verifiable compliance with sets of best practices. Some may be required by business partners as a means of ensuring data handling, such as the Visa PCI standards.

Example: COBIT configuration control monitoring

Control Objectives for Information and related Technology (COBIT) is a set of standards that the Information Systems Audit and Control Association (ISACA) and the IT Governance Institute (ITGI) introduced in 1992. IT management may subscribe to the control objectives set forth by COBIT, and require the development of monitoring procedures to maintain compliance. Few of the control objectives can be effectively monitored in real time, but a good example of one that can is Design and Support 9 (DS9), which requires "managing the configuration." In Section 4 (DS 9.4), the control specifically requires the verification and auditing of configuration information. (COBIT 4.1, ITGI, page 135.) To accomplish this, you must ensure that changes executed on critical systems and network devices have been approved and documented in a change control system.

To monitor for violation of such controls, you must reconcile detected changes to critical systems with the records in your configuration control repository. This requires access to the change logs from the devices, along with elements such as the time of the change, the component changed, and the person who made the change. To reconcile this information, you must have access to the configuration control system.

Consider COBIT configuration monitoring on a company's routers—some of the most important and sensitive devices on the network. To monitor these devices for unauthorized changes, we must first configure the routers to log a message upon changes to the configuration. On Cisco IOS routers, we can accomplish this by enabling syslog output and sending messages to an external syslog collector for monitoring and analysis.

For example, the following will set up logging to a syslog server at 10.83.4.100:

```
router> enable
Password:
router# configure terminal
router(config)# logging 10.83.4.100
```

When it's configured to enable syslog output, the router must be configured to message upon each configuration change. This will tell us when it was changed, and who changed it:

```
router(config)# archive
router(config-archive)# log config
router(config-archive-log-config)# logging enable
router(config-archive-log-config)# notify syslog
```

If it's set up correctly, the router will be logging to our collector at 10.83.4.100. Let's take a look at the setup to see whether we did it correctly:

```
router>show logging
Syslog logging: enabled (12 messages dropped, 83 messages rate-limited,
                0 flushes, 0 overruns, xml disabled, filtering disabled)
    Console logging: disabled
    Monitor logging: level debugging, 0 messages logged, xml disabled,
                     filtering disabled
    Buffer logging: level informational, 118416 messages logged, xml disabled,
                    filtering disabled
    Logging Exception size (4096 bytes)
    Count and timestamp logging messages: disabled

No active filter modules.

    Trap logging: level informational, 118420 message lines logged
        Logging to 10.83.4.100 (udp port 514, audit disabled, link up), 118420
message lines logged, xml disabled,
                filtering disabled
```

Now, every time the configuration on that device changes, it will send an alert. Here's a sampling of the kind of message it will generate upon such changes:

```
router# show archive log config all
  idx    sess         user@line      Logged command
    1    1          mnystrom@vty0    |  logging enable
    2    1          mnystrom@vty0    |  logging size 200
    3    2          mnystrom@vty0    |  hostname rtp2-prod
```

By forwarding these alerts to our monitoring system, it will receive an alert every time the configuration changes on this device. Figure 2-6 shows an example of such an alert.

 To effectively respond to incidents generated by such logs, the information must be complemented by Authentication, Authorization, and Accounting (AAA) records, which correlate employee authentication to such devices.

We must reconcile the alert in Figure 2-6 with the configuration management system to determine whether it matches an approved change record for that device. For this device, it must fall within the approved window and have been executed by the approved implementer. If the change is not an approved change, the analyst must engage the user called out in the alert message, to see whether the change can be explained. A

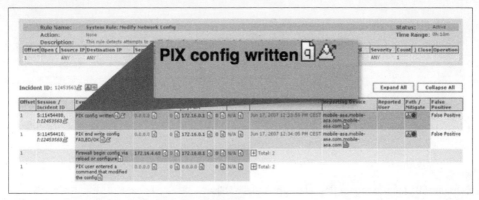

Figure 2-6. Security alert for configuration change

problem on the device may have required an administrator to troubleshoot or make temporary changes to the device. Such changes would not be reflected in an approved change request, and should be easy to reference in a trouble ticket documenting the problem. If the change cannot be reconciled, this is a policy violation and a reporting procedure must be executed.

 Alerting and responding to unexpected configuration changes is a lot of trouble. To avoid triggering incidents too frequently, tune your alerting with generous exceptions that allow for time surrounding approved change requests, documented outages, and known maintenance windows. You should also notify the support staff that their configuration changes are being monitored, and that they will be required to provide a justification for out-of-policy changes. This is like a security camera in a convenience store—it brings the positive side effect of guiding compliance with policy.

Figure 2-7 provides an example of an approved request.

Note the important elements of Figure 2-7:

- Device name
- Implementer (user ID)
- Time window (Start Time and End Time columns)
- Approval status

We can now monitor these elements by watching for device changes that fall outside this time window or were not performed by this authorized user.

 Nearly all user-based monitoring presupposes that the user ID is unique to the user. If it's a shared user ID, it will likely prove very difficult to trace the activity to an individual without a lot of extra work, such as tracing to the source IP address of the activity.

Figure 2-7. Screen capture of change management system

Example: SOX monitoring for financial apps and databases

Section 404 of SOX requires IT management to implement controls on applications that are a key part of the company's financials. This is to mitigate the potential risk of misstating the company's financial numbers.

To ensure the integrity of financial applications, especially those with direct relevance to SOX controls, you must monitor for data integrity within such applications. A rational policy would prohibit all direct database access for such sensitive applications, except for scheduled administration by administrators (and possibly data maintenance for application changes, archiving, etc.). To be practical, the allowed hosts and users, along with the approved time windows, must be documented in a policy. Security monitoring could employ network traffic analysis to watch for activity that falls outside the approved policy.

Example: Monitoring HIPAA applications for unauthorized activity

Title II of HIPAA addresses security and privacy of health data. Among many other safeguards, it states that "Information systems housing [protected health information] must be protected from intrusion. When information flows over open networks, some form of encryption must be utilized. If closed systems/networks are utilized, existing access controls are considered sufficient and encryption is optional."

To monitor for compliance with this safeguard, you could position a data capture device, such as a NIDS, on the network to ensure that data leaving the application/system is encrypted before leaving the closed network. Many NIDSs can detect unencrypted data over a supposedly encrypted channel, and could alert on discovery of such data. Tracing this to the source of the connection would allow you to log this as a policy violation.

Example: ISO 17799 monitoring

ISO 17799 (a.k.a. IEC 27002) is an information security code of practice, covering best practice recommendations on information security management for use by those who are responsible for initiating, implementing, or maintaining Information Security Management Systems (ISMSs).[*] An objective of ISO 17799 is section access control, described in Section 8, which requires that you prevent unauthorized access to information systems.

One challenge facing enterprises trying to secure systems from unauthorized access is the generic account. Shared applications such as web servers, application servers, and databases run as a generic user account, typically with limited privileges. Unless they are secured and monitored, these accounts can become weak points in implementing this policy. Administrators may need to occasionally log into these accounts to update applications. Monitoring for unauthorized access will require you to monitor system logs and audit system configurations.

Syslog from the systems you wish to monitor will allow you to detect system access and changes. To detect account access, you should configure the system to detect login and sudo access to the generic accounts. Then, you should reconcile these changes against approved change requests, as described in the previous example.

An auditing technique could involve checking snapshots of device configurations, specifically, the account registry such as `/etc/passwd`, to ensure that direct login is disabled for such accounts and that sudo is appropriately restricted.

Example: Payment Card Industry Data Security Standard (PCI DSS) monitoring

Major credit card companies developed PCI DSS as a guideline to help organizations that process card payments prevent credit card fraud, hacking, and various other security vulnerabilities and threats. A company processing, storing, or transmitting payment card data must be PCI DSS-compliant or risk losing its ability to process credit card payments.[†]

PCI DSS requires the protection of cardholder data. As an example, Requirement 4 of the standard states that you must "Encrypt transmission of cardholder data across open, public networks."

To effectively monitor for compliance, an organization could set up a NIDS to detect unencrypted data emanating from the applications used for card processing. For additional protection, additional signatures could implement a regular expression match to find credit card numbers traversing the network. You can use a regex pattern such as this:

```
^((4\d{3})|(5[1-5]\d{2}))(-?|\040?)(\d{4}(-?|\040?)){3}|^(3[4,7]\d{2})
(-?|\040?)\d{6}(-?|\040?)\d{5}
```

to detect the common numeric pattern used by credit cards. With this regular expression, a NIDS (or any packet capture device with a full copy of network traffic) could

---

[*] http://www.iso.org/iso/iso_catalogue/catalogue_tc/catalogue_detail.htm?csnumber=39612

[†] https://www.pcisecuritystandards.org/security_standards/pci_dss.shtml

catch unencrypted transmission of these card numbers. Should the NIDS detect such a pattern, it's a likely violation of the encryption policy outlined by Section 4 of PCI DSS.

Employee Policies

Compliance-based policies are developed from without, and drive an organization's policies, auditing, and monitoring. In contrast, employee policies are typically derived from the company's ethical standards or code of business conduct, and are often set by human resources, legal, and information security departments. These policies are designed to place some limits on employees to preserve ethical standards, limit financial loss, protect corporate revenue, and maintain a safe working environment.

Example: Unique login for privileged operations

To maintain accountability, an organization must be able to correlate activity to an individual employee. For the organization to do this effectively, it must require employees to use unique logins when accessing shared resources. Especially when performing privileged operations, employers must ensure that sensitive operations are attributable to an individual. To accomplish this task, an employer needs policies that require employees to use their individually assigned accounts when accessing shared resources such as Unix servers, database servers, and so on.

When employees are performing privileged operations, employers should direct the employees to first log in with their individual accounts before "switching user" for privileged operations. On Unix, sudo is the recommended command for users executing privileged operations; on an Oracle database, a user can connect as a privileged account (such as SYSTEM). Upon examining the log messages, the security analyst can trace the actions directly to the individual executing the commands. Shared accounts should never be accessible directly, as they obscure the true identity of the individual.

On a Unix server, a simple method for monitoring violations of this policy requires only that the server record each login via syslog. The monitoring application or staff must then screen for instances of the user "root" directly logging into the system, as shown in the following code snippet, and conduct further investigation about the activity:

```
Mar 28 16:19 bw-web1 sshd(pam_unix)[13698]: session opened for user root by (uid=0)
```

 Should you require security logs to investigate a malicious incident, activity will likely correlate the most damaging events to the privileged user (root or Administrator). Tracing the activity back to an individual will require that backtracking through the logs to correlate it with a login by a unique user. If the privileged user logged in directly, the investigation must take on much more complexity.

Example: Rogue wireless devices

The insecure wireless network at a Marshall's discount clothing store near St. Paul, Minnesota, may have allowed high-tech attackers to gain a beachhead in retail giant TJX Companies' computer network, resulting in the theft of information on at least 45.6 million credit and debit cards, according to the *Wall Street Journal*.[‡]

Though it's not clear whether the problem at Marshall's was a rogue wireless device or just a poorly configured wireless deployment, it's clear that wireless technology extends enterprise networks well beyond the guarded perimeter. Wireless access points are cheap, are easy to connect, and can create a dangerous back door into the organization if they are not properly configured. Security professionals must vigilantly drive rogue wireless devices out of the corporate network. Technologies now exist to allow the wireless infrastructure to defend itself by denying access to rogue wireless devices. Reliably finding and blocking rogue devices from the network requires sophisticated infrastructure. Corporate policy must require wireless devices to be properly configured and deployed, and only by the IT staff. A standard should provide details for secure configuration, and the key to successful monitoring is to watch for wireless devices that do not meet this standard. Several Wireless Intrusion Detection Systems (WIDSs) are available, which use an overlay network of RF detectors to discover wireless access points. These can be correlated to network location, allowing the network security monitor to compare the network location with those of approved wireless access points. Effective use of this solution requires a "registration" of approved wireless access points. Documenting approved, supported services, and their network location is a vital part of making policy monitoring work, and we cover it in greater depth in Chapter 3.

 WIDSs store a database of authorized access points as a basis for detection of rogue devices. WIDSs use a variety of means to identify access points, including MAC addresses, IP addresses, and RF fingerprints. The technology to detect a unique RF signature was developed at Carleton University in Ottawa, Canada, in 2006.

In Figure 2-8, the WIPS controller (a.k.a. WIDS controller; the *P* stands for *prevention*) maintains a database of authorized access points. The L3 switch has software to read the reported access point fingerprints via the connected access points. These fingerprints are stored and analyzed in the WIPS controller, which will tell the L3 switch to deny IP connectivity to the rogue access point.

[‡] *http://www.securityfocus.com/brief/496/*

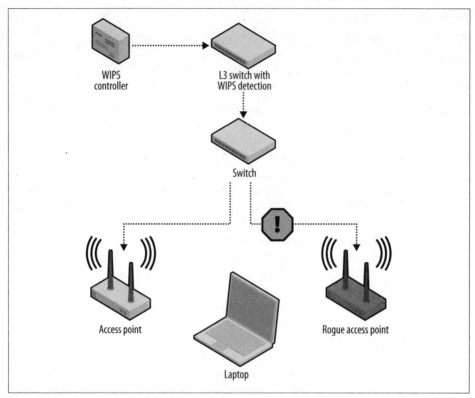

Figure 2-8. A wireless intrusion prevention system (WIPS)

Example: Direct Internet connection from production servers

In Richard Bejtlich's book, *Extrusion Detection* (Addison-Wesley Professional), Bejtlich describes the importance of watching outbound traffic, that is, connections initiated from inside the company toward the Internet. Doing so, he argues, allows the network security monitoring staff to watch for communications with known command and control servers, a sure sign of a compromised asset.

Bejtlich argues that production servers should be watched closely for their connections:

> In some cases, detecting any outbound connection at all is a sign of compromise. For example, a properly administered web server should never have to make an outbound connection to any foreign host. (By 'foreign,' I mean a machine not associated with the local organization.) DNS queries should be sent to the local DNS server. Updates should be pushed to the system from a local patch or package builder, or pulled from the local patch or package builder.§

Connections to the Internet from production servers should be rare and well documented. Software updates can be staged on local servers, and administrators should

§ *Extrusion Detection*, Chapter 3, pages 92 and 93.

use personal systems to check mail or research techniques to fix problems. If a production server has been compromised, it will soon begin to shuttle information to a server under the hacker's control.

Server policy should therefore forbid production servers from initiating Internet connections. Once network security monitoring is in place, you can set it up to catch any such activity. Initially, many of the discovered incidents will prove to be accidental usage, and can be mitigated accordingly as policy violations. Once monitoring is fully implemented, it will prove to be an early warning system for catching compromised servers and will be a surprisingly easy and effective tool for securing systems.

Session data records such as NetFlow provide the perfect tool for such monitoring, and we cover them in more detail in Chapter 3. For now, think of NetFlow as being similar to a phone bill; it lists connections between IP addresses and ports, with a record of when and for how long they occurred (see Figure 2-9). You can analyze NetFlow recorded at perimeter gateways to discover data center subnets initiating connections to Internet addresses. A single connection is a clear policy violation, and you can investigate and mitigate it accordingly.

SOURCE:PORT	DESTINATION:PORT	PACKETS	TIMESTAMP
10.83.4.112:18358	125.211.197.130:80	1	0131.01:38:24.747EST
10.83.4.112:7199	ev1s-67-15-135-138.ev1servers.net:80	2	0131.05:33:34.008EST
10.83.4.112:33495	va5.virtualappliances.net:80	26663	0131.10:25:02.338EST
10.83.4.112:33495	va5.virtualappliances.net:80	37561	0131.10:26:35.139EST
10.83.4.112:53814	221.212.220.50:80	1	0131.10:35:21.517EST

Figure 2-9. NetFlow records indicating connections

Example: Tunneled traffic

Internet Relay Chat (IRC) was developed in 1988 as an Internet chat program. IRC servers allow for many simultaneous conversations and groups via the use of channels. Since servers and channels are long-lived, users can connect and disconnect at will, and can participate in a never-ending conversation with other users on the channel. In recent years, IRC has become a popular tool for teams to communicate, as all conversation is open and readable by all users on the channel.

Because of its server/channel design and support for programmatic access, IRC has become the de facto application for hackers to remotely control their compromised systems. Commonly used for controlling botnets, IRC is widely used as the control channel for progressively sophisticated application programming interfaces (APIs). Due to its common use as a hacker control plane, default IRC network ports are commonly blocked by firewalls and reliably discovered by NIDS sensors. To circumvent these controls, hackers have begun to disguise and even encrypt the traffic. Security researcher Dan Kaminsky has famously written and spoken on the topic of tunneling information over DNS several times in the past few years, and has introduced tools such as OzymanDNS to make it easy.

Botnet IRC traffic usually has an instantly recognizable format. It contains randomly generated usernames with embedded numeric identifiers, along with an indication of geographic location. The format looks like this:

```
PASS letmein
NICK [MOO|JOR|05786]
USER XP-4132 * 0 :owned-host
MODE [MOO|JOR|05786] -ix
JOIN #
```

The botnet controller uses this information to identify and command his bots. In contrast, user-directed IRC traffic will contain more human-readable usernames and hostnames. If you have business needs that require access to IRC servers on the Internet (which prevent you from blocking IRC traffic altogether), you can deploy intrusion detection techniques to detect these patterns and block the IRC botnet traffic. This, of course, requires analysis and monitoring procedures to discern between malicious and benign traffic.

Tools that inspect network traffic can discover telltale signs of tunneling, normally by checking the traffic against the expected structure for the protocol assigned to that port. You also can apply policy-based monitoring to discover this traffic. One means for discovering such tunneling is to detect DNS requests originating from locations other than the DNS servers in the enterprise. By way of policy, clients should only use internal DNS servers for name resolution. Internet-bound DNS traffic originating from hosts other than these DNS servers would be a policy violation, and a possible sign of tunneled traffic. Upon detecting this traffic, you could then analyze it to determine whether it's truly dangerous or is an anomaly that requires further tuning of network monitors.

Here's an example of a Snort alert indicating potential DNS tunneling, requiring further investigation:

```
Apr 2818:34:15 [**] snort[1000001]: Potential DNS Tunneling [**] [Classification:
Potentially Bad Traffic] [Priority: 2] (UDP) 31.33.73.57:22652 ->10.13.55.7:53
```

Policies for Blanco Wireless

The fictitious company Blanco Wireless will serve as a platform to illustrate the stages and techniques of implementing policy monitoring. As part of account administration, Blanco must store sensitive information such as Social Security numbers and direct billing details. Due to the sensitive nature of such information, Blanco has developed several policies to protect itself and its customers' data.

Policies

Blanco employs the following policies to maintain compliance with government regulations, safeguard its most sensitive data, and provide investigative support should any of the data be compromised. These are, of course, not exhaustive. Rather, they serve as illustrations for how to apply policy monitoring.

Data Protection Policy

In keeping with California law and Blanco Wireless's commitment to customer privacy, employees are required to maintain strict confidentiality of all personally identifiable information (PII):

Scope
> This applies to all PII stored on production servers in the Blanco Wireless network.

Configuration requirements
> *Storage*
> > PII must be encrypted in storage and transmitted only over encrypted network connections.
>
> *Access*
> > Databases containing PII must be accessed only via an approved method:
> > - An application whose purpose is to broker such access.
> > - An approved database management server. Direct database access via desktop programs such as TOAD is strictly prohibited.

Database security
> Databases storing PII must be configured according to Blanco Wireless's Database Configuration Guide, which prescribes the application of all severity 1 and 2 directives contained within Pete Finnigan's Oracle Database Security Checklist.‖

Server Security Policy

The purpose of the Server Security Policy is to establish standards for the base configuration of internal server equipment that Blanco Wireless owns and/or operates. Effective implementation of this policy will minimize unauthorized access to Blanco's proprietary information and technology:

Scope
> This policy applies to all production servers at Blanco Wireless, including web, application, and database servers.

Configuration requirements
> The following directives are required of all servers at Blanco, and should be detailed in every configuration or "hardening" guide used by administrators:

‖ *http://www.sans.org/score/checklists/Oracle_Database_Checklist.pdf*

Outbound connections
> Production servers deployed into Blanco data centers may initiate connections only to other production servers within the Blanco enterprise. Connections may never be initiated from production servers to the Internet. If deployed into an approved DMZ, servers may only respond to requests in accordance with their deployed function.

Network services
> Servers in the data center must register their hosted network services in the Blanco Enterprise Management System prior to deployment. Registration is not required for approved management services such as SSH and syslog, which are necessary for administration and monitoring.

Accounts
> Servers must be configured to limit available accounts to those who have direct, administrative responsibility on each specific server. Servers must never allow direct login by nonadministrative personnel such as development support staff members or end users. Those with a need to affect application or data configuration should use the IT-supported deployment applications to effect needed changes on the servers.

Privileged access
> Direct login to the system must occur through individually assigned account IDs. Access to privileged accounts, such as root, must be permitted only via "switch user" commands such as sudo or su upon successful login. Direct login as a generic privileged account such as root is strictly prohibited.

Administration
> Remote administration must be performed only over cryptographically secured, encrypted network connections. Administrative interfaces must never be exposed directly to the Internet, but must be available only to those who have properly authenticated into the Blanco Wireless network.

Logging
> The following events must be logged to a separate log server to support investigations and monitoring:
> - Login
> - Privileged operations, including sudo and su
> - Status change for networked services (start/stop)

Implementing Monitoring Based on Policies

In the next few chapters, we will detail a method for analyzing and documenting Blanco's network, find the best areas to target our monitoring, and provide practical guidance on how to deploy monitoring specifically to watch for policy violations.

Based on the Blanco policies outlined in this chapter, here are the specific items we will monitor to effect policy monitoring:

Storage/transmission of PII
> We will monitor data center gateways to watch for signs that Social Security numbers are being transmitted over unencrypted links.

Data access
> We will monitor for unauthorized SQL*Net connections into our sensitive databases.

Outbound connections
> We will monitor for connections initiated from sensitive servers to ensure that they are approved exceptions.

Database security
> We will audit TNS listeners to ensure that they meet hardening criteria.

Network services
> We will audit open ports on servers to ensure that they are registered as required by the Server Security Policy, referenced in the preceding section.

Accounts
> We will monitor syslog for account logins and compare them against a database of system administrators to ensure that logins are proper and authorized.

Privileged access
> We will monitor syslog for direct privileged logins to servers, and monitor SQL*Net connections for direct system login to databases.

Administration
> We will audit production servers from outside the company to uncover any remote administration protocols (such as SSH, VNC, and Remote Desktop), a violation of the Server Security Policy.

Conclusion

There are a wide variety of approaches for selecting the policies to monitor. Once policies are selected, you must determine the setting—the environment in which these policies are to be applied. You'll need a reliable map of your network, one that highlights the underlying functions, applications, and users. In the next chapter, we'll explain how to develop and document a contextual understanding of your own network.

## CHAPTER 3

Know Your Network

Imagine going to battle without an understanding of the terrain, roads, buildings, weather, or even your own fighting force's tactics and capabilities. This is the situation faced by many information security professionals when they initially attempt to monitor their network environment. Knowing your network is akin to understanding your military capabilities, strengths, and weaknesses when preparing for an enemy attack. In information security, the enemy will change tactics continually, but you have a "home field advantage" because the battleground is *your network*. History proves that blindly charging into or defending the unknown will almost certainly end in defeat.

One of the best ways to express this concept comes from Richard Bejtlich, information security professional and author of *The Tao of Network Security Monitoring*. In a January 2007 post on his blog,[*] Bejtlich describes the "Self-Defeating Network" as having the following characteristics:

- Unknown
- Unmonitored
- Uncontrolled
- Unmanned
- Trusted

Although you may not have control of or influence over these characteristics, you must make every effort to Know Your Network! Doing so will help you succeed in most of your security-related endeavors. In this chapter, we will explore two primary methods of learning about a network: network taxonomy and network telemetry.

Network Taxonomy

Imagine you receive a report from your monitoring staff that "IP address 10.10.10.20 was seen performing a buffer overflow attack against IP address 10.50.10.43." What

---

[*] *http://www.taosecurity.blogspot.com/2007/01/self-defeating-network.html*

does this mean? Do these IP addresses belong to you? If so, have you even deployed that range of addresses? Are they on a production network, lab network, extranet/partner network, or data center network? Is this address space NAT'd or proxied?

The answers to these questions directly impact how you will respond to the report; they determine ownership, security policy, criticality, and whether a response is required. To efficiently process security alerts, you must build this context into the alerts data as it is generated.

Knowing your network will also improve other areas of incident response, enabling you to "separate the wheat from the chaff." You can use the network taxonomy data you've collected and enumerated for your specific environment to provide contextual information related to each security incident. You can further use it to populate object groups in your SIM and in your intrusion detection, access control, network analysis (anomaly detection), and process automation tasks.

First, however, you must classify your network types and then enumerate them in a meaningful way. Let's start with IP addresses.

Network Type Classification

IP network type classification refers to the process of identifying your organization's varying network types along with their unique attributes. This process varies widely from company to company, and even among divisions within an organization. If you were to consult 10 different network vendors you would get 10 different explanations of this process. Rather than trying to describe a "one-size-fits-all" explanation of what's involved, we'll discuss a framework for network classification based on network function.

A network's *function* is the best characteristic for defining security policy governing a network. A network's functional description should explain who the network's end users are. Each network will be configured to govern users' behavior with a variety of security policies, role-based access, and optimizations that will not fit into a simple framework. Therefore, you must concentrate on discovering only the general function of a network when applying a classification to it.

Figure 3-1 is an example of network classification.

 The network type classification principles we'll discuss focus on enterprise networks. However, you can easily apply them to service provider networks as well. Be aware, however, that when classifying networks, service providers often favor autonomous system[†] groupings instead of functional groupings.

[†] *http://www.lightreading.com/document.asp?doc_id=4054*

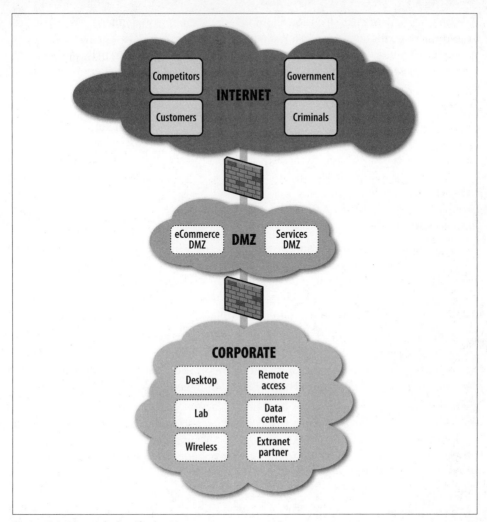

Figure 3-1. Network classification

External networks

In our network classification framework, external networks represent those that reside outside the corporate firewall. Depending on the size, needs, and characteristics of your organization, you likely have a number of networks between the Internet and your internal network. To simplify our discussion and the framework, we'll assume a medium-sized business with a DMZ (also called a *point of demarcation* or *perimeter*) network presence between the Internet and the corporate firewall.

The Internet network classification should be the last one you define; it will consist of everything that falls outside your other network classifications. This giant "network of networks" includes your customers, competitors, organized criminals, government entities, and everything in between...and you'll rarely be able to identify one from another!

The DMZ network classification describes the network (or, in some cases, collection of networks) that contains your e-commerce hosts and systems related to core business services such as SMTP and DNS. This network classification will have a few subclassifications based on the stricter security policies required for the systems exposed on it, since the primary function of the DMZ is to allow services reachable from the Internet.

Internal networks

In our network classification framework, internal networks represent those that reside inside the perimeter, behind the corporate firewall. Internal network classification is the most complex of the three main classifications; it's composed of several core subclassifications related to the following functions, most commonly found in enterprise networks:

Data center
> A dedicated, highly available network environment for critical compute services including diverse services such as code development, accounting systems, and IP telephony. Usually supported and operated by a dedicated corporate IT group.

Extranet
> Connections between your internal network and your vendors, suppliers, and partners, typically with limited access. Usually supported and operated by corporate IT, with support limited to the boundary of demarcation between the corporation and the external entity.

Remote access
> Networks providing connectivity to users from outside the corporate firewall. Access is provided via legacy dial-based services (ISDN, modem) as well as newer IP-based solutions traversing the public Internet, such as virtual private networks (VPNs). Remote access networks are usually supported and operated by corporate IT.

Lab
> Networks used for testing and development. These are typically untrusted (to the corporate network), lack security controls, and are not supported or operated by corporate IT.

Desktop and wireless
> Standardized networks that provide connectivity to employees while at a corporate worksite. Usually supported and operated by corporate IT.

Fortunately, many IT teams have already conducted much of the network enumeration and classification required for our solution. The best and most common source of such invaluable data is contained within your existing IP address management (IPAM) solution.[‡]

IP Address Management Data

Historically, gathering data about your network required software tools that discovered what was "out there" in your infrastructure by blindly scanning your IP address ranges. Commercial tools such as HP OpenView and open source software such as Cheops gather such data using a combination of Simple Network Management Protocol (SNMP) queries, supplementing the data with network port scans to discover the network. Such tools can identify device types, map network topologies, and recognize device OS and application details. However, they do not provide the contextual information needed to prioritize their collected data, except via painstaking manual annotation.

In light of the limitations of such automated discovery tools, we turn to an IPAM solution for extracting contextual data. IPAM is more than a tool; it also refers to a framework for managing and allocating the network address space for system entities. Security is not often associated with IP address management, as the tools are built primarily for the complex task of allocating IP address space within a company's diverse networks. IP address management solutions normally extend into DNS and DHCP services.

Several open source and commercial solutions exist to store IPAM data, but a useful solution for monitoring incident response must include places to store the following attributes for each IP address:

- IP subnet and mask
- Owner/contact information
- Subnet description
- Subnet function
- Subnet location
- Subnet parent
- Hierarchical presentation

Figure 3-2 shows an example of IP addresses stored in Cisco Network Registrar—a commercial IPAM solution. Example 3-1 demonstrates the representation of network hierarchy and subnet tagging made possible by an IPAM solution.

[‡] *http://encyclopedia2.thefreedictionary.com/IPAM/*

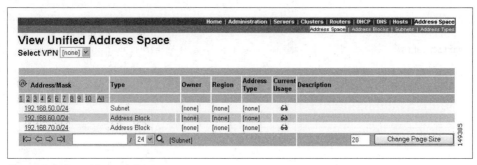

Figure 3-2. Cisco Network Registrar

Example 3-1. Example IPAM data

```
10.9.0.0/16         SITE1 Campus
|-- 10.9.0.0/19        Data Centers
|-- 10.9.32.0/19       Site 1 Desktop Networks
|   |-- 10.9.34.0/24      Building 1 3rd floor
|   |-- 10.9.57.0/24      Building 4 3rd Floor
|   |   |-- 10.9.57.0     -  Network
|   |   |-- 10.9.57.26    userid-win2k.blanco.com

Network Prefix/Length  10.9.57.0/24
Parent Block  10.9.32.0/19
Description  Building 4 3rd Floor
Type      Subnet
Status    Active
Function Desktop LAN
Location SITE1
```

If your IT networking team has done a good job with IP address management and classification, buy them a beer! They've just made your life a whole lot easier!

In Example 3-1, you saw that 10.9.0.0/16 is an address block assigned to the *SITE1 Campus*. This block contains data center subnets and desktop subnets. You can use this information to provide context for NIDS alerts, anomaly detection data, NetFlow, and anything else that provides an IP address but lacks contextual information. For example, using the IPAM data in Example 3-1, which of the following two alerts (shown in Examples 3-2 and 3-3) would you treat with higher priority?

Example 3-2. NIDS alert 1

```
evIdsAlert: eventId=1196869618127124428 severity=high vendor=Cisco
  originator:
    hostId: ids-1
    appName: sensorApp
    appInstanceId: 462
  time: 2008/01/26 15:41:54 2008/01/26 15:41:54 UTC
  signature: description=B02K-UDP id=4055 version=S2
```

```
    subsigId: 2
    marsCategory: Penetrate/Backdoor/Trojan/Connect
  interfaceGroup: vs0
  participants:
    attacker:
      addr: locality=OUT 10.100.99.244
      port: 4500
    target:
      addr: locality=IN 10.9.57.26
      port: 4500
```

Example 3-3. NIDS alert 2

```
evIdsAlert: eventId=1196869618127124428 severity=high vendor=Cisco
  originator:
    hostId: ids-1
    appName: sensorApp
    appInstanceId: 462
  time: 2008/01/26 15:41:54 2008/01/26 15:41:54 UTC
  signature: description=B02K-UDP id=4055 version=S2
    subsigId: 2
    marsCategory: Penetrate/Backdoor/Trojan/Connect
  interfaceGroup: vs0
  vlan: 0
  participants:
    attacker:
      addr: locality=OUT 10.100.99.244
      port: 4500
    target:
      addr: locality=IN 10.9.1.12
      port: 4500
```

According to the IPAM data in Example 3-2, alert 1 shows that the target of the attack is in Building 4 of Site1's desktop networks, probably a user PC. Alert 2 in Example 3-3 shows that when IPAM data is taken into consideration, the target of the attack is in a data center, making this alert a higher priority than alert 1. Although this example is greatly simplified, it still shows the power of adding context to alerts with IPAM data. To drive this point further, which of the following warnings would you rather receive?

```
"IP address 10.100.99.244 attempted a B02K-UDP attack against 10.9.1.12"
```

or:

```
"IP address 10.100.99.244 attempted a B02K-UDP attack against a datacenter server
at 10.9.1.12"
```

If possible, get access to the underlying database of the IPAM application to allow direct data queries; it's much quicker than using a GUI. It will not only save time, but it will also assist you with automating host data collection.

Even if your IPAM data is not in an application, but rather is maintained in an Excel spreadsheet, it's still a valuable context for your incident data. A spreadsheet, however, is difficult to keep up-to-date and lacks cachet as an authoritative source of data. Rather, we highly recommend an IPAM solution that is scalable and can be kept up-to-date easily.

Chapter 6 will discuss IPAM data in more detail, leveraging it for tuning your IPS and SIM tools. To get you started, here are some of the more popular IPAM products on the market today:

- BlueCat Networks Proteus/Adonis (*http://www.bluecatnetworks.com/*)
- Incognito IP/Name/DNS Commander (*http://www.incognito.com/*)
- BT INS IPControl (*http://www.ins.com/*)
- Carnegie Mellon NetReg (*http://www.net.cmu.edu/netreg/*)
- Alcatel-Lucent VitalQIP (*http://www.alcatel-lucent.com/vitalqip/*)
- IPplan (*http://iptrack.sourceforge.net/*)
- NeuStar MetaInfo (*http://www.metainfo.com/*)

Network taxonomy can assist your understanding of your network as a foundation for *practical* security monitoring. Network telemetry builds upon such knowledge, and is one of the most powerful technologies available for security monitoring. It illustrates network activity atop your network taxonomy foundation.

Network Telemetry

Telemetry conjures images of satellites and aeronautics. It is a technology that allows the remote measurement and reporting of information of interest to the system designer or operator. It's derived from a word with Greek roots: "tele" means remote, and "metron" means "measure." When we apply telemetry to the networking world, we're referring to metadata pertaining to IP communications between numerous systems. Several network equipment vendors support the ability to collect and export this network traffic metadata for analysis. The network telemetry tool we have used most extensively is Cisco's NetFlow.

NetFlow

NetFlow measures IP network traffic attributes between any two or more IP addresses based on OSI Layer 3 and Layer 4 information. Cisco initially created NetFlow to measure network traffic characteristics such as bandwidth, application performance, and utilization. Historically, it was used for billing and accounting, network capacity planning, and availability monitoring. As mentioned in Chapter 2, NetFlow records are like what you see on a phone bill (see Figure 3-3), whereas packet capture (a.k.a. network protocol analyzers, sniffers, and deep packet inspection) is like what a wiretap collects. Much like a phone bill, NetFlow tells you who called, when they called, and for how long the conversation lasted (see Figure 3-4). Though not its primary use, security is a more recent application of this key network telemetry technology. NetFlow

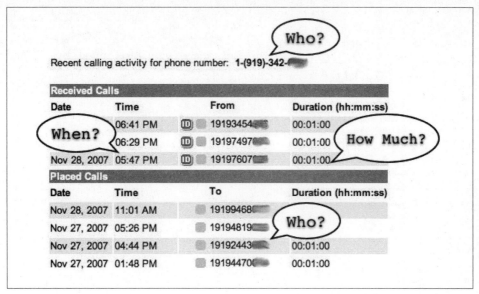

Figure 3-3. A phone bill

can provide non-repudiation, anomaly detection, and investigative capabilities unlike any other network telemetry technology.

Here's Cisco's description of NetFlow:§

> A flow is identified as a unidirectional stream of packets between a given source and destination—both defined by a network-layer IP address and transport-layer source and destination port numbers. There are several versions of NetFlow with version 5 being the most widely used.

NetFlow version 9 adds TCP flags and some additional fields, as well as a template-based format called Flexible NetFlow. For the discussions and examples in this book, we will use NetFlow version 5. However, the concepts and methods we describe should work for any NetFlow version.

NetFlow can be enabled as a feature on any network device that will store OSI Layer 3 and Layer 4 IP packet attributes in a table or cache as a record. The amount of time any given record will stay on a network device depends primarily on the amount of memory assigned for the cache and the number of new network connections being tracked (how busy the router is). You can view these records, or flows, directly from the router command-line interface or you can export them to external storage for viewing later. Figure 3-5 shows a basic overview of how these records are placed in a table and viewed or stored.

Table 3-1 shows the NetFlow version 5 header format.

§ *http://www.cisco.com/en/US/docs/ios/solutions_docs/netflow/nfwhite.html*

Figure 3-4. An example of NetFlow (http://www.cisco.com/en/US/docs/net_mgmt/netflow_collection _engine/3.0/user/guide/nfcform.html)

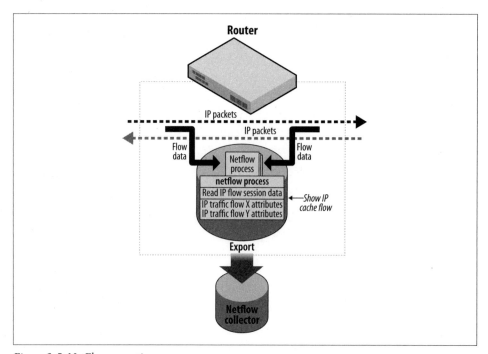

Figure 3-5. NetFlow operation

Table 3-1. NetFlow version 5 header format

Bytes	Contents	Description
0–1	Version	NetFlow export format version number
2–3	Count	Number of flows exported in this packet (1–30)
4–7	SysUptime	Current time in milliseconds since the export device booted
8–11	unix_secs	Current number of seconds since 0000 UTC 1970
12–15	unix_nsecs	Residual nanoseconds since 0000 UTC 1970
16–19	flow_sequence	Sequence counter of the total flows seen
20	Engine_type	The type of flow-switching engine
21	Engine_id	The slot number of the flow-switching engine
22–23	Reserved	Unused (zero) bytes

Table 3-2 shows the NetFlow version 5 record format.

Table 3-2. NetFlow version 5 record format

Bytes	Contents	Description
0–3	srcaddr	Source IP address
4–7	dstaddr	Destination IP address
8–11	nexthop	IP address of the next hop router
12–13	Input	SNMP index of the input interface
14–15	Output	SNMP index of the output interface
16–19	dPkts	Packets in the flow
20–23	dOctets	Total number of Layer 3 bytes in the flow packets of the flow
24–27	First	SysUptime at the start of the flow
28–31	Last	SysUptime at the time the last packet of the flow was received
32–33	Srcport	TCP/UDP source port number
34–35	Dstport	TCP/UDP destination port number
36	Pad1	Unused
37	Tcp_flags	Cumulative binary OR of TCP flags
38	Prot	IP protocol type
39	Tos	IP type of service
40–41	Src_as	Autonomous system number of the source
42–43	Dst_as	Autonomous system number of the destination
44	Src_mask	Source address prefix mask bits
45	Dst_mask	Destination address prefix mask bits
46–47	Pad2	Unused

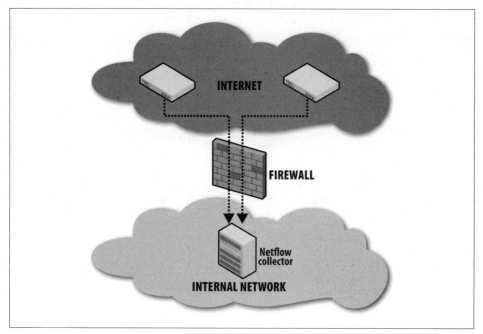

Figure 3-6. NetFlow collection at ISP gateway routers

The most important fields in Table 3-2 are the source and destination IP addresses, source and destination port, IP protocol, packets, octets, and first and last data fields. The content of the bytes in these fields of the flow record gives you the "sessionized" data necessary for effective security monitoring. Although understanding the specific byte order of a NetFlow packet is not terribly important to security monitoring, understanding how to collect the data is important. Analysis of exported NetFlow packet data will help you understand the context of any security incident.

Exporting NetFlow for collection

Many network hardware vendors support NetFlow, including Cisco, Juniper (its implementation is called J-Flow), Huawei (its implementation is called NetStream), and others. When using NetFlow, you must first decide where in the network you will collect the data. At a minimum, you *must* collect NetFlow at perimeter routers to maintain a view into the ingress (entering) and egress (leaving) traffic traversing your network. You can do this at your ISP gateway routers (see Figure 3-6) or, if you have a larger and more complex DMZ presence, at your DMZ distribution layer routers (see Figure 3-7).

Ingress and egress traffic collection of NetFlow is the key to using network telemetry successfully! You'll need this data to see what traffic is traversing your network perimeter, and to understand what direction it is flowing.

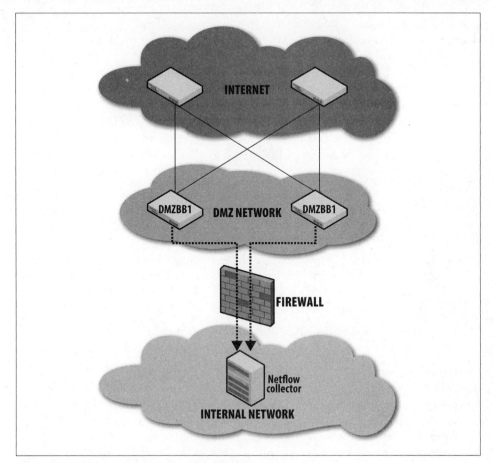

Figure 3-7. NetFlow collection at DMZ backbone routers

NetFlow collection requires two components: the NetFlow sender and the NetFlow collector. The NetFlow sender can be any networking device that creates and exports NetFlow. Many commercial and open source vendors offer collection software. The following examples discuss NetFlow export from Cisco routers and collection with the popular *flow-tools* package, which is an open source effort from Ohio State University.

Configuring Cisco routers to export NetFlow is a simple task, but the steps will vary slightly by hardware platform and NetFlow version. You should always collect bidirectional flow data; otherwise, you may end up with only half the conversations.

Example 3-4 shows a simple NetFlow configuration. It illustrates how to enable NetFlow at the global level, defining a source interface for export, and defining a destination collector IP address and UDP port.

Example 3-4. Simple NetFlow configuration for a Cisco router

```
Router1(config)#ip route-cache flow
Router1(config)#ip flow-export source Loopback 0
Router1(config)#ip flow-export destination 10.1.1.1 9999
Router1(config)#interface FastEthernet0/0
Router1(config-if)#ip route-cache flow
```

Notice that the source interface used in Example 3-4 is a Loopback interface. This is preferable, as the IP address assigned to the Loopback interface is less likely to change as networks are readdressed or modified. This IP address will probably be used in firewall rule sets to allow export of DMZ NetFlow into a collector on your internal network, as depicted previously in Figures 3-3 and 3-4. The destination address of 10.1.1.1 is the address of the NetFlow collector, which we expect to be listening on UDP port 9999.

Performance considerations for NetFlow collection

You may be concerned about the impact of NetFlow export from your network devices. Cisco has documented the performance impact of NetFlow on many of its platforms, and you can reference this information in its "NetFlow Performance Analysis" white paper, found at the following web page:

http://www.cisco.com/en/US/tech/tk812/technologies_white_paper0900aecd802a0eb9 .shtml

Based on Cisco's testing, the variable that carries the most weight on *all* platforms is the number of flows. The more flows traversing the router, the more CPU resources are used. Other variables include IOS version and whether the NetFlow processes are handled in hardware or software. In our experience, NetFlow has a negligible impact on router CPU resources. As always, however, you will want to investigate, test, and verify the impact of any change to your production router configuration.

If you find that the impact on CPU resources is too great for your environment, all is not lost: NetFlow has a feature, called Sampled NetFlow, which many Cisco routers support. Sampled NetFlow allows a router to sample one out of every *X* packets. For the purposes of using NetFlow to investigate security incidents, however, it is not recommended that you implement Sampled NetFlow; you will likely miss vital forensic data.

Where to collect NetFlow

For the security analysis we're describing, you should collect NetFlow from devices that represent a choke point or aggregation point in your network. Such a choke point delineates connection points—typically a "distribution layer" device in network parlance. Examples include the following:

A pair of redundant data center gateways
     All traffic going into and out of your data center

A DMZ backbone router
     All traffic going into and out of your DMZ

An extranet backbone router
     All traffic going into and out of your extranet

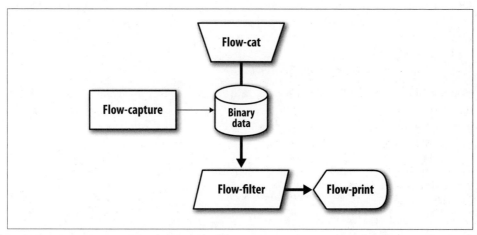

Figure 3-8. Basic flow-tools components

Ensure that you have NetFlow enabled on all appropriate router interfaces, and verify that you have the full flow mask, as illustrated in previous sections.

OSU flow-tools

OSU flow-tools contains tools to collect, send, process, and generate reports from NetFlow. An entire book could be dedicated to this one tool set; instead, we will provide simple examples of their practical application for security monitoring. Appendix A contains detailed instructions for completing a basic NetFlow collection setup with OSU flow-tools.

To effectively deploy and use OSU flow-tools, you must understand four basic flow-tools components: flow-capture, flow-cat, flow-filter, and flow-print, as shown in Figure 3-8.

Here's a brief description of what each component handles:

Flow-capture
     Listens on the defined UDP port, processes NetFlow packets, and stores the data to disk in a highly compressed binary format

Flow-cat
     Utility for concatenating the captured data; used when searching the stored data

Flow-filter
   Powerful searching and reporting utility allowing selection of specific flows based
   on criteria such as source and destination IP protocols, address, and port

Flow-print
   Utility to display flow data formatted in ASCII

The ability to determine whether a conversation between systems occurred is vital for
security investigations. Each time a system sends an IP packet through a router with
NetFlow export enabled, you have a digital fingerprint of that traffic. The following are
some real-world examples using these digital fingerprints to confirm such conversations
with high confidence. These fingerprints are vital confirmations of activity—from a
single packet attack to the leak of critical information.

Identifying infected hosts participating in botnets. Suppose that a new virus variant has been
released, and your existing antivirus product is unable to identify it. A Windows admin
in your organization has sent the following email to your team:

```
Security Team,

My server, WADC-WIN2K, has been having serious performance problems in the past 12
hours. The CPU keeps spiking and when I do a 'netstat' command I see lots of
connections to hundreds of other hosts on TCP 135. This is not normal for this
server. I ran Kaspiramicro Antivirus and didn't see any viruses listed. I know that
it was recommended for me to upgrade all of my servers because of the recent
vulnerabilities published, but I forgot this one. Perhaps it is related? Could you
take a look?

Thanks,

Srinivisan Nguyen Navratalova
Senior Systems Administrator
Blanco Wireless, Inc.
```

Your Windows security lead investigator checks the system and finds some odd-
looking *.exe* files that were written to *C:\WINDOWS\SYSTEM32* the evening before.
Some registry entries appear to run the executable on system startup. He also spots a
connection on TCP 31337 to a server in a known hacker network, according to several
security lists, at 31.33.73.57. Upon submitting the binary to the antivirus software
vendor, analysis confirms that it is indeed a new variant of a virus, one that uses the
server's latest (unpatched) vulnerability as a propagation vector. This virus is found to
be a variant of AngryMintStorm/32, known for its popularity among the organized
cybercrime group that runs the world's largest Internet Relay Chat (IRC) botnets. Your
Windows security lead investigator sends the information to you in an email:

```
Hey guys,

Looks like that server you had me look at is infected with a new variant of the
AngryMintStorm virus we've been seeing lately. It has an IRC botnet component that
allows these miscreants to control the system remotely. You should see connections
```

going to omg.i.pwnt.your.server.secretdns.org, which currently resolves to IP
address 31.33.73.57. We've got a new virus definition file on the way from our
Kaspriamicro, but there's no telling how many systems were hit with this.

Good Luck,
Jonathon "Jack" Bowers
Senior Windows Security Engineer

To identify which systems on your network were infected with the virus, you can use
NetFlow. A digital fingerprint will exist for any IP address that attempted to communicate with the virus's IRC command and control server (C&C) IP address. In such a
situation, it's common to treat any system having communicated with 31.33.73.57 on
TCP port 31337 as compromised. You should remediate the situation immediately;
there is no legitimate reason for a computer on your network to communicate with
http://omg.i.pwnt.your.server.secretdns.org. You can use the collected NetFlow and
OSU flow-tools to identify any system that has communicated with the malicious server
via your network.

First, create an access control list (ACL) file named *flow.acl* with the IP address of the
C&C. This syntax is very similar to the ACLs used on network firewalls. This file will
have access control entries that are used to match flow traffic:

```
ip access-list standard botnet permit host 31.33.73.57
```

The preceding line shows an ACL named botnet that will be used to match IP address
31.33.73.57. Now, use the flow-cat, flow-filter, and flow-print commands to search
the NetFlow collected from the perimeter DMZ backbone routers. You're looking for
digital fingerprints of connections between the IRC C&C server and systems on your
network:

```
[nfchost]$ flow-cat /var/local/netflow/files/2008-1-12/ft* | flow-filter -Sbotnet
-o -Dbotnet | flow-print -f5
```

The flow-cat /var/local/netflow/files/2008-1-12/ft* command concatenates the
compressed binary file(s) containing the NetFlow, which was specified in the file|
directory option. The flow-filter –Sbotnet –o –Dbotnet command filters the flows
based on source or destination matches, which were specified as botnet C&C servers
in the *flow.acl* file created earlier. The flow-print -f5 command outputs the matching
flow records in an easy-to-read, one-line, 32-column format.

In plain English, this command says "Show me all NetFlow sourced from or destined
to the botnet C&C IP address," or more simply, "Who is talking to the bad guys?"

Here's the output of the preceding command:

```
Start             End               SrcIPaddress   SrcP    DstIPaddress   DstP
0112.08:39:49.91 0112.08:40:34.51   10.10.71.100   8343    31.33.73.57    31337
0112.08:40:33.59 0112.08:40:42.29   31.33.73.57    31337   10.10.71.100   8343
```

You now have a digital fingerprint of IP address 10.10.71.100 talking to 31.33.73.57
at 08:39 on January 12. You need to remediate 10.10.71.100 immediately. This

single query can quickly identify all systems on your network infected with the AngryMintStorm/32 zero-day virus.

 Botnet intelligence can be gained via malware analysis with tools such as Norman SandBox,[||] conversational heuristic analysis software such as BotHunter,[#] and data shared within the security community via the Snort bleeding-edge NIDS signature database.[*]

You can extend this method to other forms of malware or phishing. For instance, the following example leverages NetFlow to identify fraud victims. Imagine the impact on your employees if they received the phishing email shown in Figure 3-9, causing the inadvertent disclosure of their bank account credentials or other sensitive information. One of your savvier employees sends you the following email:

```
Security Team,

I and many other employees received the attached email today. It looks like
phishing to me. Since so many of our employees use BigBank for their banking I
wanted to bring this to your attention.

Regards,

Frank N. Beyahns
Sales Director
Blanco Wireless
```

A quick look at the email shows that the URL presented to the user (*http://31.3.33.7/.PayPal/cmd/cgi-bin/webscrcmd_login.php*) does not belong to BigBank, but rather to a server on your familiar hacker network. The hackers have set up a website that looks just like BigBank's website so that they can harvest legitimate credentials and steal money from customers who are tricked by the phishing email.

You now know that anyone clicking on the link will leave a digital fingerprint; NetFlow will record traffic destined to TCP port 80 on IP address 31.3.33.7. In addition, BigBank let your security team know that two more sites were involved in this phishing activity at IP addresses 64.38.64.20 and 139.192.10.10. You can build a filter to match against the malicious host IP addresses:

```
ip access-list standard phish permit host 31.3.33.7
ip access-list standard phish permit host 64.38.64.20
ip access-list standard phish permit host 139.192.10.10
```

The flow-filter command has many options. In this case, you're going to filter based on your named ACL (*phish*) and destination port (80):

|| *http://www.norman.com/microsites/nsic/*

http://www.bothunter.net/

* *http://www.emergingthreats.net/*

```
[nfchost]$ flow-cat /var/local/netflow/files/2007-11-28/ft* | flow-filter  -Dphish
-P80 | flow-print -f5
```

```
Start                  End                   SrcIPaddress     SrcP     DstIPaddress    DstP
1128.09:39:49.91 1128.09:40:34.51       10.10.51.75      1250     31.3.33.7        80
1128.09:45:33.59 1128.09:46:42.29       10.10.55.12      2080     139.192.10.10 80
1128.14:15:13.05 1128.14:16:21.15       10.10.30.119     1349     139.192.10.10 80
```

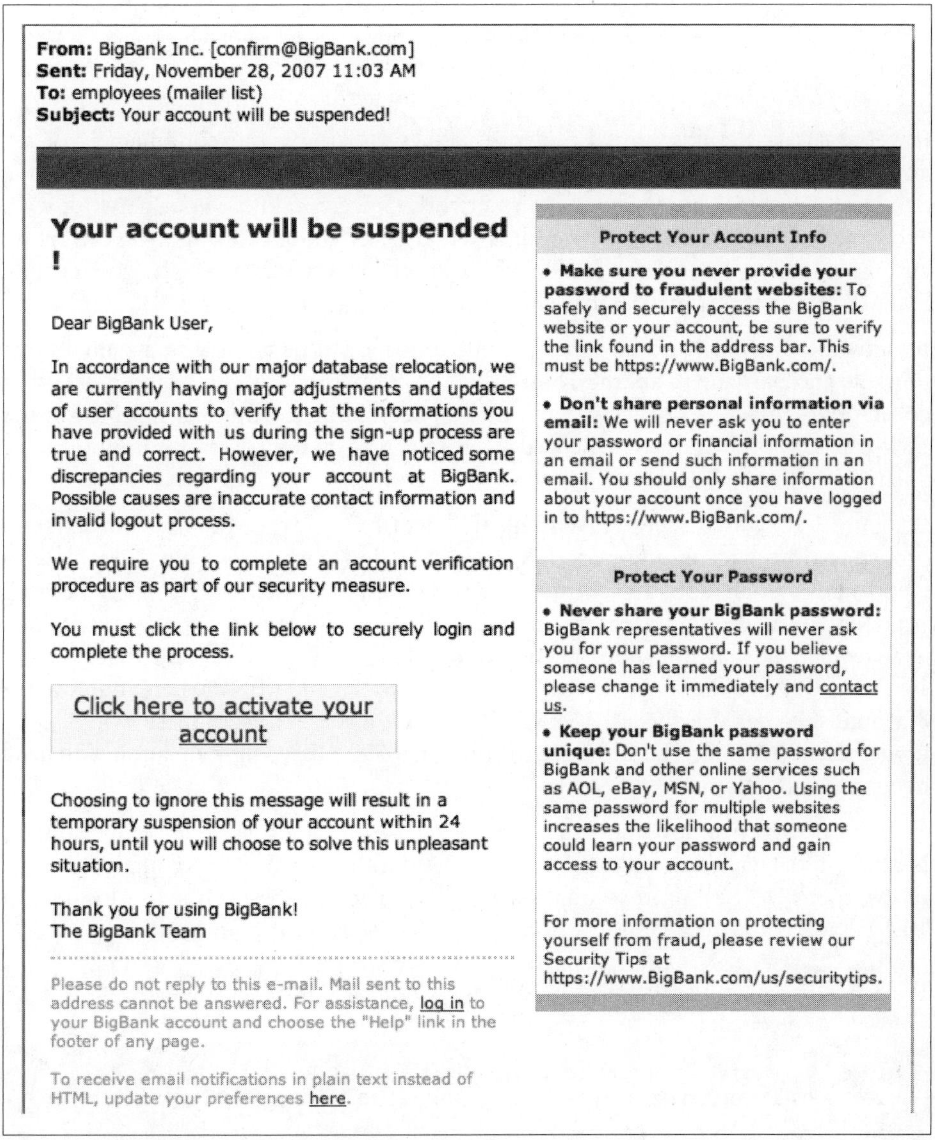

From: BigBank Inc. [confirm@BigBank.com]
Sent: Friday, November 28, 2007 11:03 AM
To: employees (mailer list)
Subject: Your account will be suspended!

Your account will be suspended !

Dear BigBank User,

In accordance with our major database relocation, we are currently having major adjustments and updates of user accounts to verify that the informations you have provided with us during the sign-up process are true and correct. However, we have noticed some discrepancies regarding your account at BigBank. Possible causes are inaccurate contact information and invalid logout process.

We require you to complete an account verification procedure as part of our security measure.

You must click the link below to securely login and complete the process.

Click here to activate your account

Choosing to ignore this message will result in a temporary suspension of your account within 24 hours, until you will choose to solve this unpleasant situation.

Thank you for using BigBank!
The BigBank Team
....
Please do not reply to this e-mail. Mail sent to this address cannot be answered. For assistance, log in to your BigBank account and choose the "Help" link in the footer of any page.

To receive email notifications in plain text instead of HTML, update your preferences here.

Protect Your Account Info

• **Make sure you never provide your password to fraudulent websites:** To safely and securely access the BigBank website or your account, be sure to verify the link found in the address bar. This must be https://www.BigBank.com/.

• **Don't share personal information via email:** We will never ask you to enter your password or financial information in an email or send such information in an email. You should only share information about your account once you have logged in to https://www.BigBank.com/.

Protect Your Password

• **Never share your BigBank password:** BigBank representatives will never ask you for your password. If you believe someone has learned your password, please change it immediately and contact us.

• **Keep your BigBank password unique:** Don't use the same password for BigBank and other online services such as AOL, eBay, MSN, or Yahoo. Using the same password for multiple websites increases the likelihood that someone could learn your password and gain access to your account.

For more information on protecting yourself from fraud, please review our Security Tips at https://www.BigBank.com/us/securitytips.

Figure 3-9. Phishing email received by employees

You need to check your DHCP, Windows Active Directory, or other logs to see who had IP addresses 10.10.51.75, 10.10.55.12, and 10.10.30.119 at the times listed. Armed with that information, you can notify those users of the phishing activity and take appropriate action with BigBank.

 If the phishing page in our example was hosted on a site that also includes popular legitimate content (such as Facebook, MySpace, iBiblio, etc.), identification of compromised systems becomes more complicated. You need to augment NetFlow with proxy server logs or other event sources that show the URLs accessed by affected users.

Flow aggregation. NetFlow can also identify policy violations, our core theme. For example, your company would probably wish to prevent data from being copied from a database server to a host outside your network. Since you know your network well, and have NetFlow deployed to your data center distribution gateways, you can set up automated reporting to send an alert, for example, when a data transfer greater than 500 MB occurs from your database host to an outside system.

In networks with high traffic volume, a file transfer can be recorded partially in one flow-file and partially in another. Since the OSU flow-tools collector (and most other collectors) writes to a file every *X* minutes as defined by the options specified in the `flow-capture` command, you will need a way to aggregate flow data over multiple files, as shown in Figure 3-10.

In Figure 3-10, you can see a 554 MB file transfer from a server to a miscreant's system occurring over a 15-minute period. To detect such a transfer, we'll use NetFlow to identify any system that transfers more than 500 MB of data in a single session. Because your NetFlow collector writes a new flow data file every five minutes, the data contained in any single file may not show that a policy violation occurred. Assume that flow-file 1 shows a 200 MB file transfer, flow-file 2 also shows a 200 MB transfer, and flow-file 3 contains the data for the last 154 MB of the file transfer. None of these would alone trigger the 500 MB threshold. To see the potential 500 MB+ policy violation, you need to aggregate the flow data.

One solution to this flow-tools limitation leverages yet another open source suite of NetFlow tools, called nfdump.[†] Using the network taxonomy data contained in the IPAM tool, we can narrow our search to Oracle database subnets, located in 10.20.20.0/24 and 10.20.23.0/24, referenced in this `flow-cat` command:

```
[nfchost]$ flow-cat /var/local/netflow/files/2008/1/5/ft* | ft2nfdump | nfdump -a -
A srcip,dstip 'bytes > 500000000 and ( src net 10.20.20.0/24 or src net
10.20.23.0/24)

Date      start    Duration Proto  SrcIP:Port      DstIP:Port      Packets Bytes
2007-1-05 12:39:11 1151.3    TCP    10.20.20.8:22   10.10.50.32:4942 234729  554.9 M
```

---

† *http://www.nfdump.sourceforge.net/*

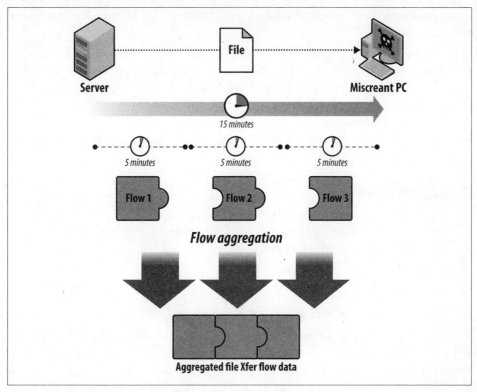

Figure 3-10. Flow aggregation of a file transfer

The preceding output shows that on January 5, 2007, at 12:39 p.m., a system using IP address 10.10.50.32 transferred a 554 MB file from an Oracle server at 10.20.20.8 via SSH (TCP 22). Follow-up on this transfer with the employee revealed that a consultant from Artists Consulting had downloaded a database containing customer information to his laptop. This is in violation of Blanco's acceptable use policy. The consultant's laptop was taken for forensic imaging and investigation. NetFlow at the DMZ perimeter was queried to determine whether the file had been copied out of Blanco's network. The following query shows all traffic for the consultant's computer at 10.10.50.32 on January 5:

```
ip access-list standard artistcon permit host 10.10.50.32

[nfchost]$ flow-cat /var/local/netflow/files/2007-1-5/ft* | flow-filter -Sartistcon
-o -Dartistcon | flow-print -f5
```

The results of this query will tell you whether the file was copied out of Blanco's network.

Repudiation and nonrepudiation. You can use NetFlow to repudiate the occurrence of a network conversation between two or more systems. A query of NetFlow for specific IP addresses during the relevant time frame can show zero results and prove that a conversation didn't exist.

Conversely, you can use NetFlow to prove the occurrence of a network conversation between two or more systems. This is very useful in situations where you suspect that a particular event has occurred and you want to prove that it did. A query of the NetFlow for specific IP addresses during the relevant time frame can show results, proving that a conversation did happen.

Note that we're using repudiation and nonrepudiation in the context of transactions happening on your network, not in the context of a court of law.

Choosing a NetFlow collector

As we already mentioned, many solutions—including commercial and open source—are available for NetFlow analysis. Here are some common features to consider when selecting a solution for NetFlow collection:

- Data compression
- Replication capability
- Storage and processing performance

The NetFlow collection software should support compression of the NetFlow. The higher the compression, the longer the data is retained. OSU flow-tools implements zlib compression which, with default settings, has shown a compression ratio of around 4:1. Although there are no known formulas for calculating disk space requirements, experience with OSU flow-tools' `flow-capture` component in a production DMZ environment is impressive. With 1.2 gigabits per second of bandwidth and a 200,000 packet-per-second (pps) data rate, a 600 GB disk can maintain approximately twelve weeks of compressed NetFlow.

The ability to relay flow data to other systems in real time is important, as many tools can use NetFlow. Examples include SIM tools such as Cisco Security Monitoring, Analysis, and Response System (MARS), anomaly detection solutions such as Arbor Peakflow, and optimization tools such as NetQoS Performance Center and Lancope StealthWatch.

To provide maximum flexibility for the NetFlow analysis solution, the collector should store data in standard, nonproprietary formats, or provide utilities to convert data to standard formats. This will enable you to use a variety of tools to analyze your stored NetFlow.

Here are some common considerations when selecting a NetFlow analysis solution:

- Speed of the query
- Storage of the raw data
- Access to the raw data

Several factors determine the speed of a query, including the capabilities of the hardware on which the analysis software is running and proper query bounding (e.g., it is probably not a good idea to query NetFlow records for all HTTP traffic from all hosts in a 24-hour period against a sizable e-commerce environment; you would quickly run out of memory and disk space). In addition, the ability to access raw flow data can allow you to develop custom tools to serve the unique requirements of your environment.

> Storing raw data in a highly compressed file format is preferable to storing it in a database. A busy network will quickly cause the database to grow by multiple terabytes within days. OSU flow-tools compression allows us to store approximately thirty days of flows for an environment with 200,000 pps sustained on 600 GB of disk space.

In summary, NetFlow is an inexpensive, easy-to-deploy, widely supported, and powerful tool that has many uses for security monitoring, incident investigation, and network forensics. The digital fingerprints provided by NetFlow are invaluable.

SNMP

Simple Network Management Protocol (SNMP) is a useful component in a well-rounded network telemetry suite. SNMP analysis can provide additional visibility into traffic patterns, network path utilization, and device health (as we'll discuss in Chapter 7). We'll take a narrow view of SNMP, limiting its use for network telemetry and security monitoring. Network interface utilization is the single most useful SNMP attribute for network telemetry; when graphed over time, it provides an easy-to-understand, visual view of your network environment.

MRTG

There are many commercial and open source software tools for collecting and analyzing SNMP data. In this section, we will explain how to use the open source tool MRTG. The Multi Router Traffic Grapher (MRTG) is free software created by Tobias Oetiker for monitoring network traffic on data network links. Here is Oetiker's description of MRTG:[‡]

> You have a router, you want to know what it does all day long? Then MRTG is for you. It will monitor SNMP network devices and draw pretty pictures showing how much traffic has passed through each interface. Routers are only the beginning. MRTG is being used to graph all sorts of network devices as well as everything else from weather data to vending machines. MRTG is written in perl and works on Unix/Linux as well as Windows and even Netware systems. MRTG is free software licensed under the Gnu GPL.

[‡] *http://oss.oetiker.ch/mrtg/index.en.html*

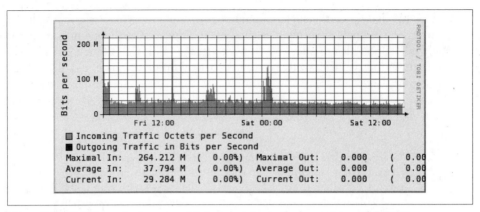

Figure 3-11. SNMP queries for network interface data graphed over time with MRTG

MRTG example. Imagine you are tasked with deploying a NIDS into a data center environment. How will you design the solution? One of the most basic requirements when deploying a NIDS involves sizing it to properly analyze the aggregate network bandwidth. SNMP provides an ability to track link utilization to discover aggregate bandwidth. In addition, network utilization patterns can provide visibility into states or occurrences of network traffic that fall outside normal ranges for the environment.

A quick glance at network utilization graphed over time can identify anomalies in activity. For example, analysis of the graph in Figure 3-11 shows that the NIDS detected a sizable spike in network traffic Saturday night. Is this normal? Should anyone be on this particular network late at night on a Saturday? This situation may warrant further investigation, possibly using NetFlow to identify large file transfers.

The data that results when you graph network traffic in this manner can be considered *meta-metadata*; that is, in contrast with NetFlow we see only aggregate utilization statistics, not individual conversations. NetFlow does not understand the concept of interface bandwidth or speed; it understands only byte (or octet) count. SNMP data can give you a high-level view of traffic patterns that may point to the need for further investigation with NetFlow, which adds further detail.

Routing and Network Topologies

You must keep network and routing topologies and policies in mind when interpreting security alerts; they allow you to infer expected traffic path traversal. To accomplish this, answer these questions regarding your routing topologies:

- Which address blocks are publicly routed?
- Which address blocks are active/deployed?
- From which ISP connection are the address blocks advertised?

If you see security alerts sourced from or destined to an address block that has not been deployed in your network, you can infer several things. If the alert shows an attack *sourced from* an inactive or yet-to-be-deployed address block, it is likely spoofed. If the alert is *destined to* an inactive or yet-to-be-deployed address block, it is likely a network scan or a noisy worm. Understanding routing topologies can also help you set expectations for traffic flow and path traversal. For example, I know the default route advertised to my Ohio sales office comes from our New York branch's ISP connection. I can infer that any outbound NIDS alerts or NetFlow showing a source IP address from my Ohio office should traverse the New York DMZ.

The Blanco Wireless Network

Blanco's security team has worked with its IT staff to better understand their company's network using IPAM data, NetFlow, and general routing information.

IP Address Assignment

Blanco has a simple address space, documented with the open source IPplan software. The subnets we will use in our examples for this and subsequent chapters are shown in Figure 3-12 and appear highlighted in the following code snippet:

```
10.10.0.0/16        Redwood City Campus
|-- 10.10.0.0/19         Data Centers
|-- 10.10.32.0/19        Site 1 Desktop Networks
|    |-- 10.10.32.0/24      Building 1 1st floor
|    |-- 10.10.33.0/25      Building 1 2nd floor
|    |-- 10.10.33.128/25  Building 2

10.10.0.0/19        Data Centers
|-- 10.10.0.0/20         Building 3 Data Center
|    |-- 10.10.0.0/25        Windows Server Subnet
|    |-- 10.10.0.128/25      Oracle 10g Subnet
|    |-- 10.10.1.0/26        ESX VMWare Farm
|    |-- 10.10.1.64./26      Web Application Servers
```

NetFlow Collection

In keeping with best practices, Blanco collects NetFlow from its Cisco routers in both the DMZ backbone and the data center gateways. Blanco uses the OSU flow-tools package to collect and analyze NetFlow for monitoring and incident response.

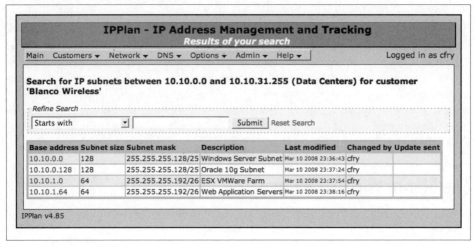

Figure 3-12. Blanco Wireless subnet data in IPplan software

Routing Information

Blanco has a class C network allocated, which is used for customer-facing web services. This network exists in Blanco's single DMZ network with two Internet connections provisioned from two competing ISPs. In addition, all network traffic destined for outside Blanco's autonomous system (AS) traverses its one DMZ network. Internally, Blanco has deployed RFC 1918 address space in the 10.10.0.0/16 block; no other portion of 10.0.0.0/8 has been deployed (see Figure 3-13).

Conclusion

Structured, documented network knowledge is foundational to context-based security monitoring. By deploying tools for documenting and understanding your network environment, you can begin to prioritize security alerts based on how they affect your network. Chapter 4 will provide a third and final foundation, guiding you to select broad targets to prioritize your monitoring against.

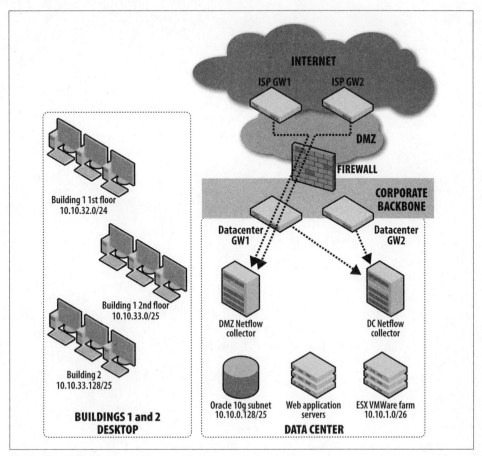

Figure 3-13. Blanco Wireless network diagram

Select Targets for Monitoring

> *Reese: Anyone who's trying to use the override would have to hack through the reactor's firewall. That would take massive computer power, which NRC could see coming a mile away.*
>
> *Jack: Is it possible that NRC could miss this due to unusually heavy traffic on the Internet?*
>
> *Reese: I don't follow.*
>
> *Jack: Well, less than an hour ago millions of computers around the world were streaming the trial of the Secretary of Defense. Is it possible that this trial was just some kind of a Trojan horse to disguise a massive attack on nuclear power plants' firewalls?*
>
> *Reese: That might be possible.*

Successful enterprise security monitoring demands focus. In this fictitious attack from Fox's popular television series *24*, the network security team (NRC) missed a targeted, critical attack due to a decoy surge in network traffic. The depicted scenario demonstrates how difficult it is to monitor effectively when all systems are given "equal" attention. Focused monitoring requires considerable tuning and quick recognition of benign traffic. For example, an Oracle 11*i*-based ERP system will generate thousands of messages per hour from its various components. Without tuning and a strong understanding of the environment, the network monitoring staff will waste their time following dead ends.

Example 4-1 contains an example of a Snort alert that could result from monitoring an Oracle system.

---

* *24*, "Episode 4 × 06: 12:00 P.M.–1:00 P.M." Original air date: January 24, 2005. Trademark & © 2005 Twentieth Century Fox Film Corporation. Originally transcribed for TwizTV.

Example 4-1. Snort alert from monitoring an Oracle system[†]

```
[**] [1:2650:2] ORACLE user name buffer overflow attempt [**]
[Classification: Attempted User Privilege Gain] [Priority: 1]
[Xref => http://www.appsecinc.com/Policy/PolicyCheck62.html]
Event ID: 62662    Event Reference: 62662
11/21/06-17:16:04.892127 172.16.0.136:34833 -> 172.16.5.12:1521
TCP TTL:64 TOS:0x0 ID:32755 IpLen:20 DgmLen:100 DF
***AP*** Seq: 0xB700F908 Ack: 0xF1594793 Win: 0x3309 TcpLen: 32
TCP Options (3) => NOP NOP TS: 2796076485 835448929
00 30 00 00 06 00 00 00 00 00 03 68 FB 01 00 00 .0........h....
00 00 00 00 00 00 00 00 00 00 00 00 00 00 00 00 ................
00 00 00 00 00 00 00 00 00 00 00 04 00 00 00 01 ................
```

Is this a critical alert? The words *buffer overflow attempt* are sure to get your attention, yet this alert is benign—often triggered by Java applications using a strange database connection string.[‡] By focusing your tuning and your monitoring, you can ignore and tune out these benign events. Across the enterprise, various logging and monitoring components generate millions of additional examples of such alerts. For effective monitoring, each alert will require detailed analysis, often involving support and application staff members to explain the anomalous traffic. This kind of tuning is an important part of security monitoring, and it's a continuous task. Policy-based monitoring can't spare you the tedium of such tuning; rather, it will narrow your focus to critical systems and to events that indicate policy violations. To apply policy-based monitoring, you must first select which systems you want to monitor.

This chapter will describe the various approaches for selecting monitoring targets. Once selected, we'll drill deeper into the targets, providing guidance for how to discover the components within them, and documenting the details necessary to configure event feeds.

Methods for Selecting Targets

To effectively select systems to monitor (i.e., your targets), you must establish your priorities. Your approach will be based on the risk or perceived value of the targets and the information within them. You can develop a taxonomy of approaches in countless ways. Here's the range we'll consider in this chapter:

Business impact analysis
Differentiating systems based on level of criticality in the context of availability

Revenue impact
Applications that drive orders and delivery

[†] See *http://www.webservertalk.com/archive251-2006-11-1737633.html*.

[‡] OSDir Mail Archive, msg#00171: "False Positive in 2650.2 (ORACLE user name buffer overflow attempt)."

Expenses impact
Systems that manage contractual obligations to partners and customers

Legal requirements
Statutes and contracts that highlight which information and systems to protect

Sensitivity profile
Systems that access privileged, restricted information

Risk profile
Systems that can't be properly protected using existing controls

Visibility profile
Systems which, if attacked or compromised, might prove embarrassing to the company or damaging to visitors

Business Impact Analysis

The process of conducting a business impact analysis (BIA) is part of the disaster recovery planning function in most enterprises. It's a methodology for identifying critical processes and systems to establish their priority for backup and disaster recovery. Many books describe methodologies for this exercise, including guides for the Certified Information Systems Security Professional (CISSP) exam. Here's a sample process taken from Roberta Bragg's *CISSP Training Guide*:[§]

1. Identify time-critical business processes.
2. Identify supporting resources (personnel, facilities, technology, computers, software, networks, equipment, vital records, data, etc.) for the critical processes.
3. Determine Maximum Tolerable Downtimes (MTDs).
4. Return to business units for validation.
5. Provide the final report, including MTDs and recommendations for next steps, to senior management.

Bragg recommends a series of interviews with business stakeholders to determine the effect of downtime or disruption on business processes. BIA breaks down the impact over time, charting the results into a table for more detailed analysis and discussion, to guide prioritization.

The key input to these prioritization discussions is the impact to the business bottom line, which invites consideration of sales, revenue, financial interest, fines/penalties, and even costs to your customers and partners. This information is then verified in steps 4 and 5. Hopefully, your company's disaster planning team has already performed a BIA. In any case, the generated list provides an excellent starting point for targeting your security monitoring.

[§] Roberta Bragg. *CISSP Training Guide* (Que Publishing, 2002), pp. 454–458.

Revenue Impact Analysis

The BIA focuses heavily on the revenue impact of disruptions, so let's analyze revenue impact a bit further. Any application used in taking or fulfilling orders, for example, is tied directly to revenue (for companies that sell goods, not services). For an e-commerce company, Bragg suggests that the MTD is exactly 0, as even tiny amounts of downtime can result in staggering losses. According to Cavusoglu, Mishra, and Raghunathan, "Firms that solely depend on the Internet as a revenue generating mechanism pay higher prices in case of a security breach than firms that have multiple sales channels. Security of IT systems for net firms is extremely important for a net firm's success."[||]

Of course, not all companies make their money selling goods. Revenue for service-based companies depends on the companies' ability to perform the task for which they've been hired. The auto body shop, the U.S. Postal Service, and eBay don't receive revenue if they can't fix, deliver, or auction your product.

When considering systems that are critical to revenue generation and recognition, order entry and fulfillment systems will have the largest impact on revenue for most companies:

Order entry systems
> Whether orders are entered directly by customers or they're taken by a sales professional, the systems used for taking orders are critical to revenue generation. Typically, many systems are involved in the process, including inventory, order status, order booking, credit card processing, and return processing systems. These systems must not only be protected from unplanned downtime, but also are targets for fraud and theft.

Order fulfillment systems
> According to U.S. Generally Accepted Accounting Principles (GAAP), revenue is not recognizable (placed on the books) until the goods or services are delivered. Therefore, manufacturing, shipping, and service scheduling/tracking systems are key parts of revenue. Although these systems are not typically exposed to the Internet as directly as order entry systems (and therefore are not as directly in the path for fraud and hacking), they are critical for maintaining compliance with regulatory requirements and revenue recognition.

Expense Impact Analysis

Applications that support payments are critical to managing expenses. If these applications are unable to function properly, your company will likely incur financial penalties. Though the cause of disruption is normally accidental, it's now becoming feasible

---

[||] Huseyin Cavusoglu, Birendra Mishra, and Srinivasan Raghunathan. "The Effect of Internet Security Breach Announcements on Market Value of Breached Firms and Internet Security Developers" (The University of Texas at Dallas School of Management, 2002), p. 14.

for malicious competitors to use distributed denial-of-service (DDoS) tools against you to impact your revenue or cause painful expenses. Such was the case in March 2008, when the gaming site Gala Coral was knocked offline for more than 30 minutes by a DDoS attack, likely at the direction of a competitor.#

Payroll and time-keeping systems directly impact expenses. Monitoring these systems can help prevent fraud and abuse, as was uncovered in an audit of Ashmont Cleaning Company, where an employee was changing system records of his work hours to receive extra overtime pay, and stole more than $30,000 before getting caught as the result of an audit (Belloli & McNeal 2006).* Two years ago, an unnamed company discovered that an employee was using its purchase order system to steal from the company by routing orders to shell companies, which the employee and her husband controlled. These cases demonstrate that monitoring financial systems such as those that process purchasing and payroll requires more than just watching for availability problems. Experts in the rules and exceptions of business processes must review reports and workflow, using periodic reports to catch problems early. System monitoring can augment human review by catching abuse of account system privileges or attempts to guess passwords for accounts with elevated system privileges.

Legal Requirements

A company may incur punitive expenses from the government or from partners in legal contracts if its systems do not perform their proper functions in terms of operating and protecting sensitive information. As dimensions of legal impact, let's consider regulatory compliance and contractual obligation and how they can affect your company.

Regulatory compliance

My neighbor manages production for a German manufacturer of industrial heat exchangers. One spring evening as we were sharing our experiences of being "called into a crisis" at the office, he topped our stories by explaining the huge penalties he faces if he's caught violating local environmental regulations. His employees must maintain high purity standards when discharging waste water used in the manufacturing plant. If an auditor discovers a breach of compliance, the company will incur shattering monetary fines and corporate officers will face personal liability, including a prison sentence, upon conviction.

Every company must comply with some amount of regulation governing its business operations. Compliance is often demonstrated in routine audits and reporting; active monitoring is seldom necessary to achieve compliance. Regulations are often developed to protect information, and such systems typically contain the most sensitive

---

See *http://news.digitaltrends.com/news/story/15992/gaming_co_hit_by_major_ddos_attack/*.

* See *http://goliath.ecnext.com/coms2/gi_0199-5592079/Fraudulent-overtime-access-to-the.html*.

information in your enterprise. Active monitoring is often required by regulation, and is a practical part of protecting regulated systems and data.

Most regulatory controls are aimed at protecting the integrity and confidentiality of financial information. The Sarbanes-Oxley Act of 2002 (SOX), which was enacted after a series of accounting scandals, specifies a set of legal controls and audits in an effort to prevent further scandals. SOX Section 404 is aimed at assessing the controls bounding financial reporting, and encourages companies to regulate and monitor the processes for storing and accessing financial information. Effective monitoring for financial systems should concentrate on the databases and applications used for such processing. This includes means for detecting unauthorized changes and abuse of privileges, as well as monitoring for database administrators and others with administrative access.

Example: Gramm-Leach Blilely Act

A U.S. regulation aimed at personal privacy, the Gramm-Leach-Blilely Act (GLBA) contains a "Safeguards Rule" which requires companies to protect non-public personal information:

> In furtherance of the policy in subsection (a) of this section, each agency or authority described in section 6805 (a) of this title shall establish appropriate standards for the financial institutions subject to their jurisdiction relating to administrative, technical, and physical safeguards—
>
> (1) to insure the security and confidentiality of customer records and information;
>
> (2) to protect against any anticipated threats or hazards to the security or integrity of such records; and
>
> (3) to protect against unauthorized access to or use of such records or information which could result in substantial harm or inconvenience to any customer.[†]

The GLBA applies only to financial institutions, but requires protection for systems that store nonpublic personal information, such as customer databases, online banking, and brokerage systems.

Example: Payment Card Industry Data Security Standard

The Payment Card Industry Data Security Standard (PCI DSS) prescribes monitoring for credit card data in the section, "Regularly Monitor and Test Networks." In Section 10.6, it specifically requires "Review logs for all system components at least daily. Log reviews must include those servers that perform security functions like intrusion detection system (IDS) and authentication, authorization, and accounting protocol (AAA) servers (for example, RADIUS). Note: Log harvesting, parsing, and alerting tools may be used to achieve compliance with Requirement 10.6." The PCI DSS requires that specific systems, including AAA servers, be monitored for abuse.

[†] U.S. Code Title 15,6801: Protection of Nonpublic Personal Information.

Example: Standards for critical infrastructure protection

Some forms of compliance are voluntary and very specific to the industry in which the company operates. Though not mandatory, compliance with such guidelines is often required by executive management to avoid external scrutiny and lawsuits. The "North American Electric Reliability Council (NERC) Critical Infrastructure Protection Committee (CIPC) Security Guidelines for the Electricity Sector"‡ provides requirements for securing, both physically and electronically, critical systems for electric utilities. The guideline prescribes detailed security configurations and monitoring for any business system that must connect to a control system. This standard requires you to discover the systems connecting to your control systems, such as trouble ticketing or inventory systems, and monitor them for security breaches.

Contractual obligation

Companies that offer packaged information technology services are often bound to contract requirements for availability, integrity, and performance. Such companies must monitor their systems very carefully, to help ensure that contract requirements are met before their customers discover a contract breach and exercise their contractual privileges, which often include financial penalties.

In recent years, large companies have turned increasingly to Application Service Providers (ASPs) to offload application processing. A common requirement specified in such contracts includes security monitoring.§ For sensitive applications and data, security monitoring is vitally important, and such contracts often require monitoring of specific segments or systems as part of the agreement.

Sensitivity Profile

Sensitive data is the most common and obvious place to target monitoring. Information may be considered sensitive because it is associated with an individual's privacy, it has competitive value (intellectual property), or it has government-labeled handling requirements (classified information).

Systems that access personally identifiable information (PII)

The thriving malware underground is fueled largely by the ability to steal, market, and sell the private information of individuals. This information has a market value because thieves can use it to create fake identities, giving them the opportunity to steal thousands of dollars from their victims via the victims' bank, credit card, or brokerage.

---

‡ NERC. *Security Guidelines for the Electricity Sector* (May 2005), p. 4.

§ Cisco Systems. *Evaluating Application Service Provider Security for Enterprises*; *http://www.cisco.com/web/about/security/intelligence/asp-eval.html* (2008).

With the advent of outsourcing and ASPs, it's becoming feasible for companies to relinquish all responsibility for storing sensitive data about employees and customers. For companies that must maintain such systems, it should be fairly obvious which applications access such sensitive information. Recent legislation in many countries outlines the definition of PII and the required protections. It usually involves a unique personal identifier combined with other data, such as a passport number stored along with the person's name. Here are examples of systems that commonly store PII:

- Payroll systems, which often contain bank account information for direct deposit of paychecks, along with tax identification numbers and Social Security numbers
- Human resources systems, which often contain Social Security numbers, immigration identifiers, and other unique identifiers for use in complying with employment law
- Systems that access credit card details, such as customer databases and purchasing systems
- Medical records systems, which contain information protected under the Health Insurance Portability and Accountability Act of 1996 (HIPAA), such as individuals' health history

Systems that access confidential information

Since 2005, reports of hackers using social engineering techniques to steal competitive intelligence have repeatedly surfaced. These techniques have involved sending targeted trojans to individuals within the victim company (commonly known as *spearphishing*), planting "back doors" that are later used to steal the data. In 2006, for example, CERT/CC warned that "The stealthy attacks have frequently been sent to a specific person at the targeted organization and show that attackers are researching the best way to convince the victim that the document containing the Trojan horse is real."[||] Data has also been stolen with more traditional attack techniques such as guessing weak passwords. SAP allegedly used such techniques in 2007, when its employees were accused of stealing volumes of Oracle's software and support materials in an attempt to gain an upper hand in engaging customers.[#]

Companies should classify proprietary information and label it for restricted distribution. Such information represents the most critical secrets a company maintains, and it can include examples such as the following:

- Product designs, including blueprints, schematics, software design specifications, and steps in a manufacturing process
- Components and assembly instructions
- Lists of customers, contacts, and order history

[||] See *http://www.securityfocus.com/news/11222/*.

[#] See *http://www.securityfocus.com/news/11453/*.

- Sales figures and leads
- Orders in process
- Plans for mergers and acquisitions
- Products/ideas under development
- Patents not yet filed or approved

Don't overlook the value of monitoring the computers and accounts of your senior executives. These systems are surely accessing highly privileged information, making them the likely targets of spearphishers.

Systems that access classified information

Handling classified information (as controlled by official markings and procedures of a government agency, bound by law) requires special handling and protections. For example, the U.S. Department of Defense directive number 5220.22-M sets forth requirements described in the National Industrial Security Program Operating Manual (NISPOM).[*] This directive requires that all TOP SECRET and SECRET information be monitored with a NIDS. It also requires special monitoring for any system connected to a classified information system, and that such connections are made via a Controlled Interface (CI), described as follows:

> 8-702. Controlled Interface Requirements. The CI shall have the following properties:
>
> a. Adjudicated Differences. The CI shall be implemented to monitor and enforce the protection requirements of the network and to adjudicate the differences in security policies.

Based on this requirement, a connection to a classified information system requires monitoring and enforcement to protect the information it contains. This serves as an excellent example of a system for which targeted monitoring is required.

Risk Profile

Due to availability requirements and vendor packaging, some systems cannot be regularly patched (and some cannot be patched at all). These systems present an increased risk to the enterprise, and you should monitor them carefully. You can use preventive controls such as firewalls and intrusion prevention systems (IPSs) to augment their security, but for sensitive or critical systems, active security monitoring is a necessary tool to further reduce risk. For example, Supervisory Control and Data Acquisition (SCADA) systems are used to control and manage a nation's critical infrastructure, including energy, water, transportation, and communication systems. In recent years, these systems have been converted to commodity operating systems and networks (such as Windows and TCP/IP), moving away from proprietary systems. Connections

[*] National Industrial Security Program Operating Manual (NISPOM), DoD 5220.22-M, Section 5-307 (February 2006).

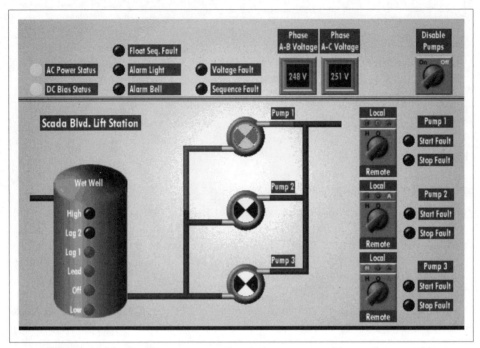

Figure 4-1. Screenshot from a SCADA water plant pumping system (see http://www.nordatasys.com/ screens.htm)

to SCADA systems from external networks have placed them in the line of fire for security threats. Weaknesses in these systems have been repeatedly demonstrated, and the role these systems play in critical infrastructure makes them extremely vulnerable to electronic warfare and terrorist attacks.

Figure 4-1 shows a screenshot from a SCADA water plant pumping system.

SCADA systems are commonly plagued by three broad vulnerabilities, as described at a Black Hat Federal Briefing:[†]

No authentication
> These systems have automated components connected and running autonomously. This makes these systems ripe for worms and other self-replicating attacks.

No patching
> Commonly due to intolerance for downtime, these systems run for many years without interruption or attention for patching.

---

† RG & DM (X-Force Internet Security Systems). "SCADA Security and Terrorism, We're Not Crying Wolf," Black Hat Federal Briefings 2006.

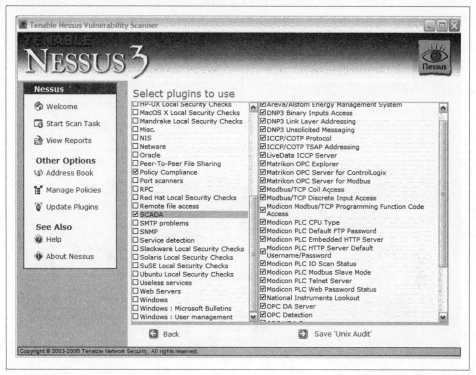

Figure 4-2. Nessus scan options for SCADA systems

No isolation/firewalling

As systems are interconnected and the network is extended, these systems are increasingly reachable via the Internet and other less-protected networks.

Because these problems are endemic to SCADA systems, security monitoring is required to mitigate the substantial risk they present. Some vulnerability scanning tools contain built-in SCADA probes, as illustrated in the Nessus screen capture in Figure 4-2.

Risk assessments

An *information technology security assessment* (commonly called a *risk assessment*) is a focused study intended to locate IT security vulnerabilities and risks. The risk assessment normally includes an evaluation of both physical and technical risks, and uses personal interviews, vulnerability scans, and on-site observation to evaluate risk. Risk assessments are aimed at evaluating an organization's compliance with a set of security standards. A common security framework used as a standard in such assessments is ISO 17799, which defines important administrative security guidelines for organizations.

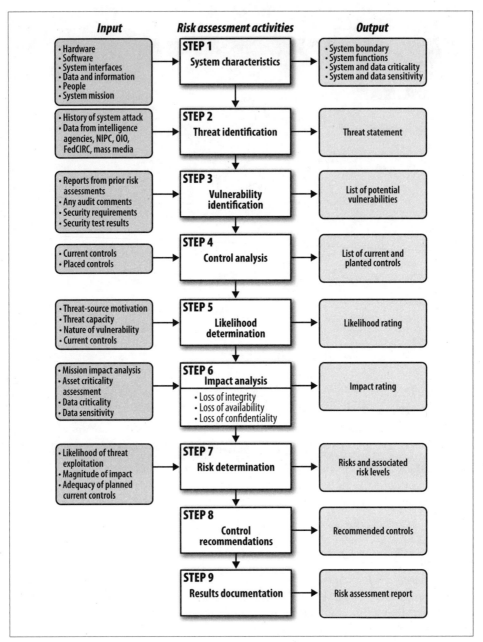

Input	Risk assessment activities	Output
• Hardware • Software • System interfaces • Data and information • People • System mission	**STEP 1** **System characteristics**	• System boundary • System functions • System and data criticality • System and data sensitivity
• History of system attack • Data from intelligence agencies, NIPC, OIO, FedCIRC, mass media	**STEP 2** **Threat identification**	Threat statement
• Reports from prior risk assessments • Any audit comments • Security requirements • Security test results	**STEP 3** **Vulnerability identification**	List of potential vulnerabilities
• Current controls • Placed controls	**STEP 4** **Control analysis**	List of current and planted controls
• Threat-source motivation • Threat capacity • Nature of vulnerability • Current controls	**STEP 5** **Likelihood determination**	Likelihood rating
• Mission impact analysis • Asset criticality assessment • Data criticality • Data sensitivity	**STEP 6** **Impact analysis** • Loss of integrity • Loss of availability • Loss of confidentiality	Impact rating
• Likelihood of threat exploitation • Magnitude of impact • Adequacy of planned current controls	**STEP 7** **Risk determination**	Risks and associated risk levels
	STEP 8 **Control recommendations**	Recommended controls
	STEP 9 **Results documentation**	Risk assessment report

Figure 4-3. NIST risk assessment process

NIST Special Publication 800-30, "Risk Management Guide for Information Technology Systems," describes nine steps for conducting information security risk assessments, as shown in Figure 4-3.

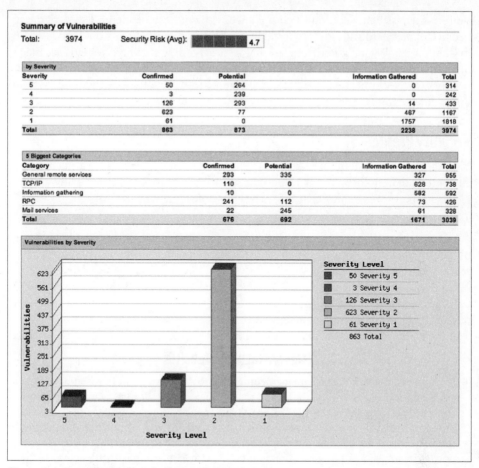

Figure 4-4. Example Qualys scan from risk assessment

This process provides structured analysis of threats, vulnerabilities in deployed infrastructure, and available controls to produce a report of security risks (gaps) and recommended controls. Where recommended controls are considered too costly or impractical, security monitoring can often provide an acceptable alternative for mitigating security risks. In the security reviews I've conducted, business units have often been unwilling to implement strict controls to mitigate risk, fearing it will slow progress on time-sensitive projects. In those cases, I've required the business unit's executive to accept the risk by signing a formal document explaining the risks of the project. This solution is effective for raising awareness, but it leaves the risks unmitigated. Security monitoring offers a unique compromise, allowing the business owner to mitigate risks by sponsoring targeted monitoring. Risk assessments commonly discover present risks via scans by specialized tools, producing reports similar to the Qualys report shown in Figure 4-4.

Your risk assessment should test compliance with your established policies, as described in Chapter 2. In addition, it should incorporate network address data, as described in Chapter 3, allowing you to aim specific tests according to where systems are placed on the network. For example, if your policy requires use of IT-sanctioned virtual private network (VPN) connections for all remote administration, you should audit the systems in the data center for rogue connections such as modems.

Visibility Profile

Your most visible systems are likely those exposed to the Internet, providing access to customers, shareholders, partners, and the press. This includes your company website, blogs, support tools, and other customer-accessible systems.

According to statistics from the 12th Annual Computer and Crime Survey,[‡] website defacements have slightly increased in recent years, but remain a very small percentage of security incidents. Many companies are generating their content dynamically, even rebuilding their static content on a nightly basis. These advances seem to reduce the need for monitoring the static web content presented by your company. However, as noted in the sidebar, "A New Attack on Websites," defacements are only one dimension of security threats for your static content.

A New Attack on Websites

Because most website defacements are intended to draw attention to the attack, they are commonly attributed to vandals and political activists. A more serious and practical concern regarding the integrity of your website involves compromise for the purpose of malware distribution. Historically, such sites were limited to the seedy side of the Internet, where victims were lured by the promise of salacious images or videos. That's now changing, as less-protected sites commonly visited and implicitly trusted by users are new targets for hackers to use in distributing malware.

As stated in the Google Technical Report, "All Your iFrames Point to Us,"[§] a sampling of millions of random URLs demonstrated that, though adult sites continued to contain the largest proportion of malicious content, several other categories had appreciable percentages of malware as well. According to the iFrames paper, two types of sites are used in malware distribution: landing sites, used to exploit or redirect a victim's browser, and malware distribution sites, used to download the payload to the victim's host.

Should an adversary compromise your site, he will likely turn it into a landing site by adding an invisible iFrame to one of the static web pages. The iFrame contains JavaScript exploit code to compromise your visitors' browsers. If your site hosts

---

[‡] Robert Richardson. "2007 Computer Crime and Security Survey"; *http://www.gocsi.com/forms/csi_survey .jhtml* (March 2008).

[§] Provos, Mavrommatis, Rajab, and Monrose. "All Your iFrames Point to Us," *http://research.google.com/ archive/provos-2008a.pdf* (March 2008).

user-contributed content such as page comments or a Wiki, the adversary can deploy exploit code directly without needing to first compromise your site.

Such techniques are commonly used in *clickjacking* and *banner ad malware* attacks. With clickjacking, the attacker overlays invisible malicious content on a page so that when the user clicks a link, he is actually clicking a URL under the hacker's control. With banner ads, attackers deploy multiple redirects via a series of banner ads, eventually directing users to a site hosting malware, which is automatically installed on the user's computer. This attack is possible because the primary (first redirect) banner ads are benign, drawing no attention when placed on leading search engines and popular sites.

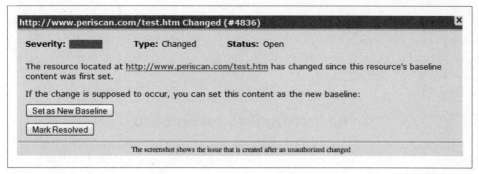

Figure 4-5. Example of website defacement detection by Periscan

Several tools and services can monitor for website defacements. These tools download each page and linked page, computing and storing a hash of the contents. They then periodically check the pages against the stored hash, calling out differences. Should the system discover a discrepancy, an administrator is notified to analyze the change and can then determine whether the change was authorized.

Site monitoring systems such as Catbird and Periscan (the latter shown in Figure 4-5) will watch your website for changes and alert you, allowing you to determine whether the change was authorized. For high-visibility systems such as your company's website, these tools allow you to augment the security monitoring of traditional tools such as a NIDS.

Practical Considerations for Selecting Targets

My Nokia smartphone drives me crazy alerting me to things that I don't need to know, that I can't do anything about, and that interfere with basic operations (such as making phone calls). One particularly annoying message, "Packet Data Started," often appears just as I'm beginning to dial a number, forcing me to acknowledge the message and restart my number dialing. Nokia thoughtfully included this feature to keep users

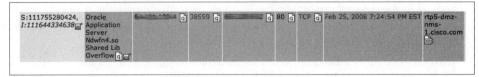

Figure 4-6. Oracle Application Server alert

without unlimited data plans informed that their phone is about to incur data charges. In my case, I have no need to see the message, since I have an unlimited data plan.

Don't configure your systems like my smartphone, collecting events for which you don't intend to take action. If you're able to fully monitor a system, but you can't do anything about the events that are generated, why bother monitoring it? Event collection is always necessary to support investigations. Even when you're not actively monitoring events, you must collect the events to support incident response. For targeted monitoring, however, events that you cannot mitigate are a distraction and should not be alerted. For example, Figure 4-6 shows an Oracle alert from a Security Information Manager (SIM) system.

The Importance of Secondary Events

"Because of the probability that an intruder will tamper with logs on a compromised system, it is important to safely collect copies of log messages in a centralized location."‖

Policy-based monitoring recommends a narrow, targeted approach to security monitoring that filters out all unrelated events. It requires deep analysis and tuning to weed out extraneous events. What should you do with the events shunned from your monitoring system? Store them in a safe place to support incident response and investigations.

When responding to a security incident, you will be focused on specific systems affected during a specific period. "Secondary" events that might normally be tuned out of a monitoring system take on new importance. These events are useful to illuminate a problem, aid in mitigation, trace activity, and attribute actions.

Collect as many events as you can store, and keep them for as long as you can. Archive all the security events you've collected to a server so that you can search them easily to support your incident response and investigation efforts. You can forward selected events in parallel to your security monitoring system for processing, where they will be analyzed or dropped based on the monitoring philosophy and procedures. Though policy-based monitoring recommends tuning out many events, it's still important to store all events (monitoring and secondary events) in archival storage for as long as possible.

‖ Richard Beijtlich. *Extrusion Detection* (Addison-Wesley Professional, 2005).

This event seems to detail an attack against an Oracle application server. If you know that you're not running Oracle application software, or that no one at the company can analyze the target systems for signs of attack or mitigate the problem, you're wasting your time alerting about the event.

Political blockades are another source of frustration for security monitoring. Although the security team may do an excellent job discovering security problems, getting the support teams to address the problems may be politically infeasible. Don't waste your time targeting such systems, if you can avoid it. Take peer-to-peer (P2P) software, for example. It's relatively easy to detect, and you can likely track down the individuals using it on the corporate network (e.g., to download movies). If management and human resources are unwilling to enforce policies governing its use, however, there's no benefit to tracking them down in the first place.

Recommended Monitoring Targets

To help you determine the best targets for security monitoring, you must build on your security policies and documented network topology, as we described in Chapters 2 and 3. Armed with those decisions and documented knowledge, you should conduct a structured assessment of the systems that comprise your company.

1. *Conduct a BIA*. Most enterprises have a team focused on business continuity and disaster preparation. Contact them and ask for the results of the most recent BIA, or ask them to conduct one in preparation for security monitoring. The BIA will produce, among other things, a list of critical IT systems. This is a good place to find targets for information security monitoring. The BIA will call out time-critical business processes and MTDs. Ordered by least amount of MTD, this list can become a priority order for applying security monitoring. Systems identified in such an assessment will likely include those responsible for revenue generation and those with high visibility profiles.

2. *Conduct an Information Technology Security Assessment (ITSA)*. This formal appraisal will analyze the security of your IT systems to determine areas of risk. It should use the policies and network knowledge that you've documented as a benchmarking standard. To that end, it will incorporate examination of regulatory compliance, contractual/legal requirements, and systems that access sensitive data. The ITSA will produce a list of action items as well as an assessment of risk presented by your IT systems. Using the results of this assessment, you can develop a list of systems that require targeted monitoring, especially where preventive controls are impractical to apply.

When you use the BIA and ITSA, a list of systems will emerge for which you can target security monitoring. The list will focus your monitoring on the business priorities and concrete risks your company faces. Based on our experience, the best targets for focused security monitoring are those that can cause the most harm, by way of data loss or revenue loss. Most companies should therefore monitor systems that do the following:

Access sensitive data
> Systems governed by regulatory compliance requirements that store intellectual property, or that store private data have enormous value, and should receive your primary attention.

Present a high risk profile
> Systems that present special risk to your company should be given careful attention for security monitoring. Normally, these systems are identified during a risk assessment or external audit.

Generate revenue
> Systems that are responsible for or directly impact revenue generation are obvious places to focus your security monitoring.

Choosing Components Within Monitoring Targets

Once you've selected the IT systems that need monitoring, you must analyze the component makeup of these targeted systems to select event feeds (which we'll cover in depth in the next chapter). To determine the component makeup, you should break down each system into its core elements, including the databases, web servers, application servers, and various hosts upon which these solutions run. Depending on the components in your solution, you might collect syslog messages from Unix/Linux servers (and from Windows servers, if they're configured with add-on packages), monitor the `AUD$` table on Oracle databases, analyze the `access_log` from Apache web servers, and so on.

Your system will also depend on complementary services such as authentication servers (LDAP, Active Directory, NIS+, etc.), caching servers, network attached storage (NAS), and so forth. Analyzing your policies will help you determine which complementary services you should monitor to complete your targeted monitoring plan. You should even consider network devices that serve access to your system; tools such as NetFlow and syslog can help trace device configuration changes, among many other things.

Example: ERP System

To illustrate the process of selecting components for monitoring, consider an installation of SAP R/3, which by definition is a three-tier architecture composed of presentation servers, application servers, and a database server. In a typical installation, the presentation and application servers would be load-balanced across two or more Linux servers. The database server is often a single Oracle database instance, load-balanced transparently using Oracle's native functionality to straddle instances across physical servers.

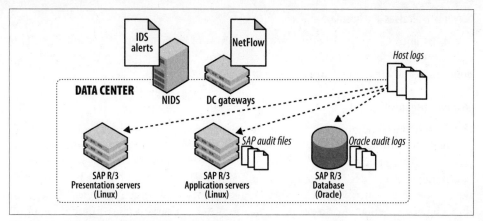

Figure 4-7. Where to collect logs for SAP R/3 monitoring

Assuming a total of five servers (two presentation servers, two application servers, and one database server), the following logs (also illustrated in Figure 4-7) provide rich event sources for security monitoring:

- Host syslog from all five servers
- NIDS logs from data center gateways
- Audit files from each application server
- Oracle audit logs from the Oracle 10g database, including specialized audit logging for master record tables
- Accounting audit trails (stored in database tables)[#]
- NetFlow logs into/from the data center

Gathering Component Details for Event Feeds

In Chapter 5, we'll detail how to begin selecting event sources from our various components into security monitoring systems. Now that we've selected our components to monitor, we have one final step to complete before we can begin to collect these events for analysis. Recall that in Chapter 3 we detailed the importance of documented network topology to provide context for security events. We'll put some of that knowledge into practice here, documenting the specific host and network information of the components in our targeted system.

[#] Dr. Peter J. Best. "Audit Trail Analysis for Fraud Control with SAP R/3." CACS 2005 ISACA Oceania Conference.

Server IP addresses and hostnames

We must enumerate the IP addresses and names of each server in our solution. This will allow us to determine the valid traffic patterns between servers and prioritize alerts containing the hostnames and IP addresses of target systems.

"Generic" user IDs

If we were to list the processes running on the servers, we would find the application components running with a generic user ID. This generic account should be "registered" to the application, and should run with very limited privileges. To monitor components effectively, we need to enumerate these user IDs. Once we build this list, we will be able to attribute behavior to registered user IDs, making it easy to see that the behavior is benign. For example, it's common to observe a large number of simultaneous connections in the database originating from the app server. We can safely ignore this event once it's clear that it's the "WebSphere" user connecting to Oracle via WebSphere's built-in connection pooling.

Generic accounts are used for running services, such as the "nobody" or "http" user that runs the Apache web server, or the "oracle" user which executes the database processes on the server. Generic accounts are also used to connect to other resources, such as the "connect as" user ID specified when connecting to the database.

Administrator user IDs

Legitimate system administration accounts must also be enumerated for similar reasons. This allows you to attribute administrative activity that may show up as security events. For example, if correlated security events show a user ID connecting to the database server and restarting the database listener, we can match the user ID with the "registered" database administrator for that database, documenting that it's in the scope of his responsibilities.

Database details

To effectively monitor the database, we must detail the database setup, enumerating the following information:

- Schemas used
- Accounts used (often the user ID for application access is different from and more limited than the schema owner account), along with account details such as the roles granted to the accounts
- Sensitive objects (tables, views, procedures)
- How activity is logged (normally logged to AUD$)
- Access controls in place (privileges granted to enumerated accounts against database objects)

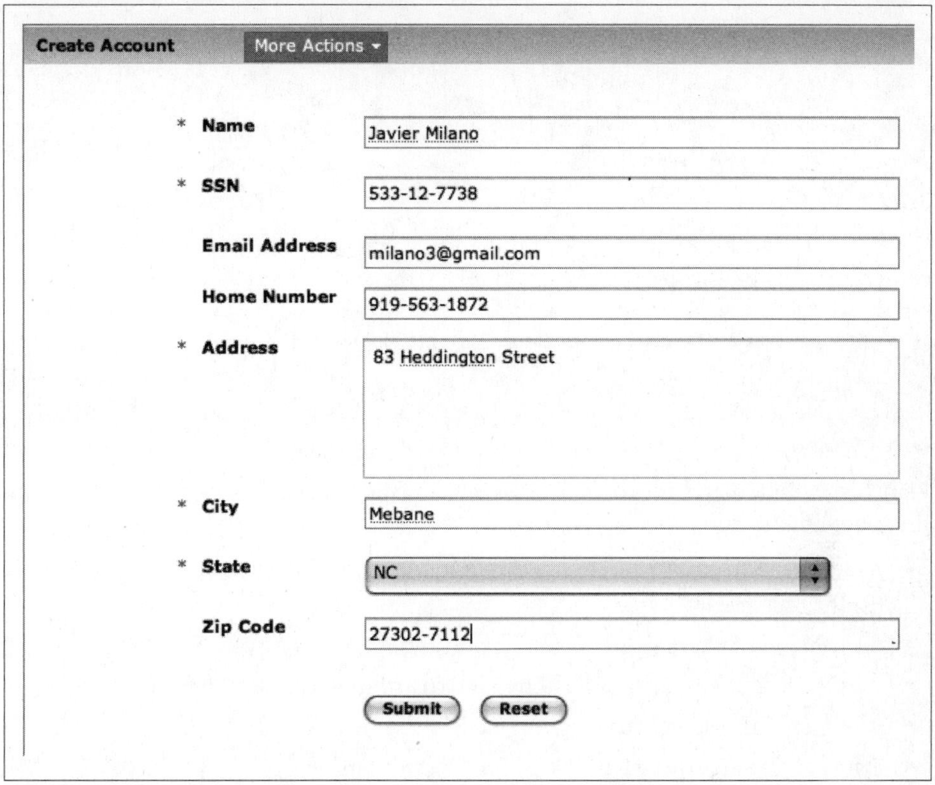

Figure 4-8. Blanco's account entry form

Access controls

Lastly, we must enumerate the access controls active in the environment. Access control systems such as firewalls and host IPS logs that can be useful for targeted monitoring. For example, if a firewall is logging DENY messages for users trying to directly access the database from outside the data center, analysis of those logs can prove useful in monitoring and defending the database. Similarly, security software, such as Tripwire and PortSentry, log messages that we can analyze to beef up our targeted monitoring capability.

Blanco Wireless: Selecting Targets for Monitoring

Like most wireless phone carriers, Blanco collects Social Security numbers from customers when setting up their accounts, illustrated in Figure 4-8. Blanco uses this information to request and report credit information from one of the large credit reporting services. As described in Chapter 2, Blanco has formed policies designed to protect such information and comply with government regulation.

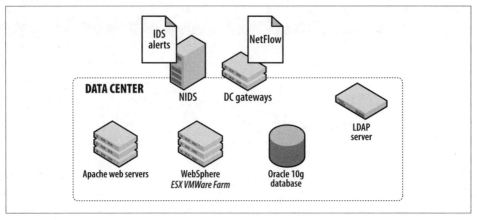

Figure 4-9. Blanco Wireless account management system

Blanco's account management system, shown in Figure 4-9, is composed of a common, three-tier architecture:

- Apache web servers running on three load-balanced Red Hat Enterprise Linux (RHEL) servers
- An IBM WebSphere Application Server running on a VMware ESX server farm
- An Oracle database (11*g*), clustered and distributed across two RHEL servers
- An OpenLDAP server running on one RHEL server
- Data center gateways (two Cisco IOS 7200 routers)
- A NIDS (one Sourcefire Snort server)

Although not pictured in Figure 4-9, load-balancing intelligence is built into the network, reducing the need for separate, specialized equipment.

Components to Monitor

In Chapter 5, we'll discuss the best event feeds to use for monitoring our target system. Our task for now, however, is to identify each component in the solution. Considering the two policies articulated in the section "Introducing Blanco Wireless" on page 10, we must configure monitoring for the Data Protection Policy and the Server Security Policy.

Data Protection Policy

To effectively monitor compliance with the Data Protection Policy, we must monitor the database for plain-text PII in storage, the network gear providing access to the database, and the database configuration, to make sure the database complies with our hardening specs. Our Data Protection Policy requires us to do the following:

- Audit data stored in the database via scheduled queries, or by monitoring the audit log of the database itself to ensure that the data is encrypted properly.
- Monitor network traffic, which is satisfied by NIDSs deployed at the data center gateway.
- Ensure that the database configuration is hardened. This will require a routine audit against the database, using a programmatic, scheduled vulnerability testing tool such as Nessus.

Server Security Policy

The Server Security Policy will require monitoring of every deployed server in our solution, including web servers, application servers, and database servers. We must also monitor the LDAP server to track account access, and must access network feeds (using NetFlow) to monitor traffic accessing the Internet from these servers.

Conclusion

Deep, proactive security monitoring is overwhelming and unproductive if it isn't targeted to specific systems. By selecting monitoring targets, you can narrow your focus to the most critical systems, making the most of your security monitoring equipment and staff. By spending the time to identify good monitoring targets, you will avoid wasting time on unproductive sources and, more importantly, improve your chances of finding the more serious security threats facing your enterprise. In the next chapter, we'll select event feeds for monitoring these selected target systems.

## CHAPTER 5

Choose Event Sources

In his book *The Paradox of Choice* (Harper Perennial), author Barry Schwartz states:

> Scanning the shelves of my local supermarket recently I found 85 different varieties and brands of crackers...285 varieties of cookies....13 sports drinks, 65 box drinks...and 75 teas...80 different pain relievers...29 different chicken soups...120 pasta sauces...275 varieties of cereal....

Schwartz examines durable goods such as electronics, then surveys life-impacting decisions regarding investments, insurance, retirement, and healthcare. Schwartz's thesis is that having too many choices can lead to anxiety, dissatisfaction, and regret. In contrast, the choices for event sources, though varied, are not nearly as complex as those lamented by Schwartz, and should by no means cause you mental distress!

Now that you've worked through the steps of defining security policies, you know your network, and you've selected your targets, you can build on that foundation by choosing your event sources. For the network, systems, and device types you are monitoring, there are several corresponding event data types from which to choose. For example, network routers can yield system status messages and access-list deny logs via syslog, interface statistics via Simple Network Management Protocol (SNMP), network telemetry via NetFlow, as well as deep packet inspection results.

Although it may be tempting to use all of these sources for security event monitoring, not all of them are appropriate. This chapter provides an overview of the various device types and their event sources, how you can collect them, and how you can inspect them for security policy violations. We've gathered the myriad choices into a subset of the best event sources to help you choose the appropriate sources quickly, without becoming overwhelmed in the sea of possible event feeds.

Event Source Purpose

To best determine which event sources to use for monitoring, you must determine *how* the event source will be used. Your purpose in collecting any event source will impact storage requirements, data retention policies, and collection intervals. An event source may be used for one or more of the following reasons:

Monitoring

Event collection consists of continuous streams of alerts recorded and *analyzed in real time or near-real time*. Correspondingly, systems selected for monitoring have a lower storage capacity and a shorter data retention policy because their window of focus is very near-term.

Incident response and investigation

Incident response and investigation typically requires a higher storage capacity and longer data retention policy. Events are often stored in a database for fast querying of recent event data (typically within one month). This time frame depends heavily on event rate and volume, with high volume and high event rates decreasing retention time and increasing storage requirements.

Regulatory compliance, legal requests, and forensics

Systems that fall under the purview of government regulation often have special compliance requirements. These include long-term, multiyear storage of event data, supporting investigations of legal matters such as lawsuits. Forensic investigations often extend to data from the distant past, requiring access to data located on tape backup, typically stored off-site. Access to this data is far from real time, as a restore from tape backup can require hours or days to complete.

Let's look at an example legal request. Say you received the following message from your legal counsel:

```
From: Dewey Cheatem (Legal Counsel)
Sent: Thursday, May 8, 2008 10:57 AM
To: CSIRT@blanco.com
Cc: Michelle Howe (Legal Counsel)
Subject: Computer Investigation Request
Importance: High

ATTORNEY/CLIENT PRIVILEGE:

Computer Security Incident Response Team,

We are currently involved in litigation from a former employee, Jermison Bue-
Snockley, who states that his co-worker logged in to his email and sent damaging
communications to friends, family, and complete strangers that resulted in a police
investigation into alleged illicit activities. We need to find out who accessed
Jermison's computers on the following dates:

October 10 2007
October 12 2007
November 4 2007
November 8 2007

In addition, Mr. Bue-Snockley claims that he was signed up for several email lists
of an adult nature from the following sites and dates:
```

```
~November 18th - lonely-adult-hookup.com
~November 20th - cannibis-exchange.com

Please investigate this incident and provide an initial writeup by the end of next
week.

Sincerely,

Dewey Cheatem, BigBucks Legal Services
```

How will you address this request? Is this data logged? For how long is it retained? Will it require a restore from backup? If you've collected all necessary event types, your response might resemble the following:

```
From: CSIRT@blanco.com
Sent: Friday, May 9, 2008 9:15 AM
To: Dewey Cheatem (Legal Counsel)
Cc: Michelle Howe (Legal Counsel)
Subject: Re: Computer Investigation Request
Importance: High

ATTORNEY/CLIENT PRIVILEGE:

Mr. Cheatem / Ms. Howe,

I've checked with our lead incident handler and we should be able to provide most
of this data by early next week. We won't be able to look directly at Mr. Bue-
Snockley's computer data for 3-5 business days as the backups have already been
taken offsite.

Regards,

Blanco CSIRT
```

The Blanco CSIRT team in this example has NetFlow, which recorded connectivity from a computer connecting to the IP addresses of the websites in question, as well as proxy logs showing the specific URLs used to register Mr. Bue-Snockley's email address to the alleged websites (plus several others that he may not yet have seen). In addition, the team has logon/logoff messages collected via syslog from all systems, including Mr. Bue-Snockley's. As it turns out, the CSIRT investigation found logon events that corresponded with the time frame of the NetFlow. It was later learned that an employee on Jermison's team logged into his computer and signed him up for the lists, in retaliation for a personal conflict.

Event Collection Methods

When selecting event sources for security monitoring, you must factor in the method for collection, since it will affect performance and timeliness. As depicted in Figure 5-1, there are two general methods for collecting events: push and pull.

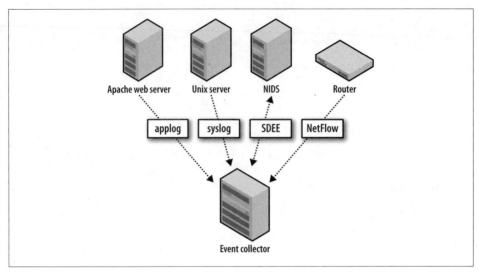

Figure 5-1. Event collection using both push and pull methods

The push method

With the push method, events are sourced from the device at specified intervals or in real time, as configured on the device itself. The event collector must be prepared to receive the events as they occur. Examples of this method include syslog messages, access-list (ACL) logs, and NetFlow.

The pull method

With the pull method, events are stored locally on the originating device and are retrieved by the collector. That is, the collector initiates collection of the event messages from the device that generates the events. Two common protocols for pulling event data are Security Device Event Exchange (SDEE) and the familiar SNMP. SDEE was developed by a working group at ICSA Labs, called the Intrusion Detection Systems Consortium (IDSC), which consisted of Cisco, Fortinet, INFOSEC Technologies, ISS, SecureWorks, Sourcefire, Symantec, and Tripwire, which provide the following information regarding the protocol:

> The Security Device Event Exchange (SDEE) specifies the format of the messages as well as the protocol used to communicate the events generated by security devices. SDEE is designed to be flexible and extensible so that vendors can utilize product specific extensions in a way that maintains messaging compatibility. SDEE builds upon the XML, HTTP and SSL/TLS industry standards to facilitate adoption by vendors and users by allowing them to utilize existing software that implements these standard interfaces.
>
> SDEE Data Format
>
> • Currently addresses the data format of intrusion detection/protection alerts
>
> • Events formatted as XML elements
>
> • Formats specified using XML schema. Supports schema validation

---

- Documented with schema annotations
- Designed to support extensions and to evolve while maintaining core compatibility
- Designed to be efficiently managed

SDEE Communication

- Extensible. Support for different transport bindings
- Currently specifies bindings to HTTP and HTTP over SSL/TLS
- Using existing technology eases adoption for providers and clients
- Support for authorization and encryption with existing HTTP and SSL/TLS
- Client initiated event retrieval

SDEE has been implemented on numerous security devices, such as firewalls, NIDSs, routers, and other network devices. It is also used on various host intrusion prevention system (HIPS) solutions, such as Cisco's CSA software. The SDEE standard, released in 2004, has been adopted primarily by Cisco, ISS, and Sourcefire, which developed and documented the standard. The IDSC was renamed the Network IPS Product Developers (NIPD) Consortium in March 2005.

The pull collection method offers some advantages over the push collection method, including event-rate control, preparsing (allowing you to specify the specific events types to pull), and guaranteed delivery. These benefits are illustrated in Figure 5-2. In contrast, most connectionless UDP-based push technologies, such as syslog, SNMP, and NetFlow, only provide "best effort" delivery. Consequently, pushed events offer less control, especially in controlling event rates; these messages are sent "fire and forget".

Event Collection Impact

Event collection can impact a system in several ways, most commonly in terms of system performance and storage requirements. Due to separation of duties, it's unlikely that you'll have responsibility for every device used in event collection. You may have direct control over the event collector, allowing you to configure storage space to meet your needs. The performance of the devices generating the events, however, is more likely under the control of IT system and network administrators. This obviously complicates the process of accessing the events, and requires careful planning to prevent disruption to your event collection.

Here are some important issues to consider when you're configuring event data feeds:

Impact on the sending device's CPU
Collect only necessary messages (many devices use a term such as *alert level*). This will minimize both the performance impact and the disk storage requirements. As we mentioned in Chapter 3, using standard templates for each type of device will speed the process for configuring devices.

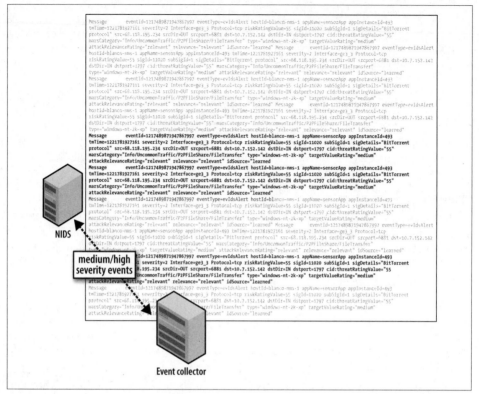

Message   eventId=1217489871947867997 eventType=evIdsAlert hostId=blanco-nms-1 appName=sensorApp appInstanceId=493
tmTime=1221781927161 severity=2 Interface=ge3_3 Protocol=tcp riskRatingValue=55 sigId=11020 subSigId=1 sigDetails="BitTorrent
protocol" src=68.118.195.234 srcDir=OUT srcport=6881 dst=10.7.152.142 dstDir=IN dstport=1797 cid:threatRatingValue="55"
marsCategory="Info/UncommonTraffic/P2PFileShare/FileTransfer" type="windows-nt-2k-xp" targetValueRating="medium"
attackRelevanceRating="relevant" relevance="relevant" idSource="learned" Message   eventId=1217489871947867997 eventType=evIdsAlert
hostId=blanco-nms-1 appName=sensorApp appInstanceId=493 tmTime=1221781927161 severity=2 Interface=ge3_3 Protocol=tcp
riskRatingValue=55 sigId=11020 subSigId=1 sigDetails="BitTorrent protocol" src=68.118.195.234 srcDir=OUT srcport=6881 dst=10.7.152.142
dstDir=IN dstport=1797 cid:threatRatingValue="55" marsCategory="Info/UncommonTraffic/P2PFileShare/FileTransfer"
type="windows-nt-2k-xp" targetValueRating="medium" attackRelevanceRating="relevant" relevance="relevant" idSource="learned"
Message   eventId=1217489871947867997 eventType=evIdsAlert hostId=blanco-nms-1 appName=sensorApp appInstanceId=493
tmTime=1221781927161 severity=2 Interface=ge3_3 Protocol=tcp riskRatingValue=55 sigId=11020 subSigId=1 sigDetails="BitTorrent
protocol" src=68.118.195.234 srcDir=OUT srcport=6881 dst=10.7.152.142 dstDir=IN dstport=1797 cid:threatRatingValue="55"
marsCategory="Info/UncommonTraffic/P2PFileShare/FileTransfer" type="windows-nt-2k-xp" targetValueRating="medium"
attackRelevanceRating="relevant" relevance="relevant" idSource="learned" Message   eventId=1217489871947867997 eventType=evIdsAlert
hostId=blanco-nms-1 appName=sensorApp appInstanceId=493 tmTime=1221781927161 severity=2 Interface=ge3_3 Protocol=tcp
dstDir=IN dstport=1797 cid:threatRatingValue="55" marsCategory="Info/UncommonTraffic/P2PFileShare/FileTransfer"
type="windows-nt-2k-xp" targetValueRating="medium" attackRelevanceRating="relevant" relevance="relevant" idSource="learned"
Message   eventId=1217489871947867997 eventType=evIdsAlert hostId=blanco-nms-1 appName=sensorApp appInstanceId=493
tmTime=1221781927161 severity=2 Interface=ge3_3 Protocol=tcp riskRatingValue=55 sigId=11020 subSigId=1 sigDetails="BitTorrent
protocol" src=68.118.195.234 srcDir=OUT srcport=6881 dst=10.7.152.142 dstDir=IN dstport=1797 cid:threatRatingValue="55"
marsCategory="Info/UncommonTraffic/P2PFileShare/FileTransfer" type="windows-nt-2k-xp" targetValueRating="medium"
attackRelevanceRating="relevant" relevance="relevant" idSource="learned"
Message   eventId=1217489871947867997 eventType=evIdsAlert hostId=blanco-nms-1 appName=sensorApp appInstanceId=493
tmTime=1221781927161 severity=2 Interface=ge3_3 Protocol=tcp riskRatingValue=55 sigId=11020 subSigId=1 sigDetails="BitTorrent
protocol" src=68.118.195.234 srcDir=OUT srcport=6881 dst=10.7.152.142 dstDir=IN dstport=1797 cid:threatRatingValue="55"
marsCategory="Info/UncommonTraffic/P2PFileShare/FileTransfer" type="windows-nt-2k-xp" targetValueRating="medium"
attackRelevanceRating="relevant" relevance="relevant" idSource="learned"
Message   eventId=1217489871947867997 eventType=evIdsAlert hostId=blanco-nms-1 appName=sensorApp appInstanceId=493
tmTime=1221781927161 severity=2 Interface=ge3_3 Protocol=tcp riskRatingValue=55 sigId=11020 subSigId=1 sigDetails="BitTorrent
protocol" src=68.118.195.234 srcDir=OUT srcport=6881 dst=10.7.152.142 dstDir=IN dstport=1797 cid:threatRatingValue="55"
marsCategory="Info/UncommonTraffic/P2PFileShare/FileTransfer" type="windows-nt-2k-xp" targetValueRating="medium"
attackRelevanceRating="relevant" relevance="relevant" idSource="learned" Message   eventId=1217489871947867997 eventType=evIdsAlert
hostId=blanco-nms-1 appName=sensorApp appInstanceId=493
riskRatingValue=55 sigId=11020 subSigId=1 sigDetails="BitTorrent protocol" src=68.118.195.234 srcDir=OUT srcport=6881 dst=10.7.152.142
dstDir=IN dstport=1797 cid:threatRatingValue="55" marsCategory="Info/UncommonTraffic/P2PFileShare/FileTransfer"
xp" targetValueRating="medium" attackRelevanceRating="relevant" relevance="relevant" idSource="learned"
eventId=1217489871947867997 eventType=evIdsAlert hostId=blanco-nms-1 appName=sensorApp appInstanceId=493
severity=2 Interface=ge3_3 Protocol=tcp riskRatingValue=55 sigId=11020 subSigId=1 sigDetails="BitTorrent
8.195.234 srcDir=OUT srcport=6881 dst=10.7.152.142 dstDir=IN dstport=1797 cid:threatRatingValue="55"
UncommonTraffic/P2PFileShare/FileTransfer" type="windows-nt-2k-xp" targetValueRating="medium"
attackRelevanceRating="relevant" relevance="relevant" idSource="learned"
Message   eventId=1217489871947867997 eventType=evIdsAlert hostId=blanco-nms-1 appName=sensorApp appInstanceId=493
tmTime=1221781927161 severity=2 Interface=ge3_3 Protocol=tcp riskRatingValue=55 sigId=11020 subSigId=1 sigDetails="BitTorrent
protocol" src=68.118.195.234 srcDir=OUT srcport=6881 dst=10.7.152.142 dstDir=IN dstport=1797 cid:threatRatingValue="55"
marsCategory="Info/UncommonTraffic/P2PFileShare/FileTransfer" type="windows-nt-2k-xp" targetValueRating="medium"
attackRelevanceRating="relevant" relevance="relevant" idSource="learned"

NIDS

medium/high
severity events

Event collector

Figure 5-2. Events pulled from a NIDS to a collector, allowing filtering as well as rate control

Event message detail

You should analyze messages generated by each event source to verify that the contents are useful and have the appropriate level of detail. For example, a login message that lacks the username and system name is not attributable; it lacks sufficient detail to allow immediate analysis and response. Such messages are not worth collecting, and they take up space without providing proportionate usefulness.

Event volume

The impact of event volume depends on the system's purpose, rate of utilization, and configured logging level. For example, a firewall that is logging deny messages via syslog can send messages at a rate that would quickly fill your collector's disk, decreasing the retention time for all of your event data.

Event logging configuration plays an important role in system performance, and can create a negative impact on the sending device's CPU. In denial-of-service (DoS) attacks, for example, a router configured with an access control entry logging denied packets could have its performance severely degraded. The impact can cascade to other devices as critical router processes such as routing itself (BGP peers dropping, etc.) are unable to function properly due to the lack of CPU resources. It is important to verify with your network hardware vendor what the CPU impact could be and whether there are ways to mitigate it, such as log rate limiting. Cisco, for example, gives the following advice when logging ACLs:[*]

> ACL logging can be CPU intensive and can negatively affect other functions of the network device. There are two primary factors that contribute to the CPU load increase from ACL logging: process switching of packets that match log-enabled access control entries (ACEs) and the generation and transmission of log messages.

You can mitigate this scenario with rate limiting and by increasing the logging interval:

> The `ip access-list logging interval 10` command limits log-induced process switching to one packet per 10 milliseconds, or 100 packets per second. The `logging rate-limit 100 except 4` command in the example limits log generation and transmission to 100 messages per second except for log levels 4 (warnings) through 0 (emergencies).

The configuration for rate limiting is quite simple; the following commands implement these suggestions for a Cisco router:

```
logging buffered informational
logging rate-limit 100 except 4
ip access-list logging interval 10
```

Cisco's NIDS solution also features a throttling mechanism to prevent a DoS attack on the sensor via its event summarization modes. The sensor will "summarize" a large burst of individual events into a meta-event that, although not specific (i.e., it doesn't include a source/destination IP), can prevent an overload from the same event. This thwarts attacks that attempt to overwhelm the security staff with alert volume, such as the "Stick" attack described by Coretez Giovanni.[†] You will still get the source and destination IPs in the first few events before the summarization starts.

Just as important as the performance impact on the sending device is the need to obtain the appropriate amount of detail in the collected messages. Too little detail and the messages are not useful; too much detail and the messages require unnecessary extra processing and storage. For example, a NIDS alert can contain data ranging from minimal contextual information to full packet capture (often called a *trigger packet*). In some situations, you may want to know exactly what packet(s) triggered the alert. You may also require the packet contents from the next few packets after the alert as well. For example, the following log message shows that host 10.0.30.209 connected to the HTTP port on 64.62.193.129. If that is all you need to know (the fact that one host connected to the other, similar to what you'll get with NetFlow), the message is sufficient with its timestamp and source/destination IP information.

```
20:29:54.829259 IP 10.0.30.209.1514 > 64.62.193.129.80
```

---

[*] See *http://www.cisco.com/web/about/security/intelligence/acl-logging.html*.

[†] See *http://packetstormsecurity.nl/distributed/stick.htm*.

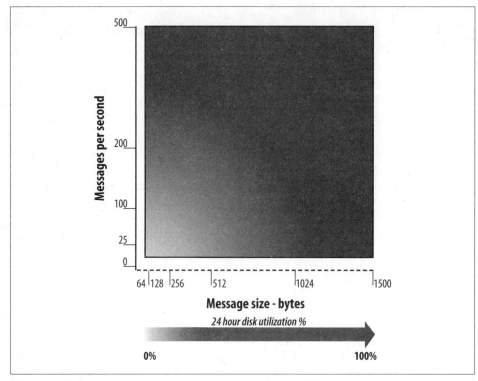

Figure 5-3. Relationship between event rate, message size, and disk utilization

However, you may want to know specifically what host 10.0.30.209 has requested from the web server. Those details need to come from the application log source, such as the `access_log` file from your proxy server:

```
20:29:54.829259 10.0.30.209 TCP_MISS/200 1393 GET http://
64.62.193.129/J05532/a4/0/0/pcx.js text/x-c DEFAULT_CASE-DefaultGroup <Busi,-
2.4,0,-,-,-,-,1,-,-,-,-,"Skipped"> -
```

Further inspection of the *pcx.js* file shows that it contained a set of commands passed to malware running on the host, instructing it to download an updated victim list for DoS attacks.

The last issue, event volume and rate, impacts your ability to retain data for the appropriate length of time, as depicted in Figure 5-3. As the event rate received and stored increases, the available disk space correspondingly decreases. Since disk resources are finite, your event collector will likely purge the alerts in a first-in, first-out (FIFO) fashion.

For example, if your event collector can hold 100 million alert messages on 50 GB of disk space and your event rate is normally 10 messages per second, it would take approximately 115 days (10 million seconds) to fill your disk (see Figure 5-4). If your rate

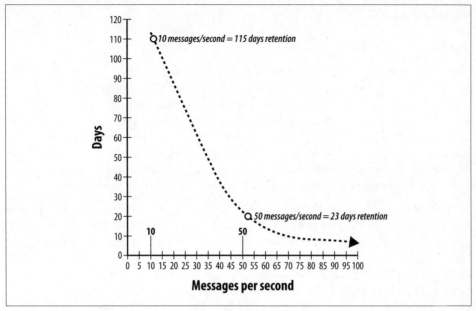

Figure 5-4. Relationship between message rate and retention time

spikes to 50 messages per second, the time to fill your disk will drop to 23 days. At 100 events per second, your retention time drops to 11 days!

This impact becomes clear when you consider an example such as a Cisco terminal server configured for TACACS+ authentication on TTY lines. The presence of noise on the async lines causes EXEC processes to be spawned and authentication attempts to be sent to the Authentication, Authorization, and Accounting (AAA) server:

```
07:44:26 aaa.blanco.com : [ID 259349 local0.warning] - User *(#$''''%^@ not found
07:45:26 aaa.blanco.com : [ID 259349 local0.warning] - User *(#$''''%^@ not found
07:45:28 aaa.blanco.com : [ID 450946 local0.warning] - User !_)*$^ not found
07:45:32 aaa.blanco.com : [ID 450946 local0.warning] - User !_)*$^ not found
07:45:48 aaa.blanco.com : [ID 259349 local0.warning] - User *(#$''''%^@ not found
07:46:33 aaa.blanco.com : [ID 624588 local0.warning] - User !_)*$^ not found
07:46:44 aaa.blanco.com : [ID 259349 local0.warning] - User *(#$''''%^@ not found
07:47:43 aaa.blanco.com : [ID 259349 local0.warning] - User *(#$''''%^@ not found
07:48:36 aaa.blanco.com : [ID 259349 local0.warning] - User *(#$''''%^@ not found
07:49:01 aaa.blanco.com : [ID 259349 local0.warning] - User *(#$''''%^@ not found
```

These errant authentication messages are essentially garbage data, filling up your log-files and wasting disk space. Such large volumes of messages can burst into your collector, severely degrading your capacity to retain log messages.

As you can see, controlling message rates from your devices is required to ensure that your data will be there when you need it, along with the necessary detail. One effective configuration technique is to allot a specific quota of disk space for each type of data source, controlling the impact of any single event source on the entire collection system.

Let's consider some specific examples of event data types, and the unique collection impact of each.

Host logs

The bulk of host logs includes OS system messages (such as those logged to */var/log/ system* or */var/log/messages*, etc.) that are written locally as configured by the system administrator. Host logs are almost always *push*ed to the collector. The event rate will vary among systems, depending on usage and logging level. A frequently used system configured to log at a very high level (such as debug logging) could cause the syslog daemon to use too many system resources. This will impact not only CPU performance, but local disk storage as well; the generated messages could fill the local system disk, causing the syslog daemon or the system itself to crash.

In Example 5-1, you can see several messages about system performance and application transactions. These messages contain critical details that you don't want to miss. Specifically, you can see user *drobbins* logging in as *root* with the sudo command. Using templates for host syslog configuration, as we will discuss in Chapter 6, can ensure that this information is logged. In this example, they were used to specify appropriate syslog settings to capture login messages for this server.

Example 5-1. Critical messages captured by correct logging configuration

```
Sep 18 03:05:24 blanco-linux installdb[80516]: started (uid 96)
Sep 18 03:05:24 blanco-linux installdb[80516]: Opened receipt database on '/' with
schema 17.
Sep 18 03:05:36 blanco-linux installdb[80516]: done. (0.007u + 0.005s)
Sep 18 19:06:02 blanco-linux sshd[84532]: Could not write ident string to UNKNOWN
Sep 18 20:59:19 blanco-linux sshd[26778]: Accepted keyboard-interactive/pam for
drobbins from 64.102.56.104 port 56475 ssh2
Sep 18 20:59:19 blanco-linux sshd(pam_unix)[26784]: session opened for user
drobbins by (uid=0)
Sep 19 21:22:40 blanco-linux sudo: drobbins : TTY=pts/1 ; PWD=/home/drobbins ;
USER=root ; COMMAND=/bin/su -
Sep 19 21:22:40 blanco-linux su[28169]: Successful su for root by root
Sep 19 21:22:40 blanco-linux su[28169]: + pts/1 root:root
Sep 19 21:22:40 blanco-linux su(pam_unix)[28169]: session opened for user root by
(uid=0)
Sep 18 22:29:13 blanco-linux syslog-ng[4791]: Log statistics;
processed='center(queued)=258910', processed='center(received)=129455',
processed='destination(messages)=129455',
processed='destination(console_all)=129455', processed='source(src)=129455'
Sep 18 22:30:07 blanco-linux ReportCrash[85189]: Formulating crash report for
process aex-pluginmanager-bin[85188]
Sep 18 22:30:07 blanco-linux ReportCrash[85189]: Saved crashreport to
/Library/Logs/CrashReporter/aex-pluginmanager-bin_2008-09-18-211606_blanco-
linux.crash using uid: 0 gid: 0, euid: 0 egid: 0
Sep 18 22:30:11 blanco-linux ReportCrash[85189]: Formulating crash report for
process aex-pluginmanager-bin[85190]
Sep 18 22:30:11 blanco-linux ReportCrash[85189]: Saved crashreport to
/Library/Logs/CrashReporter/aex-pluginmanager-bin_2008-09-18-211610_blanco-
linux.crash using uid: 0 gid: 0, euid: 0 egid: 0
```

```
Sep 18 22:30:15 blanco-linux ReportCrash[85189]: Formulating crash report for
process aex-pluginmanager-bin[85191]
```

Network IDS

Network IDS (NIDS), as we will discuss in Chapter 6, holds an advantage over other
event sources: it does not introduce extra load on the monitored systems. Each sensor,
however, has the potential to generate millions of alerts per day if it is left untuned.
You must ensure that your NIDS is properly tuned to prevent the collection and storage
of massive amounts of false-positive alerts.

You can process NIDS alerts via either a *push* or a *pull* technology, depending on its
configuration and features. Use caution when rolling out new signatures on the sensors,
however. A poorly written signature that matches expected traffic in your network can
generate so many false-positive alerts that your retention will be impacted, as we previously discussed. A well-tuned NIDS with appropriate context added from network
variables, as shown in Example 5-2 and discussed further in Chapter 6, is one of the
best sources of reliable security event data.

Example 5-2. CS-IPS alert generated by a web application server using BitTorrent

```
Message eventId=1217489871947867997 eventType=evIdsAlert hostId=blanco-ids-1
appName=sensorApp appInstanceId=493 tmTime=1221781927161 severity=2 Interface=ge3_3
Protocol=tcp riskRatingValue=55 sigId=11020 subSigId=1 sigDetails="BitTorrent
protocol" src=68.118.195.234 srcDir=OUT srcport=6881 dst=10.10.1.68
dstDir=WEBAPP_SERVERS dstport=1797 cid:threatRatingValue="55"
marsCategory="Info/UncommonTraffic/P2PFileShare/FileTransfer" type="windows-nt-2k-
xp" targetValueRating="medium" attackRelevanceRating="relevant"
relevance="relevant" idSource="learned"
```

NetFlow

NetFlow is collected via *push*, and represents a critical source of incident data with a
variety of uses for security. For instance, you can collect NetFlow in raw format to be
stored on disk, then relay it to systems that interpret trends or identify anomalies.
Because NetFlow is based on network traffic patterns, spikes in traffic, such as those
caused by a DoS attack, can negatively impact data retention. However, you can configure NetFlow collection with OSU flow-tools to drop (not store) certain traffic based
on source/destination address, source/destination ports, IP network, AS number, type
of service, prefix length, TCP flag, and other attributes. To drop traffic based on these
criteria, you can define your settings with the capture filter command. For more information, reference documentation via the `man flow-capture` command.

You should collect NetFlow at critical choke points, such as distribution gateways in
a data center and perimeter devices in your DMZ. You will find these choke points at
your network ingress/egress demarcations; they are often the division point of security
policies. In our experience with OSU flow-tools, we've found that 1.2 gigabits per second of bandwidth running at 200,000 packets per second (pps) can be stored in 600
GB of storage, allowing approximately 90 days of history.

Figure 5-5. A network without telemetry (photo courtesy of Jennifer Budenz for Photojenics)

Figure 5-5 depicts your visibility into a network without NetFlow. Without NetFlow, you are essentially blind to anything happening on your network. Did someone download the payroll database? Who uploaded a trojan file to the web server? How many times was the accidentally exposed data downloaded? The answer to all of these questions is "I don't know" without network telemetry such as NetFlow.

Application logs

Application logs can be extremely useful to collect, as they provide in-depth data about application activity between users and systems. Because application log formats vary so widely, identifying specific incidents and ruling out false positives can be challenging, even with the more popular applications such as Apache Web Server and the Squid proxy, with their large and well-established user base.

As you can see in Example 5-3, proxy server logs include varying levels of detail regarding HTTP transactions. The volume and detail of messages in a proxy server typically require third-party tools to analyze the logs, such as AWStats,[‡] Sawmill,[§] or Splunk.[‖]

[‡] *http://awstats.sourceforge.net/*

[§] *http://www.sawmill.net/*

[‖] *http://www.splunk.com/*

Example 5-3. Proxy server logs

```
1219859423.875 56 10.0.30.209 TCP_MISS/200 1085 GET
http://rad.msn.com/ADSAdClient31.dll?GetAd=&PG=IMUSVT - DIRECT/rad.msn.com
text/html ALLOW_WBRS-DefaultGroup <Adve,7.7,-,-,-,-,-,-,-,-,-,-,-> -
1219859448.869 42 10.0.30.209 TCP_MISS/200 7106 GET
http://edge1.catalog.video.msn.com/videoByTag.aspx?mk=us&ns=gallery&tag=im_f_35
-49&responseencoding=rss&p=im_f_35-49 - DIRECT/edge1.catalog.video.msn.com text/xml
ALLOW_WBRS-DefaultGroup <Stre,7.7,-,-,-,-,-,-,-,-,-,-,-> -
1219859840.488 16 10.0.30.209 TCP_MISS/200 384 HEAD
http://download.windowsupdate.com/v7/windowsupdate/redir/wuredir.cab?0808271800 -
DIRECT/download.windowsupdate.com application/octet-stream DEFAULT_CASE-
DefaultGroup <Comp,2.8,0,-,-,-,-,-,-,-,-,-> -
1219859846.256 105 10.0.30.209 TCP_MISS/200 368 HEAD
http://www.update.microsoft.com/v7/microsoftupdate/redir/muauth.cab?0808271800 -
DIRECT/www.update.microsoft.com application/octet-stream ALLOW_WBRS-DefaultGroup
<Comp,8.4,-,-,-,-,-,-,-,-,-,-,-> -
1219859857.528 20 10.0.30.209 TCP_MISS/200 368 HEAD
http://download.windowsupdate.com/v7/microsoftupdate/redir/muredir.cab?0808271800 -
DIRECT/download.windowsupdate.com application/octet-stream DEFAULT_CASE-
DefaultGroup <Comp,2.8,0,-,-,-,-,-,-,-,-,-> -
1219860033.536 53 10.0.30.209 TCP_MISS/200 1085 GET
http://rad.msn.com/ADSAdClient31.dll?GetAd=&PG=IMUSVT - DIRECT/rad.msn.com
text/html ALLOW_WBRS-DefaultGroup <Adve,7.7,-,-,-,-,-,-,-,-,-,-,-> -
1219860058.807 33 10.0.30.209 TCP_MISS/200 7029 GET
http://edge1.catalog.video.msn.com/videoByTag.aspx?mk=us&ns=gallery&tag=im_default&
responseencoding=rss&p=im_default - DIRECT/edge1.catalog.video.msn.com text/xml
ALLOW_WBRS-DefaultGroup <Stre,7.7,-,-,-,-,-,-,-,-,-,-,-> -
1219860068.892 62 10.0.30.209 TCP_CLIENT_REFRESH_MISS/200 364 GET
http://watson.microsoft.com/StageOne/Generic/mptelemetry/80072efe/endsearch/sea
rch/1_1_1593_0/mpsigdwn_dll/1_1_1593_0/windows%20defender.htm?LCID=1033&OS=5.1.2600
.2.00010100.2.0&DWVer=11.0.8163.0 - DIRECT/watson.microsoft.co
m text/html ALLOW_WBRS-DefaultGroup <Comp,8.4,-,-,-,-,-,-,-,-,-,-,-> -
1219860592.185 463 10.0.30.209 TCP_CLIENT_REFRESH_MISS/302 752 PROPFIND
http://services.msn.com/svcs/hotmail/httpmail.asp - DIRECT/services.msn.c
om text/html ALLOW_WBRS-DefaultGroup <Web-,7.7,-,-,-,-,-,-,-,-,-,-,-> -
```

Because application logs can be complex and capacious, you should only collect them from the most critical systems, including those under regulatory compliance requirements. If you're not in IT, you'll need to maintain a strong relationship with IT application owners, as you will need their cooperation and input to interpret the logs properly.

Database logs

As we will discuss further in Chapter 6, database logs are one of the most challenging event sources to collect. The most detailed, useful messages require corresponding auditing configuration in the database. In Oracle, for example, auditing features are complex and require careful configuration to produce useful results that will not harm database performance. Database messages require automated parsing for efficient collection and storage, as shown in Example 5-4. Since these systems are likely to house your most precious intellectual property and critical business data, good database logging can become one of the most powerful pieces of security data.

Example 5-4. Oracle database audit log

```
USERNAME        TERMIN ACTION_N TIMESTAMP        LOGOFF_TIME      RETURNCODE
--------------- ------ -------- ---------------- ---------------- ----------
SYS             pts/3  LOGOFF   02152013:221056  02152013:221651           0
VINAY           pts/1  LOGON    02152013:221651                         1017
SYS             pts/3  LOGOFF   02152013:221659  02152013:223022           0
SYS             pts/2  LOGOFF   02152013:222622  02152013:223508           0
VINAY           pts/1  LOGON    02152013:223022                         1017
```

Network ACL logs

ACL logs from network firewall devices can provide visibility into traffic that is dropped (deny logs) or passed (permit logs), based on the codified rules of the ACL. You must be extremely cautious when collecting ACL logs from network devices because the CPU utilization often impacts other device functions. This impact will vary among hardware platforms and operating systems, but devices that act as dedicated security hardware, such as commercial firewalls, are usually designed to handle such workload. Cisco IOS, the operating system used on most Cisco routers, allows you to define update thresholds and rate limiting to mitigate the impact of ACL logging. Due to the potential impact, however, be prepared with appropriate justification before enabling ACL logging on any devices not specifically dedicated to firewalling traffic.

Network ACL logs can also be an invaluable source of troubleshooting information. For instance, in Example 5-5, you can see why a partner's Win32 computers are not getting updates and patches from Microsoft; the traffic is being blocked.

Example 5-5. Cisco router ACL logs

```
Sep 23 18:32:39.029 IST: %SEC-6-IPACCESSLOGP: list BLANCO-XNET denied tcp
10.56.68.104(3288) -> 65.55.27.221(443), 1 packet
Sep 23 18:32:45.041 IST: %SEC-6-IPACCESSLOGP: list BLANCO-XNET denied tcp
10.56.68.104(3288) -> 65.55.27.221(443), 1 packet
Sep 23 18:33:07.173 IST: %SEC-6-IPACCESSLOGP: list BLANCO-XNET denied tcp
10.56.78.215(4108) -> 65.55.27.221(443), 1 packet
Sep 23 18:33:10.393 IST: %SEC-6-IPACCESSLOGP: list BLANCO-XNET denied tcp
10.56.78.215(4108) -> 65.55.27.221(443), 1 packet
```

Now that you have an idea of how events are collected, which event types are available, and what potential performance impact exists, let's look at how Blanco has chosen its event sources.

Choosing Event Sources for Blanco Wireless

Figure 5-6 shows the configuration of event source collection for Blanco's security monitoring. Notice that Blanco has configured NetFlow, NIDS, syslog, application logs, and database audit logs to detect policy violations affecting its selected monitoring targets.

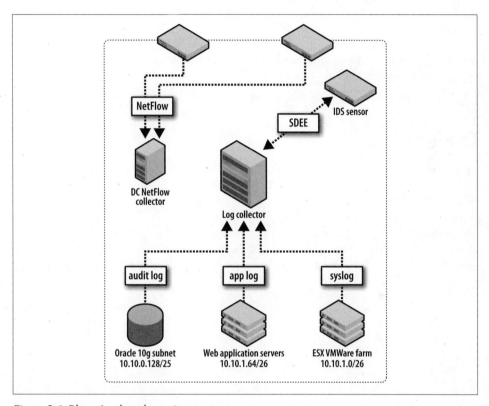

Figure 5-6. Blanco's selected security event sources

To monitor the targets selected in Chapter 4, Blanco has enabled NetFlow export from its data center routers, storing the flow data in a NetFlow collector system. Blanco's security team will use this data to identify connections sourced from critical systems toward external systems, and to identify large volume copies from database systems.

Blanco's Unix servers are configured to send messages to a syslog collection server. The security team will monitor these messages for direct privileged logins and privilege escalation via sudo. The servers are also configured to log and relay messages recording stops and starts for the web server, SSH, and database processes.

Blanco's NIDS is configured to monitor for known attacks against the Oracle suite. The security team has created custom signatures to identify:

- Unencrypted transmission of Social Security numbers (a policy violation)
- The `describe` command issued against any production database (an indication of database enumeration by someone unfamiliar with the schema)

Blanco's database administrators have configured the Oracle database servers to audit for:

- Queries against the `SSN` columns in the customer account table
- Queries against `V$` (another method for enumerating system users, processes, and connected applications)
- Direct privileged logins (`system` or `sys`)

Conclusion

Not every log message or event source proves useful for security monitoring, and even good event sources can overtax the devices you're monitoring. The work we've done to carefully choose event sources is our last *selection* step to configure policy-based monitoring. A clear understanding of how you intend to use and collect event sources will prioritize how you determine proper configuration of logging levels, select collection hardware, and set data retention policies. In Chapter 6, we will focus on strategies and methods to collect these event sources, filtering them into actionable security events.

CHAPTER 6

Feed and Tune

You awaken to find yourself adrift on a raft in the middle of the Atlantic Ocean. The sun is blazing and you are incredibly thirsty. You look around you and see that you are surrounded by cool water, but it is saltwater, not the freshwater you so desperately need. The abundance of the wrong kind of water is akin to the deluge of useless messages experienced from untuned security alert sources such as NIDS, syslog, and application logs. Instead of useful, actionable security alerts, the lifeblood of incident response, you get a mouthful of saltwater in the form of 2 million NIDS alerts a day. An untuned security event source will generate alerts irrelevant to your policies, quickly overwhelm your security monitoring staff, and reduce the availability of useful data in your collection systems. A properly tuned data source is core to your successful security monitoring, and in this chapter, we'll show you how to accomplish that.

We've defined our policies, documented knowledge of our network, and selected targets with event sources. Now we must convert this *metadata* into actionable incidents by mastering detection technology. We'll explain this central concept by first introducing a network intrusion detection framework. This framework will guide our deployment and tuning, building on the data we've gathered in previous chapters. We will follow that framework by showing how to use custom NetFlow queries with automated reporting to catch violation of security policies. We'll then explore the vast topic of syslog collection, trying to pull some useful information from what can be an overwhelming stream of data. Finally, we'll close this chapter by covering some challenges that are commonly encountered when trying to deploy these technologies in various environments.

Network Intrusion Detection Systems

Network intrusion detection is the subject of dozens of books, contentious debates within the security industry as to whether it is a dead technology, and numerous misperceptions. To define it, intrusion detection is a deep packet inspection technology that analyzes Internet Protocol (IP) packets, alerting when traffic matches malicious patterns. A network intrusion detection system (NIDS), often referred to as a *sensor*, is

101

a dedicated software or hardware technology that performs the function of intrusion detection. In our telephone analogy, a NIDS is aimed at listening for key phrases within the call itself, rather than reporting the call statistics in a phone bill, as NetFlow does. Many NIDS solutions are available, including the open source Snort, Bro, and OSSEC, and commercial hardware and software solutions from Cisco, TippingPoint, ISS, Sourcefire (the commercial version of Snort), and McAfee.

This chapter will explain how to get the most out of deploying a NIDS via a common design approach and a methodical tuning strategy based on network metadata. First, let's cover some NIDS basics, and then we'll drill deeper to explain tuning methodologies.

Packet Analysis and Alerting

In general, a NIDS device will perform some predefined action when certain criteria are met while inspecting IP packets. This may include everything from sending an alert to deploying an access control list (ACL) that blocks connectivity for the offending IP address. A NIDS primarily identifies attacks via pattern matching. This pattern matching can comprise either a single packet that matches a regular expression, such as ([Jj][Oo][Ii][Nn]), or more complex patterns requiring a sequence of matches in a particular order, as depicted in Figure 6-1. This is a greatly simplified view of how signatures work; dozens of books on intrusion detection are available that go into much more depth. For our purposes, it's important to remember that a NIDS is just a tool in your collection, not the be-all and end-all security mechanism, despite what NIDS vendors tell you.

More recent additions to NIDS capabilities include anomaly detection and OS fingerprinting. Anomaly detection works by analyzing "descriptors" of the data rather than the data itself, much like NetFlow. A baseline of "normal" is established and anything falling outside this baseline is tagged and alerted as an anomaly. OS fingerprinting works by analyzing specific characteristics of a given operating system's IP stack such that an OS can be reliably identified (similar to an "-O" switch with the familiar Nmap network scanning utility). Cisco's CS-IPS 6.x software can take advantage of this feature and adjust the confidence level or severity of the alert based on whether the attack applies to the victim OS, such as a Linux attack destined for a Windows server. A NIDS can also add further contextual information into its alerts, automatically changing confidence levels, which increases the fidelity of the alerts.

Network Intrusion Prevention Systems

A network intrusion prevention system (NIPS) is a NIDS deployed in the path of network traffic ("inline"), rather than passively inspecting it. Figure 6-2 shows a logical view of the two alternatives.

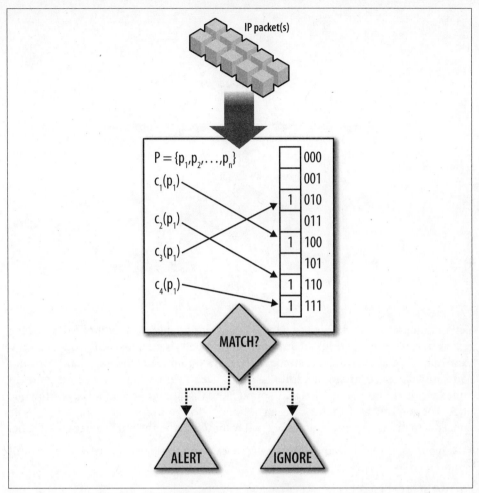

Figure 6-1. Pattern matching methodology used by a NIDS

Deploying this technology inline allows the NIPS to drop malicious traffic, hence preventing the attack and protecting end hosts. Many details must be considered before choosing between a NIDS and a NIPS. The following section provides analysis criteria to guide your decision for any given environment.

Intrusion Detection or Intrusion Prevention?

Security vendors commonly urge intrusion prevention solutions. To decide whether to deploy such a solution, you must consider many factors, including your goals for the solution, your network topology, and your availability requirements. Two core criteria dominate your criteria for deciding on a NIPS versus a NIDS: availability requirements and span of control.

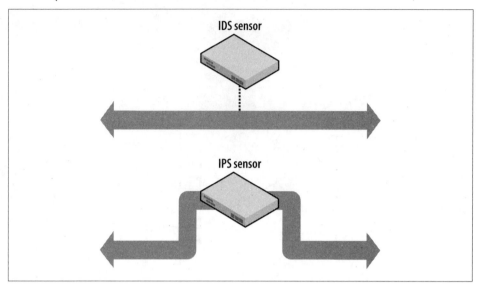

Figure 6-2. Comparison of the network deployment scenarios for NIPS versus NIDS

Let's assume you have decided to deploy your solution inline, but your IT networking team wants to know more about any potential impacts this deployment would have on availability. To answer this question, you will need to understand your hardware and software failure scenarios. In addition, you'll need to understand those scenarios in your specific environment. This may sound like a daunting task, but it is a worthwhile endeavor and much of the work is already done for you. You can apply these basic concepts to just about any technology you want to put "in the line" of network traffic.

First, your vendor will need to answer the following questions, shown here in order of importance:

1. What is your hardware's MTBF?
2. Does your solution have hardware-based "fail-open" capabilities?
   a. How long does fail-open take?
3. Does your solution have software-based "fail-open" capabilities?
   a. How long does fail-open take?
   b. Is it admin-configurable?

These variables provide some objective basis for your analysis. Now, let's veer off the beaten path a bit and play with some fun mathematics in the realm of availability theory. The method for calculating the availability of a given component or series of components is expressed in *Mean Time Between Failures* (MTBF) and *Mean Time To Repair* (MTTR). The most common way to express this availability calculation is by percentage. It is commonly referenced by network professionals using the term "9s", illustrated

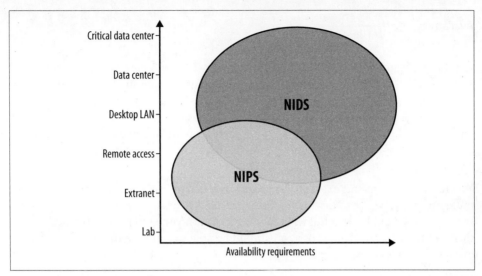

Figure 6-3. Availability's impact on NIDS versus NIPS decision

in Table 6-1. To calculate annual availability, you can multiply your targeted 9s value by 525,600 minutes per year. The second column of Table 6-1 illustrates the downtime that results.

Table 6-1. Downtime corresponding to various level of "9s" availability

Availability	Annual downtime
90% (one 9)	36.5 days
99% (two 9s)	3.65 days
99.9% (three 9s)	8.76 hours
99.99% (four 9s)	52 minutes
99.999% (five 9s)	5 minutes
99.9999% (six 9s)	31 seconds

Your availability requirements must be met by your solution; if downtime is very costly to your business environment, your NIPS solution must limit downtime. Figure 6-3 shows common availability requirements. Uptime requirements are often lowest in lab or testing environments, but very high in production environments such as data centers.

Availability

Availability is a time value calculated in terms of MTBF and MTTR. The MTBF number is provided by the manufacturer and is expressed in hours. The MTTR number, variable and dependent upon the specific network, is also expressed in hours. The simple equation is as follows:

$$\text{Availability} = \frac{\text{MTBF}}{\text{MTBF} + \text{MTTR}}$$

A device with an MTBF of 175,000 hours and an MTTR of 30 minutes has a calculated annual availability of 525,598 minutes, which equals 1.52 minutes of downtime. Appendix C provides more detail and complex examples regarding these calculations. The real challenge in computing the availability of any system or network is in understanding the MTTR. This value is unique to your environment, affected by variables such as routing protocol convergence time and/or spanning tree convergence time, depending on your topology.

You need to understand exactly what happens when an inline device fails to forward traffic properly. This can be due to power, hardware, or other environmental failure. Ideally, you would build a full test environment with your intended NIPS design and then test the different scenarios. You should be able to estimate the impact of failure by analyzing a few key variables:

Interface fail-open
> How long does it take for a set of inline interfaces to begin passing traffic after a failure? Will traffic be queued or dropped?

Layer 3 (L3) environment failures
> When your NIPS is deployed on a routed network segment, how long does your routing protocol take to converge?

Layer 2 (L2) environment failures
> When your NIPS is deployed on a physically redundant L2 network segment, how quickly will the spanning tree converge?

Nonhardware sources of downtime. We're doing these calculations based purely on hardware failure calculations, so you must also consider software failure, environmental considerations, and human error. Compared to other network devices, a NIPS has a much higher number of software updates (signatures, typically). Application of these software updates always introduces the possibility of software failure or human error that could result in an unexpected outage.

NIPS and network bandwidth. A coworker who designs networks for Cisco customers sums up this issue with the following statement: "Packet inspection capacity always trails L2/L3 forwarding capacity." This rule applies to all network devices that add processing beyond simple connection state, such as firewalls and NIPSs. NIPS vendors typically support physical interface media, but not line-rate inspection for all interfaces in the NIPS. For example, several vendors were quick to include support for IEEE 802.3ae 10 Gbps interfaces, but their systems clearly could not *inspect* 10 Gbps. With this in mind, you must keep the aggregate traffic you are trying to push through an inline system below the vendor's rated capacity. Keep in mind that traffic can be "bursty," such as when backups or database copies traverse the network. Such bursts can cause your

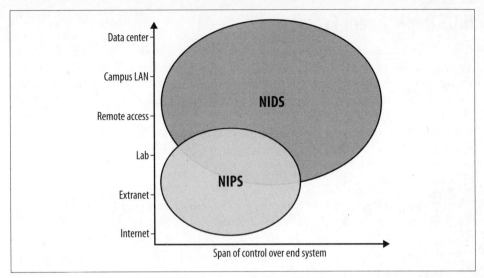

Figure 6-4. Span of control and relationship to NIDS versus NIPS

aggregate traffic to exceed the NIPS's inspection and forwarding capability, which may in turn cause it to drop traffic and create vague "network problems."

High-Availability NIPS Using Physical Redundancy

We don't intend to imply that you cannot deploy a highly available inline NIPS. On the contrary, vendors such as ISS and Cisco illustrate several designs to support high availability. Most of these designs rely on L3 or L2 network segment redundancy with the forwarding protocol's convergence time driving MTTR. This adds additional complexity, which is often more than network operators are willing to accept.

Span of control

Availability may not be the largest driver for all of your environments. Let's consider another data point: your organization's span of control over the network-connected endpoints. For example, you may have a partner or vendor on-site that supports its own servers and desktops. Because these systems are not owned or supported by your IT staff, you will have limited knowledge about the security policies governing them. On Windows systems: do users run as Administrator? Has antivirus software been installed? Are the systems promptly patched? Since these systems don't belong to you, your span of control is limited. Another example of a limited span of control scenario is a development lab where the same best practices and controls that apply in your production IT-supported environments cannot be implemented. Figure 6-4 represents this concept graphically.

NIDS Deployment Framework

Deploying a NIDS can be somewhat daunting, but if you begin with a common framework that applies to your environments, it becomes manageable and, dare we say, almost easy. This framework starts by defining a finite set of designs that should address your different network environments. For simplicity and brevity, we'll look at the DMZ, the data center, and the extranet. You can modify these designs to suit other environments as well. The key is to try to apply the framework to the environment based on your knowledge of its function and topology, as we described in Chapter 3. Implement the framework via the following steps:

Analyze
> Size your solution and select components based on the traffic requirements, function, and user base for the target environment.

Design
> Choose from your list of designs and modify for any differences in network topology or function.

Deploy
> Select and properly deploy hardware according to the design, making sure to accommodate any unique requirements.

Tune and manage
> Adjust sensor configuration settings to eliminate false positives, build network intelligence into your alerts, deploy new attack signatures, and create custom signatures.

Analyze

You must consider several factors when taking on the task of analyzing any given environment. As you will see in the examples that follow, each factor will have varying levels of impact, with aggregate bandwidth and network topology carrying the most weight.

Aggregate bandwidth
> To assess aggregate bandwidth, sum the utilization rates on your networks of interest. It's best to do this with a tool that can record utilization over time via graphs, such as the Multi Router Traffic Grapher (MRTG) discussed in Chapter 3. These graphs allow you to compare history, to help you spot the maximum traffic rates.

Network traffic mix
> Next, you need to understand the network traffic mix. By *network traffic mix*, we're talking about whether this is an Internet DMZ network, a remote access network, or a data center network, as this will likely define the security policies expected for the network. In addition, you need to know what kind of traffic traverses the network. What characterizes the traffic? Is it HTTP or HTTPS? Is it IPSEC virtual

private network (VPN) traffic? The answers to these questions will impact the location of the sensor in the network, particularly when encrypted traffic is present, as it is not possible to inspect the encrypted packet content with a NIDS. (You'll need to position it where the traffic is plain text, if that's possible.)

Network topology

Analysis of network topology requires good documentation, so it will likely require interaction with those who designed and support the environment. Important factors to consider include path redundancy and routing behavior. You need to understand whether traffic always traverses a preferred path or whether the traffic is load-balanced across multiple links. This information is necessary to help you avoid asymmetry in your traffic view, as illustrated in the sidebar, "The Trouble with Traffic Asymmetry." The network topology diagram in Figure 6-5 will serve as a model for some basic examples.

The Trouble with Traffic Asymmetry

When redundancy is designed into a routed network, traffic is often load-balanced across multiple links. Packets from a single conversation can be routed across more than one link. The NIDS's ability to match stored patterns is based on the assumption that it has inspected every packet within a conversation. When the NIDS sees only part of a conversation (because one of the redundant links is not being monitored), it cannot match the patterns contained within the rule set. To prevent such problems, you must design your solution so that the NIDS receives a copy of the entire conversation.

In Figure 6-5, you can see that gateways GW1 and GW2, which route between networks A and B, has seven links connecting the two networks. We've measured the bandwidth utilized per link over a period of one month, and represented it in Table 6-2.

Table 6-2. Bandwidth analysis for the links in Figure 6-5

Link	Speed	Average	Maximum
1	1 Gbps	280 Mbps	500 Mbps
2	1 Gbps	250 Mbps	440 Mbps
3	1 Gbps	100 Mbps	130 Mbps
4	1 Gbps	100 Mbps	130 Mbps
5	1 Gbps	10 Kbps	10 Kbps
6	100 Mbps	70 Mbps	90 Mbps
7	100 Mbps	15 Mbps	15 Mbps

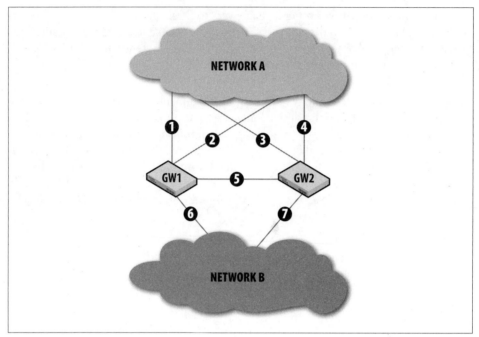

Figure 6-5. Example network topology

To inspect all traffic traversing both GW1 and GW2 from Network A, you can find the required bandwidth by calculating the sum of the *average bandwidth* used on links 1, 2, 3, and 4, which equals 730 Mbps:

280 Mbps + 250 Mbps + 100 Mbps + 100 Mbps = 730 Mbps

The NIDS solution would potentially need to handle maximum data rates above 1 Gbps to handle increasing utilization over time or spikes in traffic. If we reorient the goal for this NIDS deployment to watch all traffic from Network B through the same gateways, we can calculate the required bandwidth via the sum of the average utilization for links 6 and 7, just over 100 Mbps. Key to both scenarios is the successful capture of *bidirectional traffic* on all pertinent interfaces. Failure to do so will lead to asymmetric traffic that will confuse the sensor, as only part of a host-to-host conversation will be seen, which will ultimately decrease the likelihood of the sensor alerting on an attack.

Design

The level of standardization in your various networks will have an enormous impact on how few or how many network designs you will need. Indeed, the simplified deployment of a service into a homogeneous network environment is one of the many underestimated returns on investment of standardization.

Based on our example analysis of the environment in Figure 6-5, we know we will need an inspection capability of approximately 1 Gbps. Three primary factors will influence the specific hardware design:

Physical location
> In Figure 6-5, if gateways GW1 and GW2 are in the same physical location (such as a single rack), we probably won't have to deal with complications such as the availability of inter-building fiber cabling. If instead the gateways are geographically separated, we may need to acquire inter-building cabling, or use remote traffic copying features, such as Cisco's RSPAN.[*]

Interface options
> In Figure 6-5, we need to capture the traffic on gateways GW1 and GW2 connecting Network A to Network B. If we map interfaces 1:1 (for simplicity, we'll assume receive (Rx) and transmit (Tx) totals are less than 1 Gbps), we will require a sensor with four 1 Gbps interfaces.

Network device capabilities
> In Figure 6-5, gateways GW1 and GW2 must support the ability to copy traffic to an interface. If the gateways do not support this feature, you can use a network tap to capture the traffic. (Note that a tap is often a single point of failure and can negatively impact your availability.) Alternatively, you could capture traffic at the devices in Network A.

A Note on Taps

Despite what you might hear from vendor sales staff, a tap is a piece of hardware placed directly in the physical media path. You must consider the MTBF and MTTR of the tap hardware when determining the availability of your solution.

DMZ design

In Figure 6-6, 1 Gbps interfaces connect ISP gateways (ISP GW1 and ISP GW2) to DMZ gateways (DMZ GW1 and DMZ GW2). If our goal is to capture all Internet traffic traversing the DMZ, we must capture the interfaces connecting to links 1, 2, 3, and 4. If our ISP links to the Internet are 155 Mbps (ISP GW1) and 200 Mbps (ISP GW2), our inspection capacity must be at least 355 Mbps. A NIDS sensor with four 1 Gbps interfaces should accommodate 355 Mbps just fine. If instead our goal was to inspect traffic traversing the DMZ from the corporate network, we only need to mirror traffic for links 6 and 7 to the sensor. In either case, we must have bidirectional traffic (both Rx/Tx) for successful inspection.

This is a fairly simple example and assumes that we have no e-commerce or other DMZ networks. Let's consider a more complex setup.

[*] *http://www.cisco.com/en/US/docs/switches/lan/catalyst6500/catos/5.x/configuration/guide/span.html*

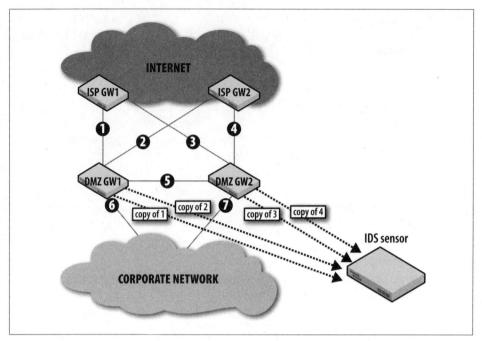

Figure 6-6. Placement of NIDS to inspect a DMZ with redundant ISP connections

Figure 6-7 depicts a DMZ environment with an e-commerce network similar to what you'd find in many organizations. This could also represent public-facing services deployed in a DMZ. Assuming that you want to inspect all ingress/egress traffic for the e-commerce and corporate networks, you would need to copy traffic from links 6 and 7 to one sensor, and copy traffic from links 8 and 9 to a second sensor. Remember again to collect bidirectional traffic on each link.

Another approach (in which you could use a single sensor) to ensure that we have a full view of traffic is to capture Rx-only on all interfaces of DMZ gateways GW1 and GW2 (that is, Rx for interfaces 1 through 9). This Rx-only method will work well in complex environments where there are a large number of network links to inspect.

Data center design

Figure 6-8 depicts a data center network connected to the corporate backbone by 10 Gbps uplinks via redundant data center gateways. Within the data center, each server network has 10 Gbps uplinks to the data center gateways. This high-bandwidth environment pushes an aggregate of nearly 1 Tbps (terabits per second) within the access layer (intra-segment traffic). Inspecting just the uplinks to the data center gateways could require 80 Gbps of inspection capacity, which is well beyond the rated capacity of any vendor's NIDS hardware today.

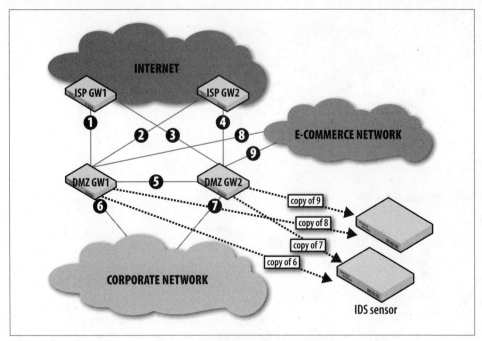

Figure 6-7. Configuration of NIDS to accommodate a more complex DMZ network

You can address this common network scenario by focusing your solution on the data center gateways, leveraging their placement as a network choke point and only inspecting the ingress and egress traffic to the data center environment. Even with this choke point-focused approach, speeds can potentially reach the 40 Gbps level. Such high-bandwidth requirements are normally met by load-balancing traffic across a farm of NIDS sensors. Several vendors—among them, Top Layer Networks—offer load-balancing solutions. Again, the most important point here is to be sure to get bidirectional traffic and ensure that the load-balancing algorithm used is deterministic so that all host–host conversations go to a single sensor.

The data center design in Figure 6-8 allows inspection of all traffic entering and leaving the data center from the corporate network and eliminates any inspection asymmetry introduced by the redundant links. The backbone uplinks from the data center gateways (links 1 through 4) are copied to a NIDS load balancer and distributed to the sensor farm. We wouldn't dare implement this inline at the data center gateways (or distribution layer), due to the high bandwidth requirements and asymmetric paths.

Extranet design

Extranet monitoring is especially challenging, as we have less control over the end systems, users, and policies. Figure 6-9 depicts extranet connectivity with four different partners, all connected via redundant WAN links. For this scenario, we'll assume that

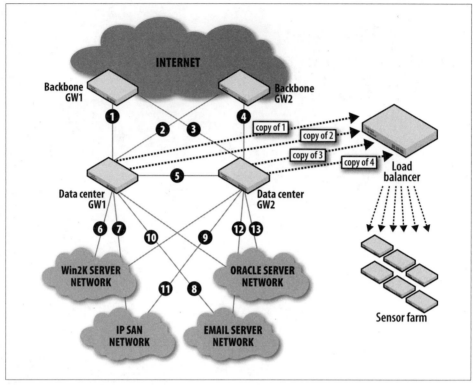

Figure 6-8. A data center network design—demonstrating choke point collection and sensor load balancing

physical and network access policies are poorly enforced, making it a good candidate for a NIPS deployment.

Network links 1 through 4 have an average aggregate bandwidth utilization of 90 Mbps. To maintain the redundancy of the network links, you can deploy a single sensor with four pairs of 100 Mbps interfaces (eight total interfaces). This inline sensor—a NIPS— is configured via specific rules to protect the corporate network from attacks sourced from these partner networks. The downside? The NIPS sensor is now a single point of failure, adding network provisioning and priority support to the responsibilities of your team.

Deploy

If you've analyzed your needs and designed your solution according to our advice, you should now be well prepared to deploy your NIDS. In this section, we'll share our experience with some often overlooked "gotchas" that can delay your installation.

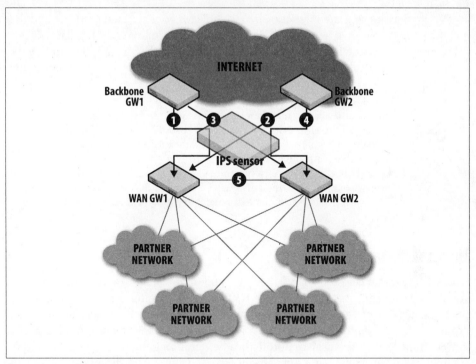

Figure 6-9. Sensor placement and connectivity for extranet

Asymmetric routing

As discussed throughout this chapter, network path redundancy, a common feature of high-availability design, introduces multiple paths and can confuse your NIDS with traffic asymmetry. You must address this in your design to prevent asymmetry from affecting your NIDS.

Jumbo frames

If jumbo frames are enabled on the network segments you're monitoring, make sure your selected NIDS hardware supports them.

Application acceleration

Network optimization solutions such as Cisco's Wide Area Application Services (WAAS)[†] are used to accelerate application performance over the WAN. To provide such acceleration, they modify TCP settings and compress data, which causes packets to appear "garbled" to the NIDS. If such optimization has been deployed on your target networks, you must ensure that the NIDS' traffic collection is outside the optimized path.

---

† *http://www.cisco.com/en/US/products/ps5680/Products_Sub_Category_Home.html*

Physical media

Verify that appropriate interfaces are available for your selected platform and that the correct media types are present. For example, if your NIDS has LC-type connectors for the fiber 1 Gbps interface, make sure the install location has LC connections available, or has LC-SC, LC-MTRJ, or other appropriate patch jumpers.

 You will also need to maintain agreements with the network support organizations to ensure that your data capture sources are reliably maintained through troubleshooting and hardware/software upgrades. Having a NIDS as a standard part of your network architecture can be extremely beneficial, because when new technologies, topologies, or designs are considered, the NIDS will be a part of that consideration. Chapter 7 introduces techniques for maintaining these important event feeds.

Tune and Manage

Once you've completed the analysis, design, and deployment of your NIDS solution, you must begin the ongoing process of tuning and managing the solution. Without tuning, your sensors will generate vast numbers of false positives, overwhelming monitoring staff, and eventually causing the NIDS to be ignored. Many vendors claim their NIDS solutions tune themselves automatically, reminding me of late-night television commercials where engines are run without oil or red wine stains disappear before your eyes. It's simply not true: tuning is necessary for the lifetime of the NIDS deployment.

Tune at the sensor

To begin tuning your NIDS, evaluate the most frequent alerts directly on the sensor. Cisco's IPS software versions 5 and 6 allow you to look at the sensor statistics with the command `show statistics virtual`:

```
blanco-dc-ids-1# show statistics virtual
Virtual Sensor Statistics
    Statistics for Virtual Sensor vs0

Per-Signature SigEvent count since reset

        Sig 3159.0 = 12
        Sig 5829.0 = 17
        Sig 5837.0 = 22
        Sig 5847.1 = 2
        Sig 6005.0 = 281
        Sig 6054.0 = 49
        Sig 6055.0 = 7
        Sig 3002.0 = 2045681
```

Notice that signature number 3002.0 has fired 2 million times since the sensor was reset (which was probably at the last power cycle). Signature 3002.0 is a *TCP SYN Port*

Sweep. Based on the description (which we looked up on Cisco's website), it could easily be attributed to a "benign trigger" (a false positive), such as the network activity generated by network management tools. We'll need to look further to determine what's causing this signature to fire. On the sensor, we can track down which IP addresses have been causing this alert to fire in the past minute via the show event alert command:

```
blanco-dc-nms-1# show event alert past 00:01:00 | include 3002

evIdsAlert: eventId=11732550926195158843 severity=high vendor=Cisco
  originator:
    hostId: blanco-dc-nms-1
    appName: sensorApp
  time: 2007/04/23 18:50:47 2007/04/23 18:50:47 UTC
  signature: description=TCP SYN Port Sweep id=3002 version=S2
    subsigId: 0
    marsCategory: Info/Misc/Scanner
    marsCategory: Probe/FromScanner
  interfaceGroup: vs0
  vlan: 0
  participants:
    attacker:
      addr: locality=IN 10.6.30.5
    target:
      addr: locality=IN 10.9.4.4
      port: 80
```

The command output points to 10.6.30.5 as the source of this traffic. Because you know your network, you're aware that this is a network management device. You can now tune the sensor to suppress alerts for this signature when the source matches the address of the network management device:

```
blanco-dc-nms-1# conf t
blanco-dc-nms-1(config)#
service event-action-rules rules0

filters insert drop_mgt_system_alerts
signature-id-range 3002
attacker-address-range 10.6.30.5
victim-address-range $IN
actions-to-remove produce-alert
```

The preceding configuration stanza suppresses alerts from signature ID 3002, but only when the source IP address matches 10.6.30.5. Later in this chapter, we will explain how to use network and host variables, enabling us to apply powerful tuning across our NIDS deployment.

Tune at the SIM

If you have a Security Information Manager (SIM), you can leverage it to further tune your NIDS. Many vendors sell SIM products, including ArcSight, netForensics, and Cisco. Query your SIM for the most frequent events over a 24-hour period, then investigate the cause, beginning with the most frequent events (the really noisy stuff). Wash, rinse, and repeat. Once you're satisfied that you've suppressed as many false positives as possible (and you're satisfied with your data retention), you're halfway there.

You can use the SIM and the sensor to verify the impact of new signature rollouts. For example, if you pushed out a custom signature that had poorly written regex, you could match on traffic that is benign and cause thousands of false positives. You can make this verification at the sensor or at the SIM, with verification at the SIM becoming increasingly easier as the number of sensors you have grows.

Network variables

In Chapter 3, we demonstrated the power of network taxonomy and telemetry to add contextual understanding to your IP address space. You can turn this enumeration of network types into "network variables" that you can use in your NIDS configuration to provide context to your alerts. Several NIDS products support this capability, including the open source Snort software. To configure your NIDS properly, begin by creating network variables from the network metadata you've gathered. To add more granular context, create host variables using the same criteria. Network and host variables will provide the context needed to create actionable NIDS alerts. Figure 6-10 depicts a simple IP address allocation: Campus, Data Center, Partner, DMZ, and Remote Access networks.

Using the subnets referenced in Figure 6-10, let's create our network variables in Snort, placing them in the *snort.conf* configuration file:

```
var DC_NETWORK 172.16.16.0/20
var PARTNER_NETWORK 172.16.8.0/23
var RA_NETWORK 172.16.32.0/20
var CAMPUS_NETWORK 172.16.0.0/22
var DMZ_NETWORK 172.16.4.0/23
```

Let's take a step backward—without these variables defined, our NIDS alerts will only display raw IP information:

```
attacker:
  addr: locality=IN 172.16.9.25
  port: 4888
target:
  addr: locality=IN 172.16.17.220
  port: 80
```

See the need for context? All we can see from this alert is that IP address 172.16.9.25 tried to attack 172.16.17.220. How can we prioritize this alert from the other 50 alerts rolling in? Once network variables are configured in the NIDS, our alerts get friendly:

```
attacker:
  addr: locality=PARTNER_NETWORK 172.16.9.25
  port: 4888
target:
```

```
addr: locality=DC_NETWORK 172.16.17.220
port: 80
```

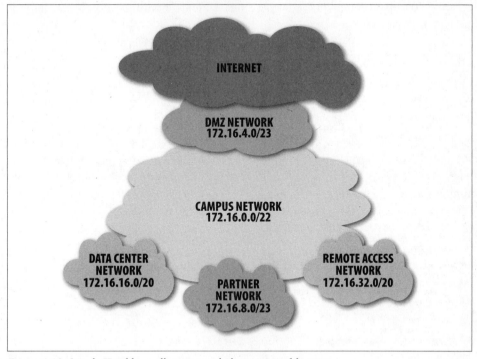

Figure 6-10. Simple IP address allocation with description of function

This alert shows clearly that a host in the partner network (PARTNER_NETWORK) attacked a host in the data center (DC_NETWORK)! Think of all the `nslookup`s and `traceroute`s you just saved yourself. As an added bonus, this information can also be used directly as query criteria in your SIM. For example: "show me all alerts from PARTNER_NETWORK."

The power of these variables is just as obvious for tuning your NIDS. You can use them to reference entire subnets, lists of subnets, lists of hosts, or a combination of both with a single variable.

Tuning with host variables

Host variables are slightly different from network variables: they reference only a single IP address at a time. Network variables that define ranges of IP addresses are most useful for contextual information and for some "meta-tuning" such as applying broad tuning policies to entire subnets and blocks of addresses. We still need something more granular to properly tune the NIDS, as most false positives will be related to specific application traffic running on a finite set of hosts. Host variables provide this level of granularity for tuning false positives. Typically, lists of IP addresses for servers of the same kind, such as DNS servers or email servers, are the most useful. For example, the last time I checked, we had more than 70 DNS servers in our environment. Rather than creating 70 tuning statements or even a single statement with a list of 70 servers, it is much easier to create a variable with the 70 server IP addresses and reference that variable in the tuning statement. With a common service such as DNS, it is likely that you'll have more than one tuning statement referencing DNS servers, so a variable saves you even more time, as all you need to do when a new DNS server is brought online is to add the new IP address to the variable. All tuning referencing that variable will now be applied to the new IP address as well!

Let's take a look at an example. Previously, we saw that a network management server was causing signature 3002 to fire. We know there are several other management servers as well, so we need to create a single variable for them and reference it in our NIDS tuning. By doing so, we can be assured that all the management servers have the proper tuning statements applied:

```
blanco-dc-nms-1# conf t
blanco-dc-nms-1(config)#
service event-action-rules rules0
variables MGT_SYSTEMS address
10.6.30.5,10.6.30.6,10.30.6.7,10.50.1.5,10.50.1.6,10.50.1.7

filters insert drop_mgt_system_alerts
signature-id-range 4003,3002,2100,2152
attacker-address-range $MGT_SYSTEMS
victim-address-range $IN
actions-to-remove produce-alert|produce-verbose-alert
```

Let's assume that we found three other signatures that were being triggered by the network management servers (4003, 2100, and 2152). The preceding tuning statement will drop alerts for all IP addresses defined in the MGT_SYSTEMS variable. Should IT deploy a new management system, you need only add its IP address to the variable. New signatures that fire false positives sourced from management systems can be tuned with this variable as well.

A Note on Documentation

One very easily overlooked aspect of NIDS tuning is documentation of your tuning efforts. Will you remember six months from now why you tuned IP address 10.44.3.56 for signature 4488? Probably not, so you need to discipline yourself to document every tuning statement and variable. Ideally, you will reference cases that led you to apply such tuning in the documentation itself. This will make things much easier should you switch vendors or deploy new sensors in a similar network environment.

Initially, our team used flat files with RCS revision control, but as the number of sensors and NIDS environments increased the scalability of flat files quickly eroded. We now use Bugzilla to track our NIDS tuning and it has worked very well (*http://www.bugzilla.org/*).

Custom signatures

The last NIDS topic we'll cover involves custom signatures. These are rules that you create and add to your NIDS, which allow you to react quickly to new threats in your environment. For example, let's say you find a piece of malware on your network that tries to resolve a domain hosting a command and control IRC server: tk.thirtyfiv.org. If you want to identify other systems infected with this trojan, you can deploy a signature that will fire when the regex for this *very* specific string of text is seen in a DNS query. On a Cisco IPS sensor, the configuration for this signature is as follows (notice the regex string for tk.thirtyfiv.org):

```
sig-description
sig-name IRC BOT DOMAINS
sig-string-info IRC BOT DOMAINS
sig-comment IRC BOT DOMAINS
exit
  engine atomic-ip
   specify-l4-protocol yes
    specify-payload-inspection yes
    regex-string
(\x03[Tt][Kk]\x0b[Tt][Hh][Ii][Rr][Tt][Yy][Ff][Ii][Vv]\x03[Oo][Rr][Gg]}
    exit
   l4-protocol udp
    specify-dst-port yes
     dst-port 53
```

You'll want to tune this custom signature to drop your DNS servers as a source of attack; they may query the root server to resolve the IP and place it in its cache.

A properly tuned NIDS deployment is one of the most powerful security tools. It can provide high-fidelity, actionable security events to your incident response team. Just remember, you'll get out of it what you put into it.

System Logging

One of the most challenging sources of event data that you will want to collect comes from the wonderful world of system logging, or *syslog*. Syslog information is particularly useful in environments where much of the application traffic is encrypted and cannot be analyzed by traditional packet inspection. In fact, syslog may be the only visibility you have in many cases.

In addition to being an operational and security best practice, core to several security standards and government regulations including the Federal Information Security Management Act of 2002 (FISMA), the Sarbanes-Oxley Act of 2002 (SOX), the Gramm-Leach-Bliley Act (GLBA), the Payment Card Industry (PCI), the Health Insurance Portability and Accountability Act of 1996 (HIPAA), and others is the collection of system log events.

In the Unix world, syslog is a standard for forwarding log messages in an IP network. Syslog messages are records of events occurring on a system. These events can take several forms, such as a record of a user logging in, a service starting, and even custom messages sent from applications running on the system.

According to the latest version of the IETF working group discussion,[‡] the format for a syslog message is suggested to be:

{PRI} {VERSION} {TIMESTAMP} {HOSTNAME} {PROCID} {MSGID} {STRUCTURED DATA}

That is, the priority of the message, version of the syslog protocol, timestamp (as specified by RFC 3339), hostname, process identifier, message identifier (used only for filtering purposes), and structured data where the contents of the message are contained. Syslog messages can and should be filtered to include only specific priorities. To do this effectively, we need to understand how the priority number is calculated. According to RFC 3164:

> The Facilities and Severities of the messages are numerically coded with decimal values. Some of the operating system daemons and processes have been assigned Facility values. Processes and daemons that have not been explicitly assigned a Facility may use any of the "local use" facilities or they may use the "user-level" Facility. Those Facilities that have been designated are shown in the following table along with their numerical code values.

Numerical Code	Facility
0	kernel messages
1	user-level messages
2	mail system
3	system daemons
4	security/authorization messages (note 1)
5	messages generated internally by syslogd
6	line printer subsystem
7	network news subsystem
8	UUCP subsystem
9	clock daemon (note 2)
10	security/authorization messages (note 1)
11	FTP daemon
12	NTP subsystem
13	log audit (note 1)
14	log alert (note 1)

‡ *http://www.syslog.cc/ietf/drafts/draft-ietf-syslog-protocol-23.txt*

Numerical Code	Facility
15	clock daemon (note 2)
16	local use 0 (local0)
17	local use 1 (local1)
18	local use 2 (local2)
19	local use 3 (local3)
20	local use 4 (local4)
21	local use 5 (local5)
22	local use 6 (local6)
23	local use 7 (local7)

Table 1. syslog Message Facilities

Note 1 - Various operating systems have been found to utilize Facilities 4, 10, 13 and 14 for security/authorization, audit, and alert messages which seem to be similar.

Note 2 - Various operating systems have been found to utilize both Facilities 9 and 15 for clock (cron/at) messages.

Each message Priority also has a decimal Severity level indicator. These are described in the following table along with their numerical values.

Numerical Code	Severity
0	Emergency: system is unusable
1	Alert: action must be taken immediately
2	Critical: critical conditions
3	Error: error conditions
4	Warning: warning conditions
5	Notice: normal but significant condition
6	Informational: informational messages
7	Debug: debug-level messages

Table 2. syslog Message Severities

The Priority value is calculated by first multiplying the Facility number by 8 and then adding the numerical value of the Severity. For example, a kernel message (Facility=0) with a Severity of Emergency (Severity=0) would have a Priority value of 0. Also, a "local use 4" message (Facility=20) with a Severity of Notice (Severity=5) would have a Priority value of 165. In the PRI part of a syslog message, these values would be placed between the angle brackets as <0> and <165> respectively. The only time a value of "0" will follow the "<" is for the Priority value of "0". Otherwise, leading "0"s MUST NOT be used.

Here is an example of a syslog message from a Linux-based system, which illustrates the use of this format:

```
Apr 20 04:16:50 bbx-vip-1.blanco.com ntpd [4024]: synchronized to 10.13.136.1
```

Notice that the Priority field is not included, as it is not required or configured on this particular system. When you break down the preceding code based on the IETF format, you get the following:

Timestamp: `Apr 20 04:16:50`

Hostname: `bbx-vip-1.blanco.com`

ProcID: `ntpd [4024]`

Structured data: `synchronized to 10.13.136.1`

This message tells us that the `ntpd` process on server `bbx-vip-1.blanco.com` synchronized its time to 10.13.136.1 on April 20 at 04:16:50. Is this message useful in the context of security monitoring? The answer is no, which is true for the vast majority of messages you're likely to receive from any given host. Depending on how syslog is configured, you may find the volume of messages overwhelming. Therein lies the challenge to collecting syslog data for security monitoring. As with NIDSs, the separation of "the wheat from the chaff" determines whether syslog will be a useful event source or a noisy distraction.

Key Syslog Events

To make the collection of syslog data manageable, first we must focus on some key syslog events. For security monitoring, we are interested in four types of events:

- Authentication events
- Authorization events
- Daemon status events
- Security application events

It should be noted that different flavors of Unix/Linux store their logfiles in different locations and use different filenames. Be aware of which files you expect to contain authentication logs, authorization logs, system messages, and other data. As an example of this diversity, here are the locations of the su log messages for each of the following Unix variants:

FreeBSD: */var/log/messages*

HP-UX: */var/adm/sulog*

Linux: */var/log/messages*

Solaris: As defined in */etc/default/su*

This diversity in log location is where you should address two important issues upfront. First, applying standardization to a set of servers running the same OS will make it much easier to collect syslog data from them. Take advantage of standardization by

---

implementing a syslog configuration template on all servers of a given *nix distribution. Second, you can't be an expert in everything. You will likely need help from the IT sys admins. Buy them a beer, thank them for standardizing as much as they can, and be up front about what you're trying to accomplish.

Authentication events

Authentication events record access to a system or application, generally referred to as logon and logoff messages. These are a primary source of security monitoring data because they provide timestamped attribution of account usage by userid. A set of logon and logoff messages for a single userid can show when the user logged in (and subsequently logged out), giving a time frame for when the account was in use. These messages may help you uncover some unexpected events, such as privileged accounts accessing systems at unusual times or from unusual systems:

```
Apr 25 20:22:16 xsrv.blanco.com sshd(pam_unix)[15585]: session opened for user root
by root(uid=0)
```

From this syslog message, we can see that a session was opened for the **root** user account on xsrv.blanco.com at 20:22:16 on April 25. Perhaps this is outside what is considered normal because it is after business hours, or perhaps xsrv.blanco.com is a server that contains very sensitive information. You may want to investigate unusual login messages. Access by service accounts (such as *www* or *apache*) is normal, but access from other accounts might be unusual and require investigation.

Authorization events

Authorization events record changes of privilege level for a given userid, such as changing to the **root** user via the **su -root** command, or via the superuser-do facility as in **sudo su - root**. The following message is an example of an authorization event:

```
Apr  4 21:25:49 xsrv.blanco.com sudo:   rajesh : TTY=pts/4 ; PWD=/users/rajesh ;
USER=root ; COMMAND=/bin/su -
```

The userid **rajesh** attempted to become the "root" user by issuing the command **sudo su -**. Such messages would be completely normal if **rajesh** was a system administrator whose job was to manage the server. However, if user **rajesh** is an intern or an administrative assistant, further investigation is likely warranted: we could query our logs for userid **rajesh** to see whether there is any other suspicious activity.

Daemon status events

Daemon status events record a change in state for a given daemon, typically start and stop messages. These messages alone do not necessarily indicate suspicious behavior. You must interpret the messages within the contexts of time of day and userid. For example, consider the following:

```
Apr 27 13:11:03 blanco-nnc sshd(pam_unix)[2862]: session opened for user cfry by
(uid=0)
```

```
Apr 27 13:11:10 blanco-nnc su(pam_unix)[2901]: session opened for user root by
cfry(uid=44642)
Apr 27 13:11:30 blanco-nnc sshd: sshd -TERM succeeded
Apr 27 13:11:30 blanco-nnc sshd:   succeeded
```

We see that user `cfry` connected to server `blanco-nnc` just after 1:00 p.m. He then
proceeded to open a root session, and soon after, the SSH daemon, `sshd`, was stopped
and started. Is it normal for services to be stopped and started on this server at 1:00
p.m.? Is `cfry` a sys admin? Querying our logs further, our investigation finds that userid
`cfry` had recently downloaded and installed a trojaned SSH daemon that captures all
keystrokes and logs them to a file. Monitoring daemon status events, in this case, allowed us to discover the suspicious activity that drove deeper investigation.

Security application events

Security application events record activities of applications installed specifically to perform a security function, such as Tripwire, Samhain, PortSentry, and Cisco Security
Agent (CSA). These file integrity and host-based NIDSs can be a source of valuable
incident response data.

Syslog Templates

Let's assume you know the kinds of messages you want to receive. How do you ensure
that you receive them from each system in your infrastructure? If you are a large enterprise that runs many different operating systems, you will need to have a standard
syslog configuration template if you hope to collect log messages consistently and reliably. The template will likely vary by server function and location, such as a DMZ
web server versus an internal web server. Also, you may choose to log more detailed
levels on your most critical servers. The following is an example of a host configuration
file for a DMZ server running Solaris:

```
# Copyright (c) 1991-1998 by Sun Microsystems, Inc.
# All rights reserved.
#
# syslog configuration file.
#
# This file is processed by m4 so be careful to quote ('') names
# that match m4 reserved words.  Also, within ifdef's, arguments
# containing commas must be quoted.
#
*.err;kern.notice;auth.notice              /dev/sysmsg
*.err;kern.debug;daemon.notice;mail.crit   /var/adm/messages

*.alert;kern.err;daemon.err             operator
*.alert                        root

*.emerg                     *

# if a non-loghost machine chooses to have authentication messages
# sent to the loghost machine, un-comment out the following line:
```

```
#auth.notice              ifdef('LOGHOST', /var/log/authlog, @loghost)

mail.debug                ifdef('LOGHOST', /var/log/syslog, @loghost)

#
# non-loghost machines will use the following lines to cause "user"
# log messages to be logged locally.
#
ifdef('LOGHOST', ,
user.err                  /dev/sysmsg
user.err                  /var/adm/messages
user.alert                'root, operator'
user.emerg                *
)
#
# $Id: syslog.conf template,v 1.5 2005/02/30 rajavin Exp $
#
local2.notice    /var/log/sudolog
local2.notice    @dmzsyslog.blanco.com
local3.info      /var/adm/ssh.log
local3.info      @dmzsyslog.blanco.com
local4.info      /var/adm/tcpwrap.log
local4.info      @dmzsyslog.blanco.com
local7.info      /var/adm/portsentry.log
local7.info      @dmzsyslog.blanco.com
*.err;kern.debug;daemon.notice;mail.crit    @dmzsyslog.blanco.com
auth.notice      /var/log/authlog
auth.notice      @dmzsyslog.blanco.com
```

Key Windows Log Events

Microsoft operating systems can write to different Event logfiles that are divided into application, system, and security logs. Unfortunately, it's not easy to retrieve these logs from the system without the use of third-party software such as InterSect Alliance's Snare.[§] In addition, if you are trying to view the logs on anything other than an end system, it is nearly impossible to do so with the EventViewer provided in Windows. Getting the log messages out of the EventViewer and into a standard syslog format will allow us to use them for security monitoring. The events listed in the following sections are the kinds of messages you will want to record for security monitoring and for incident response.

 Much of the information in the following sections is based on the excellent information put together by Randy Franklin Smith, which you can access at the Ultimate Windows Security site.[ǁ]

[§] *http://www.intersectalliance.com/projects/SnareWindows/*

[ǁ] *http://www.ultimatewindowssecurity.com/encyclopedia.aspx*

Windows authentication

Numerous Windows event IDs are devoted to authentication messages—referred to as "logon" and "logoff" messages. Table 6-3 lists the different Windows authentication event IDs, their applicable OS versions, and a description of the event.

Table 6-3. Windows logon and logoff events

Event ID	OS version	Description
528	All versions	Successful logon
529	All versions	Logon failure: unknown username or bad password
530	All versions	Logon failure: account logon time restriction violation
531	All versions	Logon failure: account currently disabled
532	All versions	Logon failure: the specified user account has expired
533	All versions	Logon failure: user not allowed to log on at this computer
534	All versions	Logon failure: user has not been granted the requested logon type at this machine
535	All versions	Logon failure: the specified account's password has expired
536	All versions	Logon failure: the NetLogon component is not active
537	All versions	Logon failure: the logon attempt failed for other reasons
538	All versions	User logoff
539	All versions	Logon failure: account locked out
540	Windows XP, Windows 2000, Windows Server 2003	Successful network logon
552	Windows Server 2003	Logon attempt using explicit credentials

Windows authorization

Several Windows event IDs are devoted to authorization messages, used to record access to privileged services or privileged actions. Table 6-4 lists the different Windows authorization event IDs, their applicable OS versions, and a description of the event.

Table 6-4. Windows authorization events

Event ID	OS version	Description
577	All versions	Privileged service called
578	All versions	Privileged object operation
601	Windows Server 2003	Attempt to install service
602	Windows Server 2003	Scheduled task created
608	Windows Server 2003	User right assigned
609	All versions	User right removed
612	All versions	Audit policy change

Of course, all of the event IDs change with Windows Vista and Windows Server 2008 (see Table 6-5).

Table 6-5. Windows Vista and Windows Server 2008 logon events

Event ID	Description
4624	An account was successfully logged on
4625	An account failed to log on
4648	A logon was attempted using explicit credentials

Windows process status events

Windows process status events record the action of starting and stopping processes on a Windows system. Table 6-6 provides a list of such events. Note that recorded events will likely be voluminous. You will need to filter them to save only those that are critical to server availability, integrity, or confidentiality.

Table 6-6. Windows process status events

Event ID	OS version	Description
592	All versions	A new process has been created
593	All versions	A process has exited
594	All versions	A handle to an object has been duplicated
595	All versions	Indirect access to an object has been obtained

Windows domain controller events

Windows domain controller events record events unique to domain controllers, usually on a system functioning solely for that purpose. This includes events recording policy and group changes, security software (Kerberos), and authentication messages. Table 6-7 provides a list of relevant domain controller events, and Table 6-8 provides a list of relevant Kerberos events. Table 6-9 provides a cross-reference for converting error codes (which are recorded in decimal format) to hexadecimal. It also serves as a reference for common error messages you may receive.

Table 6-7. Windows domain controller events

Event ID	OS version	Description
617	All versions	Kerberos policy changed
632	All versions	Global group member changed
636	All versions	Local group member changed
643	Windows 2000	Domain policy changed
	Windows Server 2003	Domain policy changed
660	All versions	Universal group member changed

Event ID	OS version	Description
672[a]	Windows Server 2003	Kerberos success and failure
675[b]	Windows 2000	Preauthentication failed (Kerberos)
680[c]	Windows 2000	Account used for logon by %1
	Windows Server 2003	Logon attempt
681 [d]	Windows 2000	The logon to account: %1 by: %2 from workstation: %3 failed
	Windows Server 2003	The logon to account: %1 by: %2 from workstation: %3 failed

[a] From page 83 of RFC 1510, *http://www.ietf.org/rfc/rfc1510.txt*.

[b] Also from page 83 of RFC 1510, *http://www.ietf.org/rfc/rfc1510.txt*.

[c] Windows Server 2003 uses event ID 680 instead of 681.

[d] From *http://support.microsoft.com/kb/273499/en-us/*: "Note that the error codes in the Event Log message are in decimal form, but they are actually hexadecimal values." You can translate the values from decimal to hexadecimal by using the Calculator tool in Windows 2000, or by viewing Table 6-7. The most common error codes you may receive are defined in Table 6-7.

Table 6-8. Kerberos error codes

Error code	Cause
6	Client not found in Kerberos database (no such username)
18	Client's credentials have been revoked (account disabled)
23	Password has expired
24	Preauthentication information was invalid (incorrect password)

Table 6-9. NTLM error codes

Error code	Hexadecimal value	Cause
3221225572	C0000064	User logon with misspelled or bad user account
3221225578	C000006A	User logon with misspelled or bad password
3221225581	C000006D	User logon has incorrect username
3221225583	C000006F	User logon outside authorized hours
3221225584	C0000070	User logon from unauthorized workstation
3221225585	C0000071	User logon with expired password
3221225586	C0000072	User logon to account disabled by administrator
3221225875	C0000193	User logon with expired account
3221226020	C0000224	User logon with "Change Password at Next Logon" flagged
3221226036	C0000234	User logon with account locked

Collecting Windows Server Events in Syslog Format

One of the primary challenges to collecting Windows events from a server is getting the events out of the proprietary Event Viewer and into a standard format such as syslog. A common way to do this is via third-party software such as Snare. Snare converts the events into a syslog-compatible format and has features to allow an administrator to specify which event IDs will be forwarded to a syslog collector. The Snare format for a Windows Administrator logon event looks like this:

```
Dec 12 18:27:22 dc.blanco.com MSWinEventLog 1 Security
39226 Dec 12 18:27:22 2008 538 Security Adminstrator User
Success Audit DC Logon/Logoff User Logoff: User Name:
Administrator Domain: BWIR Logon ID: (0x0,0x404843F) Logon
Type: 3 39211
```

Windows security application events

Antivirus logs can be an essential tool in detecting and mitigating outbreaks in a timely and precise fashion. Imagine this scenario: a miscreant creates a virus variant and intends to target executives at your company (a practice that is often called *spearphishing*) by sending them an infected file via email with some specially crafted social engineering content. Unfortunately, some of your executives clicked the file and a few of them ran the virus file. One of the more technically savvy executives sends an email to report the issue:

```
Security Team,

I received an email yesterday that had a suspicious attachment. The email contained
some references to an upcoming product and appeared to be from one of our vendor
partners. I didn't open the attachment and my antivirus didn't alert on it
initially. But this morning the AV program says that the file has a virus but it
couldn't clean it. Please have a look at my computer when I return next week. I
spoke with a few other executives and they received the email as well.

Thanks,

Mikael Shekotzi
Vice President, CFO
Blanco Wireless, Inc.
```

Luckily, you are collecting your antivirus logs into your syslog collector and can query for activity on this executive's computer, called *mshekotzi-wxp*, immediately. You find that your antivirus product detected the virus but couldn't clean it:

```
Tue_Apr_29_12:10:03_EDT_2008|mshekotzi-wxp|172.16.8.12|Administrator|2008-04-29
16:06:27|On-Demand
Scan|W32/Sdbot.gen.an|trojan|c:\WINDOWS\system32\Explorer\xAO.exe|5.2.0|4.0.5283|Cl
ean-Delete Error|Unresolved
```

A quick query of your syslog data for file *xA0.exe* reveals that at least seven other executive officers at Blanco received the email, including the CEO and CTO. In addition, one of the executive administrative assistants opened a second email from the same sender that included a Word document. Her computer showed a CSA message that lets us know that "something bad" has probably happened:

```
Tue_Apr_29_13:40:05_EDT_2008|ddmilas-wxp|10.6.20.245|186|833|2008-04-30
01:36:20|The process 'C:\Program Files\Microsoft Office\OFFICE11\WINWORD.EXE' (as
user BLANCO\ddmilas) attempted to access a resource which resulted in the user
being asked the following question. 'The process C:\Program Files\Microsoft
Office\OFFICE11\WINWORD.EXE is attempting to invoke a system function from a
buffer. Do you wish to allow this?' The user was queried and a 'Yes' response was
received.
```

We now know which executives received the email, which executives' computers were able to detect and delete the virus, and which were not. By analyzing the CSA log messages we can see which employees' systems were likely trojaned, because they answered "yes" to the pop-up CSA prompt. These logs allow us to prioritize remediation efforts appropriate to the scope of the spearphishing attack.

Syslog data can be extremely beneficial, but collection and analysis appear quite daunting due to the number and variety of possible messages recorded by systems. Windows events can be extremely difficult to collect in a useful way given the complexity of the operating system's implementation (Hex codes, Kerberos codes, different codes for different OS versions), the proprietary format (export to CSV doesn't adequately address this), and the sheer volume of events that a single server can generate. However, if we follow the guidance given in Chapter 4 (to choose our target systems), and restrict the events we are collecting and analyzing to include only security events, the collection process becomes much more manageable. Start with critical Windows servers, create a workable logging policy, and then apply that same policy to other critical Windows servers of the same type.

Application Logging

Though they are more complex, application logs are an excellent source of security event data. Depending on the level of customization allowed, application logs can be correlated with other logs to provide insight into specific event types, and can be a valuable source of forensic data. Several applications now support logging directly into syslog and provide a range of logging levels. Apache Web Server is a good example of this capability. URL access logs (Apache `access_log`) are an incredibly powerful source of forensic data for security monitoring. Imagine a scenario where your web application team found that a misconfiguration may have exposed some confidential data:

```
Security Team,

We received an email from a customer claiming that we exposed his contact data via
our webserver hosted on www.blancowireless.com. We checked into his claim and it
```

appears to be valid. I'm not sure how to respond to this situation, there may be
more information exposed as well. Can you help us look at the logs?

Thanks,

Jayson Alodnom
Web Administrator
Blanco Wireless, Inc.

A quick phone call with Jayson finds that the web administrators are logging the
`access_log` file locally on the server and there should be a couple of weeks' worth of
history in there. Looking through the logs we find that several downloads of a spreadsheet occurred because someone posted it to a customer collaboration blog hosted on
blancowireless.com. The first entry shows a 2 MB file being uploaded to the blog:

```
37.33.7.57 - - [28/Apr/2008:08:31:11 -0700] "POST /blancoblog/submit.php HTTP/1.1"
200 2045589 "-" "Mozilla/4.0 (compatible; MSIE 6.0; Windows NT 5.1;)"
```

The following two `access_log` file entries show downloads of the Excel spreadsheet by
two different IP addresses:

```
33.80.7.20 - - [29/Apr/2008:01:08:55 -0700] "GET /blancoblog/php/uploads/G8-exec-
home-phone-numbers.xls HTTP/1.0" 200 2045589
```

```
17.12.44.88 - - [29/Apr/2008:01:48:11 -0700] "GET /blancoblog/php/uploads/G8-exec-
home-phone-numbers.xls HTTP/1.0" 200 2045589
```

A full query of the logs shows that at least 20 other downloads occurred. In addition,
the IP address 37.33.7.57 that uploaded the file appears to have uploaded a few other
files, but queries don't show download activity. Querying other system logs, we see
that 37.33.7.57 was trying to exploit various vulnerabilities, for which Blanco's system
administrators had already patched. It was decided to block the IP address from reaching Blanco's network, which should mitigate further attacks.

Database Logging

One often-overlooked source of incident data comes from the audit logs in a database.
The `SYS.AUD$` table in Oracle can be a source of extremely useful security incident
information.

> When discussing database logging with your database administrators,
> you may find that much of this information is already being logged as
> part of regulatory compliance with SOX, HIPAA, or the European Un-
> ion Directive on Privacy and Electronic Communications. Getting ac-
> cess to these logs should be considerably easier than convincing the
> DBAs to turn on logging just for you.

According to the documentation for Oracle 10g,[#] an Oracle database has four general types of auditing:

Statement auditing

> Watching SQL statements, privileges, objects, and so on. The audit information is written to either `SYS.AUD$` or the operating system as syslog, as configured in the `AUDIT_TRAIL` initialization parameter.

Fine-grained auditing

> Watching for specific activities, such as time of day, user-based rules, specific tables being updated or selected, or a Boolean condition check for a combination of rules. These are written to `SYS.FGA_LOG$` or to an XML file residing on the operating system. This is configured in the `DBMS_FGA.ADD_POLICY` parameter.

Privilege auditing

> Watching for user `SYS` and anyone connecting with `SYSDBA` or `SYSOPER` privileges by logging these activities to syslog on Unix or the Event log on Windows. This is configured in the `AUDIT_TRAIL` parameter.

Schema object auditing

> Focused auditing based on a specified schema object, such as `SELECT` on a sensitive object. This type of auditing applies to *all* users of the database. The audit information is written to either `SYS.AUD$` or the OS syslog, as set in the `AUDIT_TRAIL` initialization parameter.

 Be careful when attempting to audit actions on a database. Query time and disk utilization can be negatively impacted by an overzealous auditing configuration, such as auditing `SELECT` statements on a commonly used database. In addition, the `AUD$` table is in the `SYSTEM` tablespace, which will cause the database to hang when filled to capacity. Therefore, it is critical to have a purge strategy in place for the `AUD$` table.

The default auditing configuration for Oracle records database startup and shutdown, connections from privileged accounts, and changes made to the database structure. Oracle's documentation[*] provides configuration guidance with examples. Here are a few examples of activities you may want to record:

- `DESCRIBE` statements on production databases, which indicate reconnaissance by someone unfamiliar with the database structure
- `SELECT` statements for sensitive fields in a database, such as employee compensation or medical records
- Database connections for privileged accounts outside of normal maintenance hours

---

[#] *http://download-east.oracle.com/docs/cd/B14117_01/network.101/b10773/auditing.htm#DBSEG125*

[*] *http://download.oracle.com/docs/cd/B28359_01/network.111/b28531/toc.htm*

Auditing messages can be recorded in a table, to an XML file on the local system, or to syslog on the local system. The recording location is set as an initialization parameter for the database. Here is an example of both the XML and syslog formats for an AUDIT message. It shows user JEBEDIAH has issued a SQL query on sensitive database fields (select * from medical.provider where provider = :h).

Here's the message in XML format:

```
<xml version="1.0" encoding="UTF-8">
    <Audit xmlns="http://xmlns.oracle.com/oracleas/schema/dbserver_audittrail-
10_2.xsd" xmlns:xsi="http://www.w3.org/2001/XMLSchema-instance"
xsi:schemaLocation="http://xmlns.oracle.com/oracleas/schema/dbserver_audittrail-
10_2.xsd">
    <Version>10.2</Version>
    <AuditRecord>
        <Audit_Type>1</Audit_Type>
        <Session_Id>224655</Session_Id>
        <StatementId>10</StatementId>
        <EntryId>1</EntryId>
        <Extended_Timestamp>2008-04-08T08:46:10.77845</Extended_Timestamp>
        <DB_User>JEBEDIAH</DB_User>
        <OS_User>oracle</OS_User>
        <Userhost>blancodb1</Userhost>
        <OS_Process>32389</OS_Process>
        <Terminal>pts/2</Terminal>
        <Instance_Number>0</Instance_Number>
        <Object_Schema>MEDICAL</Object_Schema>
        <Object_Name>PROVIDER/Object_Name>
        <Action>103</Action>
        <Returncode>0</Returncode>
        <Scn>6447496045</Scn>
        <SesActions>---------S------</SesActions>
        <Sql_Text>select * from medical.provider where provider = :h</Sql_Text>
    </AuditRecord>
```

Here's the message in syslog format:

```
Apr 10 08:46:10 oradba Oracle Audit[28955]: SESSIONID: "224655"
ENTRYID: "1" STATEMENT: "10" USERID: "JEBEDIAH" USERHOST: "blancodb1"
TERMINAL: "pts/2" ACTION: "103" RETURNCODE: "0" OBJ$CREATOR: "JJRM" OBJ$NAME:
"PROVIDER" SES$ACTIONS: "---------S------"
SES$TID: "6447474" OS$USERID: "oracle"
```

To pull or push these messages from the database host, you must use either XML or syslog. You can export syslog from the database host by configuring the host's syslog daemon, but XML will require additional scripting. We recommend the use of syslog for simplicity. You can accomplish this with the following configuration steps:

1. Set initialization parameters (in *init.ora*):

   ```
   AUDIT_TRAIL=OS
   AUDIT_SYSLOG_LEVEL=USER.ALERT
   ```

2. Configure */etc/syslog.conf* to write to a separate logfile for audit logs:

   ```
   user.alert /var/log/audit.log
   ```

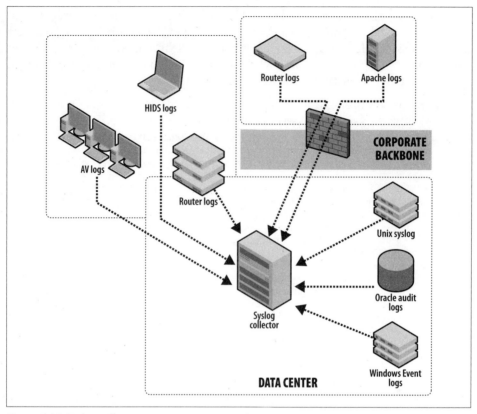

Figure 6-11. Syslog collection

This configuration will separate the messages generated by Oracle auditing from the messages generated by the system; otherwise, the audit trail messages will be logged to */var/log/messages* by default.

Collecting Syslog

Syslog collection solutions can be as simple as a server running a syslog daemon, or as complex as an infrastructure with multiple layers of forwarding and filtering between servers. Many open source and commercial tools are available to build a solution. Syslog collection for large enterprises typically makes use of a well-indexed database to provide fast query times. As mentioned previously, you can configure each host to forward syslog messages to a central collection server, as depicted in Figure 6-11.

Using the standard syslog protocol, you can collect from a variety of sources, including antivirus and host intrusion detection system (HIDS) logs on your desktop network, events from your network devices, and server and application logs. Windows Event logs, as mentioned previously in this chapter, require a forwarding mechanism such as Snare to send in syslog format.

If your environment is larger than what a single syslog collector can handle, you may need to deploy regional syslog collectors that relay the messages to a centralized collector, as depicted in Figure 6-12.

syslog-ng is a popular syslog collector and relay. It provides content-based filtering and the ability to use connection-oriented TCP as the transport in place of the default UDP, which is connectionless. The central collector, depicted at the bottom of Figure 6-12, is often a software solution that provides fast queries for large volumes of data, such as those offered by LogLogic[†] and Splunk.[‡] These packages typically load the messages into a well-indexed database that is optimized for fast query performance. In addition to security monitoring reports, they also offer specialized "canned" reports for regulatory compliance, operational issues, and business reporting. For example, our team queries antivirus logs every four hours to find systems reporting a virus that is detected but unresolved:

```
Thu_May__8_10:30:09_EDT_2008|SAL-W2K|172.16.64.95|NT AUTHORITY\SYSTEM|2008-06-08
13:58:09|OAS|Vundo|trojan|C:\WINDOWS\system32\sstts.dll|5.2.0|4.0.5290|Clean-Delete
Error|Unresolved
```

The preceding message tells us that there is a trojan on SAL-W2K that our antivirus software cannot clean; therefore, a desktop PC support technician should remediate or rebuild the system immediately. We can now query the rest of our logs for activity sourced from the machine's NetBIOS name (SAL-W2K) or IP address (172.16.64.95). The following are example CSA logs from this machine:

```
Mon_May__21_06:10:01_EDT_2008|SAL-W2K|172.16.16.64|1691|833|2008-06-08 15:37:16|The
process 'C:\Program Files\Internet Explorer\iexplore.exe' (as user BLANCO\SAL)
attempted to access a resource which resulted in the user being asked the following
question. 'A process is attempting to invoke C:\Documents and Settings\SAL\Local
Settings\Temporary Internet Files\Content.IE5\7GF6TOJ3\registry-clean-
expert[1].exe, which has not previously been seen on this system. Do you wish to
allow this?' The user was queried and a 'Yes' response was received.
```

Blanco employee Salmon Fydle's system logged a CSA message, showing that an executable tried to launch from his browser's cache. Unfortunately, he answered "yes" when CSA asked him whether he wanted to allow this activity.

From the following message, we can see that the machine is likely *rootkitted* (entirely compromised with malware):

```
Tue_May__22_01:50:03_EDT_2008|SAL-W2K|172.16.16.64|186|547|2008-06-07 00:00:51|The
process 'C:\Program Files\HaX\Hax\Hax.exe' (as user BLANCO\SAL) attempted to call
the function VirtualHax from a buffer (the return address was 0x8700ced). The code
at this address is 'fc506a04 68001000 0051ff93 891c0010 8a07a880 74042c80 8807598d
45fc50ff' This either happens when a process uses self-modifying code or when a
process has been subverted by a buffer overflow attack.  The operation was allowed.
```

[†] *http://www.loglogic.com/*

[‡] *http://www.splunk.com/*

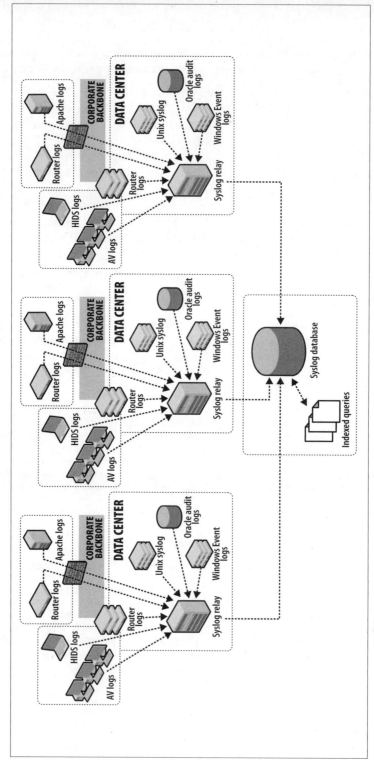

Figure 6-12. Syslog collection with relay and database indexing

CSA is doing its job, knocking down modules as they try to load, as shown in the following message:

```
Tue_May__22_06:30:08_EDT_2008|SAL-W2K|72.163.165.229|46|762|2008-06-06
15:58:42|Kernel functionality has been modified by the module sprs.sys. The module
'sprs.sys' is used by entries in the System syscall table.  The specified action
was taken to set detected rootkit as Untrusted.
```

Finally, CSA stops a connection from being made to a likely command and control server or a site hosting additional malware. You also can use this IP address in a NetFlow query to identify any other systems that may have successfully connected to IP address 207.46.248.249. At the very least, we need to get SAL-W2K off the network!

```
Tue_May_22_07:00:08_EDT_2008|SAL-W2K|172.16.16.64|54|452|2008-04-22 16:27:12|The
process 'C:\WINDOWS\explorer.exe' (as user BLANCO\SAL) attempted to initiate a
connection as a client on TCP port 80 to 207.46.248.249 using interface
Wired\Intel(R) PRO/1000 MT Mobile Connection. The operation was denied.
```

The following syslog entries from a Linux server show a user, cfry, trying to escalate privileges to the root user using the su – command, with several failures followed by a successful su message:

```
Apr 28 21:17:25 blanco-lnx su(pam_unix)[9710]: authentication failure; logname=
uid=1000 euid=0 tty=pts/0 ruser=cfry rhost=  user=root
Apr 28 21:17:27 blanco-lnx su[9710]: pam_authenticate: Authentication failure
Apr 28 21:17:27 blanco-lnx su[9710]: FAILED su for root by cfry
Apr 28 21:17:27 blanco-lnx su[9710]: - pts/0 cfry:root
Apr 28 21:17:30 blanco-lnx su(pam_unix)[9711]: authentication failure; logname=
uid=1000 euid=0 tty=pts/0 ruser=cfry rhost=  user=root
Apr 28 21:17:31 blanco-lnx su[9711]: pam_authenticate: Authentication failure
Apr 28 21:17:31 blanco-lnx su[9711]: FAILED su for root by cfry
Apr 28 21:17:31 blanco-lnx su[9711]: - pts/0 cfry:root
Apr 28 21:17:36 blanco-lnx sudo(pam_unix)[9712]: authentication failure; logname=
uid=0 euid=0 tty=pts/0 ruser= rhost=  user=cfry
Apr 28 21:17:45 blanco-lnx sudo:    cfry : 3 incorrect password attempts ;
TTY=pts/0 ; PWD=/home/cfry ; USER=root ; COMMAND=/bin/su -
Apr 28 21:17:52 blanco-lnx su[9713]: Successful su for root by cfry
Apr 28 21:17:52 blanco-lnx su[9713]: + pts/0 cfry:root
Apr 28 21:17:52 blanco-lnx su(pam_unix)[9713]: session opened for user root by
(uid=1000)
```

Perhaps user cfry is a sys admin who had the Caps Lock key activated the first few times he tried to become root. Maybe cfry is a sys admin who is violating process by not using the sudo command to become root. Or maybe cfry is a trainer at the on-site gym and shouldn't even be logged in to a shell session on a Linux server! The more context you can add to your messages, the more useful the event source. In this next section, we'll highlight the power of NetFlow to provide context to your event logs.

NetFlow

As we've asserted throughout this book, NetFlow is a free and powerful tool, and should be one of the most powerful tools in your security tool belt. NetFlow

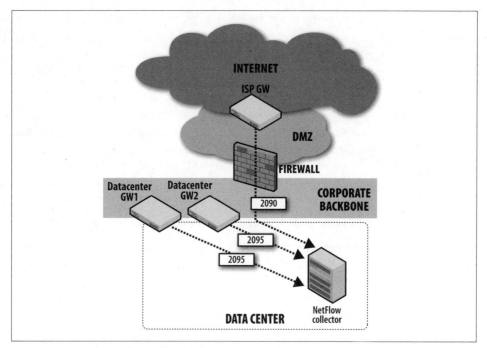

Figure 6-13. Simple NetFlow collection

deployment is fairly simple. If you have a large enterprise, aggregating your data and performing queries across data sets can add complexity, but it can be scripted with some simple Perl. NetFlow is an invaluable forensic investigation tool that you can query on demand. The examples that follow are built on OSU flow-tools, which we discussed in Chapter 3.

Figure 6-13 depicts a simple NetFlow collection in a small network environment. Notice that for ease of operation and separation of data, we're running two flow-capture instances on a single NetFlow collector. The ISP gateway router is configured to export flows to the collector on UDP port 2090 and the data center gateways are configured to export on UDP 2095. The collector has one process listening on UDP 2090 for ISP gateway flows, and the other is listening for the DC gateway flows.

This flow-capture command:

```
/usr/local/netflow/bin/flow-capture -w /var/local/flows/isp-data -E90G -V5 -A1134
0/0/2090 -S5 -p /var/run/netflow/isp-flow-capture.pid -N-1 -n288
```

contains several command-line flags, which will do the following:

- Capture ISP gateway flows to the */var/local/flows/isp-data* directory (make sure the NetFlow user can write here!)
- Begin rolling over once there is 90 GB of flow data (i.e., if you had a 95 GB drive)
- Collect and store data in NetFlow version 5 format

- Tag flows with your AS number (e.g., AS1134)
- Listen and capture on UDP 2090 (note: you may have to poke a hole in your firewall because flow collection is in your DMZ and your collector is probably inside the firewall)
- Log a `stats` message every five minutes
- Specify the process ID *isp-flow-capture.pid* in location */var/run/netflow*
- Set the nesting level to YYYY-MM-DD/flow-file (see `man flow-capture` for options)
- Create a flow file 288 times per day (every five minutes)

This provides visibility into ingress and egress traffic at the ISP interconnect layer, so any network traffic coming into or leaving the corporate network is logged. To continue with our example in Figure 6-13, we are collecting data center gateway flows on port 2095 to a different data directory:

```
/usr/local/netflow/bin/flow-capture -w /var/local/flows/dc-data -E90G -V5 -A1134
0/0/2095 -S5 -p /var/run/netflow/dc-flow-capture.pid -N-1 -n288
```

This provides visibility into ingress and egress traffic at the data center gateway layer, so any network traffic coming into or leaving the data center networks is logged. You can run queries against these two setups by simply specifying the appropriate data directory.

OSU flow-tools NetFlow Capture Filtering

You may have a shared backbone router that combines data center networks with other networks, instead of a dedicated data center gateway. This doesn't prevent you from collecting only data center NetFlow, should you not care to log the other traffic. You can accomplish this with the OSU flow-tools `flow-capture` command combined with an option to use a filter configuration file, *filter.cfg*, located in */usr/local/netflow/var/ cfg*. The following will allow for capture of the 10.14.19.0/24 network:

```
filter-primitive dc-address-mask
  type ip-address-mask
  permit 10.14.19.0 255.255.255.0
filter-definition dc-only
  match dc-address-mask
```

Finally, the command to make use of this capture filter with `flow-capture` looks like this:

```
/usr/local/netflow/bin/flow-capture -F dc-only -w /var/local/flows/dc-data -E90G
-V5 -A1134 0/0/2095 -S5 -p /var/run/netflow/dc-flow-capture.pid -N-1 -n288
```

The preceding command will log all flows that match the filter definition and will drop all of the other unwanted flow data.

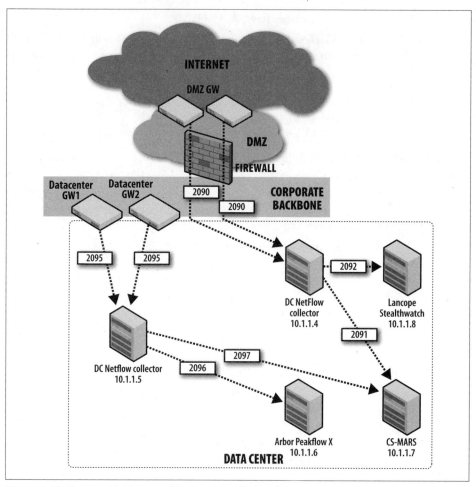

Figure 6-14. Copying NetFlow to other devices with flow-fanout

OSU flow-tools flow-fanout

We often recommend sending NetFlow to any device that can use it. To accomplish this, we can use the flow-fanout tool from the flow-tools suite. Figure 6-14 shows the export of NetFlow from DMZ and data center routers to separate NetFlow collectors. The flows are then copied to three solutions that can perform anomaly detection and performance analysis on the data: Arbor's Peakflow X, Cisco's CS-MARS, and Lancope's StealthWatch.

The `flow-capture` flags will be the same as the ones we used for the example depicted in Figure 6-13. To use flow-fanout, we must "insert" it between the routers sending data and the flow-capture process. This sends a copy to localhost for logging and a copy to the external devices. The configuration changes a bit as follows:

```
/usr/local/netflow/bin/flow-fanout 0/0/2090 0/0/2089 10.1.1.4/10.1.1.7/2091
10.1.1.4/10.1.1.8/2092
```

You can interpret the preceding DMZ NetFlow collector config as "take flows seen on UDP port 2090 and copy them to localhost:2089, CS-MARS:2091, and Lancope:2092". Next, we need to tell the collector to listen on 2089 and capture as appropriate:

```
/usr/local/netflow/bin/flow-capture -w /var/local/flows/data -E90G -V5 -A1134
0/0/2089 -S5 -p /var/run/netflow/dflow-capture.pid -N-1 -n288
```

You can interpret the following DC NetFlow collector config as "take flows seen on UDP port 2095 and copy them to localhost:2094, Arbor:2096, and CS-MARS:2097".

```
/usr/local/netflow/bin/flow-fanout 0/0/2095 0/0/2094 10.1.1.5/10.1.1.6/2096
10.1.1.5/10.1.1.7/2097
```

Next, we must tell the collector to listen on 2094 and capture:

```
/usr/local/netflow/bin/flow-capture -w /var/local/flows/data -E90G -V5 -A1134
0/0/2094 -S5 -p /var/run/netflow/dflow-capture.pid -N-1 -n288
```

Now, from a single source of NetFlow, you can share NetFlow with as many other devices as you want! This is our preferred method, as we have both the raw flows kept for forensics and the live feeds to multiple tools, each using the data in different ways.

Blanco's Security Alert Sources

Blanco Wireless has several sources for security alerts, including NIDS, syslog, application logs, database logs, host antivirus logs, host NIDS logs, router and firewall logs, and NetFlow (see Figure 6-15).

NIDS

Blanco Wireless has NIDS installed, and is inspecting the backbone uplinks on the data center gateway routers (connections 1, 2, 3, and 4). Analysis of the network traffic shows an average of 12 Mbps with spikes of up to 60 Mbps. Blanco will install a single Cisco IPS 4255 sensor with four interfaces running IPS software version 6.0. The routers are configured to provide a copy of each interface's *bidirectional* traffic. This setup provides a view of ingress/egress data center traffic, but does not capture intra-data center traffic, as is desired.

Blanco's security team has taken advantage of the information gathered in its Internet Protocol Address Management (IPAM) software and makes use of network locale variables in tuning the sensors (note that the "slash notation" is broken down into ranges of addresses to represent subnets):

```
variables DESKTOP_NETWORKS 10.10.32.0-10.10.63.255
variables WINDOWS_SERVERS 10.10.0.0-10.10.0.127
variables ORACLE_SERVERS 10.10.0.128-10.10.0.255
variables VMWARE_SERVERS 10.10.1.0-10.10.1.63
variables WEBAPP_SERVERS 10.10.1.64-10.10.1.127
```

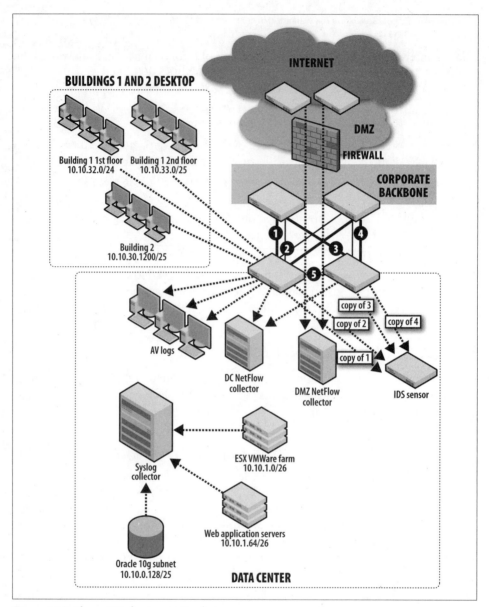

Figure 6-15. Blanco Wireless's security alert sources

Because Blanco handles sensitive customer information, it has written a custom NIDS signature to watch for unencrypted Social Security numbers on the wire:

```
signatures 60001 0
!
sig-description
sig-name SSN_POLICY
sig-string-info SSN HANDLING POLICY VIOLATION
sig-comment CLEARTEXT SSN
exit
  engine string-tcp
    event-action produce-verbose-alert
    specify-min-match-length no
    regex-string ([0-9][0-9][0-9]-[0-9][0-9]-[0-9][0-9][0-9][0-9])
    service-ports 1-65535
      exit
```

This signature will match on regex for the U.S. Social Security number format ###-##-#### if it's seen on any TCP ports.

Syslog

Blanco's Linux servers are configured to send all authentication events, authorization events, and daemon status events to syslog servers. Blanco's Windows 2000 servers have a Snare agent installed and configured to forward events in syslog format, including authentication and authorization.

Apache Logs

Blanco's web applications run on Apache Web Server. The system administrators have configured Apache (according to guidance in O'Reilly's *Apache Cookbook* by Ken Coar and Rich Bowen) to log errors and authentication events to syslog. This was accomplished by configuring *httpd.conf* with the following parameter:

```
ErrorLog syslog:user
```

and with this Perl script to grab authentication events and send them to syslog:

> Logging your access log to syslog takes a little work. Add the following to your configuration file:
>
> ```
> CustomLog |/usr/local/apache/bin/apache_syslog combined
> ```
>
> where apache_syslog is a program that looks like the following:
>
> ```
> #!/usr/bin/perl
> use Sys::Syslog qw( :DEFAULT setlogsock );
>
> setlogsock('unix');
> openlog('apache', 'cons', 'pid', 'user');
>
> while ($log = <STDIN>) {
>         syslog('notice', $log);
> }
> closelog;
> ```

This allows the security team to see when the application stops and restarts as well as when users log in to the application.

Database Logs

Blanco's database administrators have configured their Oracle 10g environment to send system messages and audit events directly to syslog. This includes database start and stop events, as well as auditing of all activities occurring with `SYS` and `OPS$ORACLE` accounts. On Blanco's production databases, connections to these accounts should have an associated Change Request or note from the database administrator making the connection.

Antivirus and HIDS Logs

Blanco's employee desktop and laptop computers are configured to send their antivirus logs and their host intrusion detection logs to a centralized collector where they are stored. Blanco has created automated queries to identify antivirus messages with the word *Unresolved*, as well as messages from the HIDS showing that a user has disabled the antivirus or HIDS software.

Network Device Logs

All of Blanco's network devices are logging to the syslog server so that changes to their configurations are recorded.

NetFlow

As shown in Figure 3-13 in Chapter 3 as well as in Figure 6-15, Blanco collects NetFlow from its DMZ and its data center environments. In addition, Blanco runs automated reports to search for policy violations, including indications that data is being copied out of the environment.

Conclusion

The heart of security monitoring—configuring systems to record, forward, and collect security events—culminates the preparation of all the previous chapters. This chapter provided guidance on how you can carefully configure systems that fit your infrastructure, and then tune them so you can detect the real security events. In the next chapter, we'll explain how to keep things humming. Once you've gone to all this trouble to configure your events, you don't want them to go missing, now do you?

## CHAPTER 7

Maintain Dependable Event Sources

In "Stalking the Wily Hacker," Cliff Stoll describes his investigation of a major security breach at Lawrence Berkeley Laboratories. According to the account, the hacker took pains to avoid leaving tracks of his intrusion: "Whenever possible, he disabled accounting and audit trails, so there would be no trace of his presence...."[*]

Security events such as user activity logs, network intrusion detection system (NIDS) alerts, server logs, and network device records are indispensable footprints, allowing security investigators to trace activity and monitor for problems. Without reliable event sources, monitoring is a futile exercise—there's no way to discern *lack of activity* from *unrecorded* activity.

Figure 7-1 displays a router traffic graph, generated by Multi Router Traffic Grapher (MRTG) to show traffic throughput for a series of network interfaces. It illustrates traffic received by eight NIDSs in a production environment. There's clearly a problem with one of the sensors—it's no longer receiving any traffic.

This may be a planned outage. Perhaps the sensor was just placed into service, or its SPAN was disconnected from the router for scheduled maintenance. It's possible there's a malicious explanation for this outage, but as is true with much of security monitoring, the explanation is likely mundane. Regardless of the source for this outage, you'll be blind to security alerts while the sensor is offline. What can you do to catch these problems, keeping downtime to a minimum?

Consider other gaps—systems or network segments of which you're not even aware. If you have a relatively large network, it's probably not constant; new networks and systems are being added monthly or even weekly. This illustrates another blind spot: new areas of the network and new systems where security intrusions could go unnoticed; you probably aren't yet collecting events from these systems. Without these events, there's nothing to trigger alerts in your monitoring system. How can you prevent such gaps while watching for substantive changes to your environment?

[*] Stoll, C. 1988. "Stalking the Wily Hacker." *Communications of the ACM* 31(5): p. 484.

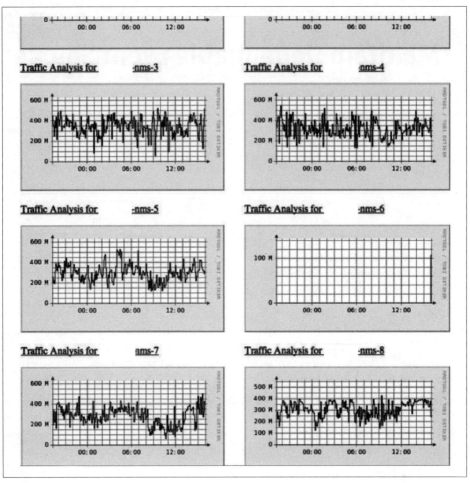

Figure 7-1. Router graph generated via MRTG, illustrating a dramatic drop in traffic for one of the monitored routers

To maintain reliable security monitoring, you must not only deploy the proper event sources, but also monitor the event sources to catch interruptions. In addition, you must keep watch for new systems deployed into your environment to ensure that events are properly recorded. This chapter will introduce you to tools and processes to keep security events continually recorded. We'll describe how to maintain proper device configurations, how to keep an eye on your event feeds, and how to maintain agreements with the support staff.

Maintain Device Configurations

One of the most effective means for keeping event sources working reliably is to manage configurations on the devices themselves. Recall that Chapter 5 provided guidance for configuring security event feeds. For example, a NIDS deployed passively requires a copy of the network traffic via a router switch port analyzer (SPAN) port, and a Unix server hosting an Apache web server should be configured to log authentication events to an event collector via its *syslog.conf* file. Consistent event collection depends on specific configuration directives on the source systems. If a network engineer removes a SPAN or a system administrator overwrites the *syslog.conf* settings, event feeds will suddenly stop. To minimize such errors, this section introduces the following techniques:

- Maintain documented agreements with device administrators.
- Where possible, leverage an automated configuration system to ensure that all systems maintain proper configuration for sending events.

Create Service Level Agreements

Device administrators (those who maintain servers, network equipment, and databases) hold responsibility for keeping things running smoothly and securely on the devices they support. They also hold *superuser* privileges on these devices, allowing them to make changes to configurations as they see fit. Consequently, the event feeds upon which you depend will require their cooperation to configure these devices and keep them functioning properly.

You may have a strong rapport with these administrators, and believe you can depend on them to keep your event feeds running smoothly. However, organizations change—a boss is promoted, a colleague reassigned—and can disrupt your informal agreements. To ensure commitment to your goal, we recommend you document your configuration requirements in formal agreements. Such agreements are best expressed in a contract called a *service level agreement* (SLA), formed between two parties: you (the client party), and the administrator's organization (the service provider party).

When building an SLA, be sure to clearly represent the following:

Rationale
    Why is the agreement necessary? What value does it protect for the business?

Specific, required actions for each party in the agreement
    This is the heart of the SLA, to document what's expected in a way that can be quantified. It's not reasonable to document what's required of only one party. Each party must bear some responsibility.

Time period in which the agreement will be in effect
    (Almost) nothing lasts forever.

Signatures of accountable managers for each party to the agreement
These can be ink or electronic signatures. The point is to ensure that you've reached a final agreement so that you can put it in effect and hold each party accountable.

You'll need a separate SLA for each organization you engage. If your company is organized like most are, this means you'll have one SLA per type of event source. Table 7-1 outlines the types of configuration directives you'll want to maintain via the SLA and the commonly used names for the organizations you'll probably need to engage.

Table 7-1. Configuration directives to maintain dependable event sources, and the teams to engage for SLAs

Event source	IT organization	Configuration support
NIDS alerts	Network engineering/ administration	• SPAN ports on routers and switches that feed NIDSs • Network flow logging from routers to flow collectors • Selected security event types to log • Network device logging to event collectors
Server events (syslog, etc.)	System administration/ hosting	• Selected security event types to log • Log destination (to your event collectors) • OS support for network flow collectors • OS support for event collectors
Database events	Database administration (DBA)	• Selected security event types to log • Accounts and privileges to read security events from audit table or logfile • Log destination (to your event collectors)
Application events (web servers, app servers, etc.)	Application administration (webmasters, etc.)	• Selected security event types to log • Log destination (to your event collectors) • Add-on scripts to push events to your collectors (if necessary)

Back It Up with Policy

Just as Chapter 2 described, policy is the foundation for effective security monitoring. Before you build an SLA, establish a device logging policy that documents expectations for the following:

- Which devices must log events (which devices are "in scope" for the policy)
- Which event types must be logged
- Where events must be logged (a "collection server" for security events)
- Who must have access to such logs (be sure to include your security team members)

This policy provides the foundation for building an SLA and maintaining a configuration template, which we'll illustrate in the next section.

SLA Sections

To build your SLA, include the following sections:[†]

Service description
> This is where you should document the scope of the service being offered. By scope, we mean to define the bounds of the service, indicating that you are committing to only certain devices, certain parts of the globe, and so forth. For the purpose of security event monitoring, you should describe exactly which devices are included in the scope of support and what event feeds you are expecting to be maintained.

Roles and responsibilities
> This is where each participant is named, both the service provider and the service client. For the purpose of event monitoring, this should name the group that maintains the device and exactly what is expected, including maintenance of event feeds and configuration directives. You are the client of such an agreement.

Requesting service
> This is where the process for making requests is documented. For security event feeds, this should document how the client (you) is expected to make requests of the device owner, and how the device owner is to make you aware of service outages or configuration changes.

Hours of operation
> This is where you should document expectations regarding expected up time of event feeds and support staff.

Response times
> This is where you should document the expected turnaround times for reported issues with event feeds.

Escalation
> Document how cases will be escalated, including to whom they will be escalated, when, and under what conditions. This section should also include information about how requests are prioritized.

Maintenance and service changes
> Document the expected maintenance schedule (e.g., "every Sunday from midnight to 3:00 a.m."), as well as a process for communicating changes to the event feeds.

Pricing
> If your company uses a chargeback system, or if an outside organization maintains your event feeds, you may need to document the pricing for various services in this section. This should include a process for how rates are set, as well as a catalog of charges that the client should expect.

[†] UC Santa Cruz Information Technology Services Services Agreement, 2008.

Reporting, reviewing, and auditing
> Document the start/end dates for your agreement, and include a regular review process and owner. Note the dates in this section for the next review, the previous review, and so on. This section should also note the official electronic "home" of this document.

Associated policies and processes
> It's important to link this agreement to specific policies about event recording, configuration management, and security.

You'll find a sample SLA for supporting NIDS feeds in Appendix B.

Automated Configuration Management

SLAs are an effective means of maintaining agreements, but they're only as reliable as the human beings who maintain them. An important supplement to maintain sound configuration for collecting security events is to maintain your device configurations with automated tools. For example, if you run Red Hat Enterprise Linux (RHEL) servers, you're probably already using the Red Hat Network (RHN) to download and apply package updates. You also can use RHN to push configuration files to managed servers. Such a configuration service allows administrators to deploy packages based on a "template" for system configurations, ensuring that all managed systems have correct settings applied for firewall settings, logging, user authentication, and so on. For Windows servers, Active Directory (AD) domains allow server configurations to be maintained and managed with Group Policy Objects (GPOs). You can even develop your own tools with a bit of shell scripting and some SSH trusts.

For example, to maintain reliable security events from your Unix servers, use a template like the following one for *syslog.conf*, to ensure that the correct events are logged and sent to your log collection server (in our example, the collection server is at 10.83.4.102):

```
# Sample section of syslog.conf to enable remote logging
local2.notice    /var/log/sudolog
local2.notice    @10.83.4.102
local3.info      /var/adm/ssh.log
local3.info      @10.83.4.102
local4.info      /var/adm/tcpwrap.log
local4.info      @10.83.4.102
local7.info      /var/adm/portsentry.log
local7.info      @10.83.4.102
*.err;kern.debug;daemon.notice;mail.crit        @10.83.4.102
auth.notice      /var/log/authlog
auth.notice      @@10.83.4.102
```

At Cisco, for example, we use something called *autoconfig templates*. This allows us to deploy a set of approved templates to our network devices. To ensure that we have the security feeds we need, we could build a "security event template" to make sure

NetFlow and event logs are sent to the appropriate event collectors. A template for NetFlow feeds might look like this:

```
# Setup NetFlow export to our NetFlow collector at 10.83.4.99
ip flow-export source Loopback0
ip flow-export version 5
ip flow-export destination 10.83.4.99 2055
```

A template for syslog events would look like this:

```
# Setup logging for certain events to our event log collector at 10.83.4.102
logging facility auth
logging facility daemon
logging trap informational
logging host 10.83.4.102
```

If you wish to use off-the-shelf products to automate the configuration of your network devices you could use Cisco Network Compliance Manager, or Cisco Security Manager which manages configuration of security devices.

Monitor the Monitors

If you've worked in information security for long, you've noticed a phrase emerge over the past few years: "watching the watchers". The idea is to keep an eye on your privileged users—the ones maintaining the systems for common users. We must apply the same concept here: to make sure the systems used for conducting security monitoring are reliably maintained. Without that assurance, critical security events may be lost or deliberately suppressed.

To effectively monitor the health of your monitoring system, you must first set a benchmark for "normal" activity. As Æleen Frisch writes in *Essential System Administration*: "As with most of life, performance tuning is much harder when you have to guess what normal is. If you don't know what the various system performance metrics usually show when performance is acceptable, it will be very hard to figure out what is wrong when performance degrades. Accordingly, it is essential to do routine system monitoring and to maintain records of performance-related statistics over time."[‡]

You'll use this benchmark to compare recent activity and determine whether anything has changed, and whether that change requires attention. For example, if you know that your NIDS normally sustains 400 Mbps of traffic, a sudden, sustained drop to 5 Mbps should cause you to take note and look for problems on the network or the devices. If you normally receive 150 messages per hour from your Windows domain controller, you'll want to be notified if the rate has dropped to 0 in the past 60 minutes.

In this section, we'll discuss how to keep your monitoring systems running smoothly by tracking the system health (CPU, memory, disk, etc.), as well as each event feed.

[‡] Frisch, Æleen. 2002. *Essential System Administration*, Third Edition. Sebastopol, CA: O'Reilly Media, Inc.

We'll discuss each type of system (NIDS, server, and database), along with specific checks for each type of system, to keep them reporting reliably.

Monitor System Health

The systems that generate and feed events necessary for security monitoring must be monitored themselves; if they're not functioning properly, they can't continue sending events. System load, disk space, and built-in hardware sensors should be observed to provide early warning of present or imminent failure. To monitor overall system health, observe the following system indicators, measuring them against your "normal" benchmark.

Monitor system load

Take snapshots of system load at regular intervals (spaced a few seconds apart) to trend and watch for spikes. This includes snapshots of CPU performance such as what you can see with uptime, procinfo, or w:

```
[mnystrom@blanco-rich-1 ~]$ uptime
 07:25:11 up 32 days, 17:04,  1 user,  load average: 0.01, 0.02, 0.00
```

It turns out that different types of systems compute this number differently. Linux does not take into account the number of processes waiting for the CPU, whereas HP does. Therefore, you'll want to understand how the number is calculated before you set alerting thresholds. However, it's fair to say that if the system is running normally when the load is less than 1, seeing it spike to 4 or 5 indicates that something has drastically changed, and you'll want to look into what's causing the spike.

Monitor memory

Watch memory to ensure that you aren't exhausting all of your free or swap memory. It's good to check memory utilization against what's "normal," but some processes grow over time. At the very least, check to make sure you don't run out of physical or swap memory. On a Unix machine, you can check this with commands such as top, free, and meminfo.

Monitor disk space

Watch available disk space to ensure that there's adequate room to store collected events. Keep an eye on space utilization in the partition where you're collecting data, and where the system must keep disk space available to function properly. You can check available disk space on a Unix server with the command df. Beyond just having disk space available, you'll also want to ensure that the space is writable.

Monitor network performance

Check network performance and throughput to ensure that security events aren't over-whelming your network interface. You can check this on Unix (as root), with the `ifconfig` command:

```
bash-3.00$ sudo ifconfig
Password:
eth0      Link encap:Ethernet  HWaddr 00:1E:0B:34:9F:D7
          inet addr:10.83.4.102  Bcast:10.83.4.255  Mask:255.255.255.0
          inet6 addr: fe80::21e:bff:fe34:9ee7/64 Scope:Link
          UP BROADCAST RUNNING MULTICAST  MTU:1500  Metric:1
          RX packets:20892745 errors:0 dropped:0 overruns:0 frame:0
          TX packets:12713946 errors:0 dropped:0 overruns:0 carrier:0
          collisions:0 txqueuelen:1000
          RX bytes:2754879057 (2.5 GiB)  TX bytes:1151366228 (1.0 GiB)
          Interrupt:209
```

Verify that you're not seeing errors on the interface by inspecting the *errors* section of the output.

To continually monitor your systems, you should program these commands to run at frequent intervals, benchmarking them against normal values. We'll describe an approach for accomplishing this later in "Automated System Monitoring" on page 167.

Now that we've discussed how to monitor the health of your systems, we'll address how you should monitor each type of device to ensure a continual stream of events.

Monitor the NIDS

When functioning properly, a NIDS is one of the best event sources for security monitoring. To function properly, a NIDS must have bidirectional visibility to the network segments it monitors; it must be able to fully inspect every single packet on the wire. To maintain your NIDS so that you have an uninterrupted stream of events, you must be sure that a number of areas are working properly: monitor the traffic feeds, sensor processes, and recent alerts generated to ensure that the NIDS is performing as expected.

Monitor traffic feeds (uplinks)

To ensure that you're getting traffic to your NIDS, watch the ports feeding into it. If your NIDS is configured to receive traffic via a SPAN port, watch the SPANs to ensure that they're still pointed to your NIDS. (Occasionally a network engineer will "steal" the SPAN port to troubleshoot other problems. She may forget to reset the configuration for your NIDS.) Alternatively, if you've deployed your NIDS in the line of traffic (inline), watch the traffic rates to ensure that nothing has been interrupted. It will be obvious if your NIDS is no longer receiving traffic, as all downstream traffic will also be interrupted.

MRTG is an excellent open source tool for watching traffic volumes. It uses Simple Network Management Protocol (SNMP) for status updates on the monitored device. If MRTG shows a sudden drop in network traffic for your NIDS, it's likely that you've lost a traffic feed.

To ensure that your routers are still configured to send traffic to your NIDS, you must watch the SPAN configuration on the routers themselves. If you analyze the configuration of the monitor sessions on the router, you should see that it remains configured to mirror traffic to your NIDS. The best way to ensure that it's working properly is to document the output of the working configuration, and compare it to the running configuration at regular intervals. For example, here's the output of `show monitor` on an IOS 12.2 router:

```
blanco-dc-gw1>show monitor
Session 1
- ---------
Type                    : Local Session
Source Ports            :
    Both                : Gi1/1
Destination Ports       : Gi3/11


Session 2
- ---------
Type                    : Local Session
Source Ports            :
    Both                : Gi1/2
Destination Ports       : Gi3/12
```

In this example, a NIDS is connected to port Gi3/11 on *Session 1* and Gi3/12 on *Session 2*.

Monitor sensor processes

Even if traffic is reaching your NIDS, you must be sure it can process the events. The NIDS will have some processes responsible for receiving and analyzing events, which must be kept running to continue analyzing traffic and raising alerts. You should watch the sensor processes to be sure they're running normally. For example, on a Cisco NIDS, the Analysis Engine must be running for the sensor to process events. In a Snort deployment, it's the `snort` process that's critical. You may wish to add further checks to ensure that the required processes are not in a "zombie" state, and that they're getting sufficient CPU time.

Monitor alerts

If your router is sending traffic to the NIDS, and the processes are running normally, everything is probably working fine. One further check that you can add is to ensure that alerts are being generated. To do so, watch the alerts coming from the NIDS to ensure that you've received at least one alert within the past few minutes. On many networks, a properly tuned device will still generate events very frequently, so if you've not seen a single event within the past 30 minutes, something is definitely wrong.

Monitor Network Flow Collection

As we described in previous chapters, Cisco NetFlow is a popular open standard for recording network flows. We recommend capturing such flows for analysis, for monitoring, and as a secondary source to support investigations. To ensure that your network flows are flowing, monitor the collection servers to make sure you're getting the amount of data you expect from the places you expect. You should monitor the system used to collect the flows, the processes that collect and store the flows, the network traffic along the segments in your network, and the routers sending NetFlow to your collection system.

 We recommend collecting NetFlow from routers that act as choke points on your network. Typically, such choke points are deployed where you're already doing traffic filtering, such as the corporate Internet connection, data center gateways, and gateways to specialized networks for partners or labs.

Monitor system health

Most importantly, the network flow collector must itself be watched to ensure that it can receive, store, and relay flows properly. This requires "health monitoring," as we expounded earlier in this section. Health monitoring checks that the collector can keep up with incoming data, and that the disk space and permissions are properly configured so that captured flows can be properly stored.

Monitor traffic feeds from routers

There's more than one way to monitor for flows coming in from each router you're expecting. It's most important to watch that the sending routers are configured to send flows to your collector. On each router, verify that the `ip flow export` command is properly configured. For example, here's the NetFlow configuration on a Cisco IOS 12.2 router. It's configured to export NetFlow v5 to our collector at 10.83.4.99 on port 2055.

```
blanco-dc-gw1>show ip flow export
Flow export v5 is enabled for main cache
  Exporting flows to 10.83.4.99 (2055)
  Exporting using source interface Loopback0
  Version 5 flow records, peer-as
  327844689 flows exported in 10928453 udp datagrams
  -- output clipped for brevity --
```

You should also confirm that NetFlow is being exported from the proper interface (in the preceding example, it's exporting via the Loopback0 interface). If you check this again in a few seconds, you should see the number of exported flows increasing, indicating that it's still exporting properly.

Monitor collector network configuration

Now that you've checked the configuration from the routers, you should also check the collector to be sure it's listening to receive flows, and that they're being received. Assuming the collector is running Unix, simply use netstat to check that the collector is listening for NetFlow traffic on the proper port by "grepping" for the correct listening port:

```
[mnystrom@blanco-dc-nfc-1 ~]$ netstat -l | grep 2055
udp        0      0 *:2055                    *:*
```

You'll also want to see whether you're receiving traffic from each router. One technique is to create iptables rules on the collector itself, adding an entry for each router from which you expect to receive NetFlow. For example, if you want to monitor the amount of traffic you've received from two gateway routers, add ACCEPT rules for each router to the iptables INPUT chain:

```
[root@blanco-dc-nfc-1 ~]# iptables -vL INPUT
Chain INPUT (policy ACCEPT 9875 packets, 14M bytes)
 pkts bytes target     prot opt in     out     source        destination
-A INPUT -s 10.83.4.1 -p udp -m udp --dport 2055 -j ACCEPT
-A INPUT -s 10.83.4.2 -p udp -m udp --dport 2055 -j ACCEPT
ACCEPT
COMMIT
```

 A typical use for iptables is to filter traffic by including a DROP statement somewhere in the chain, to dictate that any traffic not explicitly allowed should be blocked. Because you're using iptables only to keep count of traffic from each source, you don't need to include a DROP rule in the configuration file unless you want to filter traffic.

The iptables chain in the preceding code is "accepting" connections from gateways 10.83.4.1 and .2 (corresponding to blanco-dc-gw1 and gw2, respectively). You can periodically run iptables -VL INPUT, to see how many bytes and packets have arrived from each accepted host in the chain. Simply compare those numbers with the ones from a few minutes ago to prove that you're getting traffic from each source:

```
[root@blanco-dc-nfc-1 ~]# iptables -vL INPUT
Chain INPUT (policy ACCEPT 9875 packets, 14M bytes)
 pkts bytes target prot opt in  out  source        destination
  159  230K ACCEPT udp  --  any any  blanco-dc-gw1 anywhere udp dpt:2055
 4692 6776K ACCEPT udp  --  any any  blanco-dc-gw2 anywhere udp dpt:2055
```

The preceding output proves that you've received 159 packets and 230,000 bytes since the last flush of the counters. Once you've checked these numbers, flush the counters so that you can see whether you're accumulating flows at the next read. You can do this easily with the "zero counters" option on the `iptables` command (indicated in the following code by the -Z option):

```
[root@blanco-dc-nfc-1 ~]# iptables -vxL -Z INPUT
Chain INPUT (policy ACCEPT 273 packets, 130896 bytes)
 pkts bytes target  prot opt in  out  source          destination
  43 64156 ACCEPT  udp  --  any any  blanco-dc-gw1  anywhere udp dpt:2055
  11 16412 ACCEPT  udp  --  any any  blanco-dc-gw2  anywhere udp dpt:2055
Zeroing chain 'INPUT'
```

Monitor collection directories

To prevent a problem where routers are sending NetFlow but you're not able to store it, check the directories where NetFlow is stored to be sure permissions are set properly. For example, to check the */apps/netflow* directory on a Unix box, check that the *write* bit is properly set for the user writing the flows:

```
[mnystrom@blanco-dc-nfc-1 data]$ ls -l /apps/netflow
total 12
drwxr-xr-x  243 netflow infosec 12288 Jul 28 09:41 data
```

In the preceding example, you can see that the `netflow` user (the owner of the file) has full permissions on the `data` file, so the file system is properly configured. This is a good place to verify that datafiles have been written to the collection directory within the past few minutes.

Monitor collection processes

Once you've verified that the system can receive flows and that data is coming from the routers, you should ensure that the processes used for collecting and storing (and, if applicable, relaying) NetFlow are running, and that they haven't failed or gone into a zombie state. To check processes, run a command on the operating system to see whether all the correct processes are running. Of course, you'll first need to know which processes should be running, and how many of them.

```
[mnystrom@blanco-dc-nfc-1 ~]$ ps -ef | grep netflow
netflow  29982    1  0 2007 ?        1-09:34:16 /usr/local/netflow/bin/flow-
capture -w /apps/netflow/data -E54G -V5 0/0/2056 -S5 -p /var/run/netflow/flow-
capture.pid -N-1 -n288
netflow  29999    1  0 2007 ?        05:32:35 /usr/local/netflow/bin/flow-fanout
0/0/2055 0/0/2056 10.71.18.5/10.71.18.6/2055
```

In the preceding example, one flow-capture and one flow-fanout process is running. With OSU flow-tools, these processes are used to receive and store data to the local system, and relay them out to other systems.

Maintain flow retention

Many collection tools provide a means for keeping storage within the bounds of available disk space by rotating out older data. With OSU flow-tools, the flow-capture process allows you to set the *expire size* or *expire count* for flows. These settings allow you to set a limit on how many flows you want to keep, or how much space you want to use for storing flows. Assuming, for example, that you want to keep as much data as possible within 1 TB of disk space, you could use the option `-E 1024G` on flow-capture. This option tells flow-capture to throw away the oldest flows in order to keep within the 1 TB (1,024 GB) disk space limit.

The knowledge that you have a full tool chest is useless without the accompanying knowledge of which tools are contained within. Likewise, you'll want to know just how far back your NetFlow records go, so you can support necessary investigations and monitoring. If your collection directories are named by date, your job is an easy query against directory names. If not, simply finding the date of the oldest directory in your collection should show you how far back you can query NetFlow records.

Watch for New Systems

In a large enterprise, it's difficult to keep abreast of the new systems deployed. If routing changes, systems are moved, or new systems are added to provide load balancing, your monitoring will be blind to those events until you add their events to your systems. The network engineering team, for example, may deploy an additional router to handle load on the network, bring up a new data center, or deploy a new Internet Point of Presence (PoP). The system administration team may replace a Linux server with a virtual machine, or the DBAs may load-balance the database instance across multiple servers. Discovering these infrastructure changes is critical and complex. Here are a few ideas for uncovering these changes.

Change management. Most enterprises have a means of documenting important changes to the environment. This is often in the form of change requests that are then communicated, reviewed, and approved by appropriate teams and representatives. More sophisticated systems even allow users to register interest in particular hosts or devices, queuing notification when changes are scheduled. This can be a useful means of noting simple changes to the environment, such as configuring a router so that it peers with a new router. Such changes can serve as triggers for you to reach out to the responsible team so that you can get your security event feeds configured.

Network scans. Network scanning tools discover the devices present on network segments, often including additional probes to determine how the devices are configured. These scans can turn up new devices that might otherwise be missed, allowing you to catch new systems and determine whether they should be in the scope of your security monitoring.

Use network scans to watch for new routers and systems appearing, especially within subnet ranges that correspond to the ranges targeted for monitoring. Your company will probably use centrally managed scanning systems, but here's an example of what you can discover with a simple ping scan from Nmap:

```
thor$ nmap -sP 10.3.1.0/24

Starting Nmap 4.50 ( http://insecure.org ) at 2008-08-09
17:07 EDT
Host corp-dc-gw1.blanco.com (10.3.1.1) appears to be up.
Host webserver (10.3.1.18) appears to be up.
Host webserver-bkup (10.3.1.19) appears to be up.
Host new-webserver (10.3.1.20) appears to be up.
Nmap done: 256 IP addresses (7 hosts up) scanned in 1.589
seconds
```

This scan looked for hosts on the 10.3.1.0/24 network segment. Assuming this network segment is in range of your targeted monitoring, you can keep a list of known hosts on this segment, watching for new ones appearing. Once you see new hosts, determine what information you might need to collect from them to maintain full coverage for security monitoring.

Relationships. In "Parents: The Anti-Drug," a series of public service announcements, parents are encouraged to spend time talking to their teenagers to detect signs of drug abuse. The point is that personal conversations are clearly the most reliable way to uncover information. As painful as this analogy sounds (talking to your network administrators about capacity planning is not the same as talking to your kids about drugs), if you hope to detect important changes to an environment, you should regularly engage with IT staff. This will help you uncover what's changing and what they're planning for the environment. At Cisco, a strong relationship with IT Networking has helped InfoSec discover new PoPs under deployment, new data centers, and important organizational changes.

Monitor Event Log Collectors

Like network flow collectors, event log collectors run software for gathering and forwarding event logs. To keep events flowing to security monitoring systems, and to ensure that downstream systems are not kept waiting for events routed through event log collectors, monitor system health as well as the health of collection and relay processes. Most importantly, you'll need to watch the event flow coming from originating devices to prevent event gaps in your monitoring.

Monitor system health

Monitor system health using the same approach used for NetFlow collectors. Verify that the collector is functioning properly and has enough memory, that load is sufficient for processing, and that the disk can handle more incoming data.

Monitor collection processes

For event collection to work properly, the system processes used for receiving and storing events must run constantly, listening for relayed events. For example, when using syslog-ng for collecting event logs, the syslog-ng process must be listening for relayed syslog, normally via the standard syslog port of UDP/514. To check whether the process is running and listening on the correct port, use netstat to check for running UDP listeners and what processes are bound to those ports. You can do this with the -a option to show all connections, along with the -p option to show programs bound to ports:

```
[mnystrom@syslog-blanco-1 ~]$ sudo netstat -ap | grep syslog
tcp 0    0 0.0.0.0:514          0.0.0.0:*         LISTEN      1813/syslog-ng
udp 0    0 0.0.0.0:514          0.0.0.0:*                     1813/syslog-ng
udp 0    0 10.83.4.102:32851 10.71.180.220:514 ESTABLISHED 1813/syslog-ng
udp 0    0 10.83.4.102:32873 10.70.149.28:516  ESTABLISHED 1813/syslog-ng
unix 10  [ ]  DGRAM             4663    1800/syslogd         /dev/log
```

 You must run this command as a privileged user (root on Unix), to see the status of ports < 1024.

Based on the output from the preceding netstat -ap command, we can see that syslog-ng is listening for syslog, as we expect.

syslog-ng can handle listening for incoming syslog as well as storing it and relaying it to other servers. This is accomplished within one process, so there's no need to monitor other processes on this host. Alternative event collection systems may use more processes in collecting and storing events. For example, Splunk, a commercial flexible analysis tool for events, requires processes for receiving events, helper processes, a watchdog process, and a web server.

Monitor collection directories (logs)

You must watch the systems that are originating events to the log collector to ensure that they're still sending data. There are a number of ways to oversee these event streams to ensure that they're still flowing, but the most painless method is to watch the growing logfiles, checking for recent events from each system.

Begin with a list of hostnames from which you're expecting events, and then check the event logs for recent events from such systems. Count any recent event as a "heartbeat" from the source system, indicating that it's still sending events. There's no need to evaluate the type of message that arrived from the source system; its recent timestamp is enough to indicate that the event feed is functioning. To check for a recent message from a source, search through the directory of collected logs. This may be a simple exercise if the directory is organized by event source, but if you're using syslog-ng, you'll have to slog through the mass of data to find the recent messages.

Let's say it's August 9 at 2:59 p.m., and you want to check for a message from the *webserver-1* server within the past hour. Using egrep (extended grep) on a Unix system, you can construct this search to find something within the hour of 14:00, across all logfiles in the current directory:

```
egrep "Aug 9 14:.*webserver-1" /apps/logs/all-*
```

The egrep command tells the Unix server to run a regular expression match against the files. The .* between the date and the server name is a regular expression telling egrep to ignore everything between the date format and the server name. Even a single message within the past hour is an indicator that the server is running and sending events to the collector, as we expect.

> This works only if the sending server and the event collector are time-synchronized. If they're not, none of the monitoring in this chapter or book will work for you, as you can't correlate events. To synchronize time on your servers, use Network Time Protocol and a common time offset (we suggest GMT).

Monitor network traffic

Watch the network interface card (NIC) for messages arriving from the source system. The setup works as we described in "Monitor Network Flow Collection" on page 157. Create an iptables configuration with an ACCEPT rule for each source server. Monitor the accumulated packets for each rule in iptables, flushing each time you check the table.

Audit configurations

Technically, auditing isn't active monitoring, but the servers originating events to your collector require a configuration that will capture the correct events and relay them to the proper collector. To maintain the correct configuration on systems, deploy an auditing solution that can check its logging configuration against a reference template. Check for the following two configuration directives in the system's log configuration:

- Is the relay set to the IP address of your event collector?
- Are proper event types being logged?

A simple script to access the source server and grep the *syslog.conf* might include a check such as this:

```
$ ssh webserver-1 grep 10.83.4.102 /etc/syslog.conf
*.*                         @10.83.4.102
```

This checks the *webserver-1* server for the presence of the 10.83.4.102 collection server in the *syslog.conf* file, and finds it in the response.

> Scripts that remotely check configuration values require setup of public key authentication to the target server prior to execution. Take precautions to protect the private keys, and never permit connections to production servers from nonproduction hosts, as those keys are less protected.

Maintain log retention

Just as we described in "Monitor Network Flow Collection" on page 157, it's vital to make sure your event collection doesn't overrun the available disk space. You can monitor this by watching available disk space (covered in "Monitor system health"), but you'll need to proactively rotate your collected logs, expiring the oldest content to make room for new events. This feature is not native to `syslog-ng`, so you'll need complementary tools to accomplish it. The most common pairing is logrotate, a freely available Unix utility authored by Erik Troan of Red Hat. This utility is scheduled to run as a daily cron, archiving logfiles by rotating, compressing, and deleting them.§

Monitor Databases

Databases can be critical sources of security events, especially on systems that store sensitive data. To ensure that they keep a continuous flow of messages, monitor the processes that record events in the database, and monitor the storage locations for the events, to make sure new messages are showing up. This section explores techniques for monitoring database settings for auditing and logging.

Monitor Oracle

You can configure Oracle to record a wide variety of events. To make certain Oracle is properly capturing an audit trail, you must ensure that events are being logged properly and that audit settings are properly set. As an additional precaution, configure the database to capture administrative events to audit DBA activity.

Maintain Oracle systemwide audit settings

To enable event logging in Oracle (Oracle calls it "auditing"), you must set the `audit_trail` parameter in the *init.ora* file. The database references this core configuration file at startup, and specifies whether to log events to the Oracle database (`audit_trail = db` or `audit_trail = true`) or to a logfile (`audit_trail = os`) on the host file system.

As an added step, routinely check the configuration files to be sure the Oracle database remains properly configured for logging. From the database, you can ensure that systemwide auditing is turned on by checking the **v$parameter** table:

```
select NAME, VALUE from V$PARAMETER where NAME like 'audit%';

NAME                              VALUE
------------------------------
audit_trail                       DB
audit_file_dest                   ?/rdbms/audit
```

§ See *http://linuxcommand.org/man_pages/logrotate8.html* for more information.

Here you can see that the administrator has configured *init.ora* with `audit_trail = db`, and that audit data will be written to the database's audit area (`SYS.AUD$`).

Monitor Oracle audit events

Should you decide to collect events to the file system, it's easy to relay those logs into your event log collection server. However, if you want Oracle to record events to the `SYS.AUD$` table, you must keep watch over that table to confirm that new events are arriving regularly. For example, here's a simple query to check for new events arriving every five minutes:

```
select count(*) from SYS.AUD$
where (current_timestamp - aud$.timestamp#) > 5*1/24/60
```

If the query returns a count greater than zero, you've confirmed that some events have been received within the past five minutes. To be sure you've received audit events of a certain type (for a specific table, column, user, etc.), simply add criteria to the `where` clause in the preceding query.

Maintain Oracle audit settings on objects

If events are captured in the `SYS.AUD$` table (or the file system, depending on how Oracle is configured), you can have confidence that the system is configured to properly log events. However, because configuration changes can disrupt the flow of events, it's useful to monitor Oracle's audit settings to be sure you're capturing audit events.

When you configure auditing on a table, Oracle stores the setting in metadata. The `DBA_OBJ_AUDIT_OPTS` view lists these settings, cross-referencing all objects with audit settings for every possible statement. You should regularly query this view to verify that audit settings are correct. For example, to ensure that auditing is still enabled for successful and unsuccessful queries against the `CUSTOMERS` table (where Social Security numbers are stored), issue the query:

```
select SEL from dba_obj_audit_opts
where object_name = 'CUSTOMERS';
```

If it's properly configured for auditing, it should return:

```
SEL
---
A/A
```

This shows that auditing is enabled for both successful and unsuccessful `SELECT` statements against that table.

Monitor administrative privileges

It's considered a best practice to ensure that event logs are immutable so that a malicious user cannot cover her tracks by modifying them. Because a DBA has superuser privileges, she will always be able to modify the `SYS.AUD$` table. Two simple configuration directives will record DBA activity and provide a record of any attempt to remove data from the auditing table.

First, set a directive to capture all changes to the `SYS.AUD$` table. Connect as `SYSDBA` and modify the `SYS.AUD$` table with this statement:[||]

```
audit ALL on SYS.AUD$ by access;
```

This will ensure that every operation against the `SYS.AUD$` table—including delete and truncate—are inserted into the `SYS.AUD$` table as audit entries. If a DBA tries to cover her tracks by deleting entries from the table, those actions will be logged into the table itself!

You should also provide an off-database log of DBA activity. To do so, turn on file-based auditing of DBA actions by adding this configuration directive to *init.ora*:[#]

```
AUDIT_SYS_OPERATIONS = TRUE
```

This will configure Oracle to log all `SYS` operations (including `SYSDBA` and `SYSOPER`) to the operating system logfile, which, if the system is configured correctly, is off-limits to the DBAs.

Monitor MySQL Servers

The current version of MySQL (5.x) has limited options to enable auditing. SQL query statements are logged in the "general query" logfile. This is enabled if you specify the `--log` option when starting the database. To ensure that messages are still being written to the general query log, simply watch recent entries to the *mysqld.log* query logfile, which shows recent events:

```
080228 15:27:50   1170 Connect  user@host on database_name
                  1170 Query    SET NAMES "utf8"
                  1170 Query    SELECT something FROM sometable WHERE some=thing
                  1170 Quit
```

Watching this file allows you to verify that queries are still being written to the logfile.

Use Canary Events to Monitor Sources

Here's an additional tool to monitor event sources: generate "canary" events and watch for them downstream. You can use a canary event like a heartbeat to verify that events are being captured, relayed, and collected properly. For each event source described in this chapter, we've outlined an example of how to generate and find canary events. Note that for these illustrations, *coalmine* is a server used for executing scripts to generate canary events.

NetFlow. Pick a router sending NetFlow to your collector. Now pick a server with an Internet Protocol (IP) address on the other side of that router (between *coalmine* and

---

[||] Loney, K., and B. Bryla. 2005. *Oracle Database 10g DBA Handbook*. Oracle Press.

[#] Oracle Corporation. 2002. *Oracle9i Database Administrator's Guide*.

the IP you're testing). Run a script on *coalmine* to ping that IP address at a regular interval. On the NetFlow collector, regularly query the stored NetFlow records to look for the canary event. The query will be very specific and efficient, as it's searching for an exact match on source and destination IP address, along with the exact protocol (ICMP).

Here's an example using flow-cat and flow-filter, which are part of OSU flow-tools.[*] In this example, *coalmine* uses IP 10.10.0.12. We're building a query in the *flow.acl* file, searching the NetFlow directory using flow-filter to find only the canary events:

```
[blanco-nfc]$ cat flow.acl
ip access-list standard canary-flow permit host 10.10.0.128
host 172.17.54.31

[blanco-nfc]$ flow-cat /apps/netflow/data/2008-09-18/ft* |
flow-filter -r1 -Scanary-flow
```

NIDS. Find a host that requires traversal by a router monitored by each NIDS, and generate an alert by scripting a ping from *coalmine* to that host's IP. On the NIDS, build and deploy a custom signature to detect your canary connection. Now, your monitoring tools can watch for the canary alert downstream (in the Security Information Manager [SIM] or wherever your NIDS alerts are collected).

Host Logs. On every monitored host, deploy a script that generates a canary event every few minutes. On the event collector, query for the canary event from each host at a regular interval.

Database Audit Events. Pick a table to monitor. Deploy a script to query the target table every few minutes, using a well-protected test account. Monitor the audit log for queries by the test user against the specific table.

Automated System Monitoring

So far, this chapter has illustrated manual techniques to monitor and maintain event feeds for NIDS, event collectors, and databases. However, automation is the key to sustaining a continuous stream of events for security monitoring. In this section, we will examine a few commercial and open source tools available for network and system monitoring, applying them to keep dependable event streams for security monitoring.

Traditional Network Monitoring and Management Systems

Network monitoring systems are types of network management systems. Monitoring is conducted by agents running on "end stations" (the systems being monitored). These end stations are observed by management entities that are programmed to respond to

---

[*] National Chi Nan University. OSU flow-tools documents; *http://163.22.3.90/flow-doc/* (accessed September 18, 2008).

the agents.[†] These tools are designed to monitor system health, though new functions are constantly being introduced into such software.

Network monitoring has been around for decades, notably in the form of HP OpenView Network Node Manager (NNM), which uses SNMP (along with other technologies) to maintain visibility into system health. OpenView presents a dashboard overview of all managed devices, using varying colors to illustrate their health and event status. Competitors include IBM Tivoli Monitoring, CA Unicenter TNG, and Microsoft SMS. It's hard to pin a name on such products because many of them handle provisioning, health monitoring, inventory, and configuration. Such tools have been used to manage host operating systems, network devices, application software, and databases. In recent years, a number of free open source products have matured to the point that they are now viable alternatives to commercial network monitoring systems, including such tools as Nagios, OpenNMS, Pandora, and Zenoss.

 As the systems we've described here offer much more than network device monitoring, it's hard to call them "network monitoring" solutions. We couldn't find an accepted term that describes more than that, so we'll just call them "system monitoring" solutions for the duration of this chapter.

How system monitoring works

System monitoring solutions maintain a dashboard that allows an "at-a-glance" view of device status. They track the health and event status of each system using a variety of inputs, and contain the following elements:

- Agents that assess the health of managed devices (via SNMP, scripts, local agents, etc.)
- A state retention database to track the health information recorded for each system
- A monitoring console, which provides an overview of up-to-the-minute device status

Agents can run on the monitored device, such as an SNMP agent reporting to a system monitor or an installed agent. Alternatively, the central monitoring server can probe the device to evaluate output and record the health of the component. Figure 7-2 depicts a traditional network monitoring system.

The agents that run in a system monitoring solution check the health of a component or end station. They typically run a script containing commands much like the ones we've described in this chapter. For example, an agent could SSH into a server and run a command, evaluating the output to determine whether the system is performing

[†] Castelli, M.J. 2001. *Network Consultants Handbook*. Indianapolis: Cisco Press.

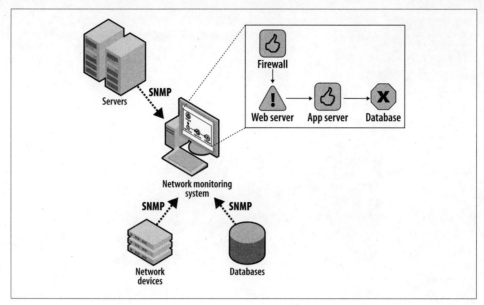

Figure 7-2. A traditional network monitoring system showing a dashboard representing the availability of each device

within prespecified boundaries. Alternatively, the agent may run on the monitored device itself, triggering an SNMP trap when CPU utilization crosses an upper threshold.

To leverage such a system for your targeted monitoring event sources, you should configure it to monitor the following:

- System health of every device reporting events
- Status of accumulating events from each sending device
- Status of accumulating events on event receivers
- Health of each event collector
- Health of each component in detection systems

The status of each item should be represented on the network monitor dashboard, allowing you to observe "at a glance" those areas that require administrative attention.

How to Monitor the Monitors

You've likely seen monitoring systems displaying a dashboard on large screens in offices and data centers. What value, however, is such a display without action? Someone must be assigned responsibility to not only view the alerts, but also—and more importantly—take action to address the problems highlighted on the dashboard. Monitoring the status of security event feeds is a task best assigned to the team already conducting security monitoring. These staff members depend on event feeds from the monitored systems, and are in the best position to notice when they go offline.

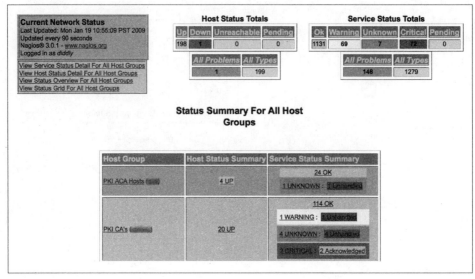

Figure 7-3. The Nagios dashboard showing the status of groups of devices, linking to a detailed status for each

Many of the system monitoring solutions provide built-in case handling and notation capabilities, allowing staff to track the status of alarms. To use these effectively, establish monitoring procedures that include attention to the system monitoring solution, with documented, assigned responsibilities. Good case handling procedures will allow staff to see the status of such alarms without mistakenly troubleshooting the same problems, duplicating their effort.

Monitoring with Nagios

Nagios, formerly known as NetSaint, is a feature-rich system monitoring package. It displays current information about system or resource status across an entire network. In addition, you can configure it to send alerts and perform remedial actions when problems are detected.‡

Figure 7-3 is a screenshot of Nagios's dashboard, giving an overview of the systems being monitored, along with an indication of the status for each device.

Nagios lists an overall status for hosts and services, along with a summary for each group of servers. When you click on a specific host, Nagios displays a detailed status page for the host (shown in Figure 7-4). This detailed status page specifies monitored aspects, provides a set of available commands for monitoring the host, and provides an interface to make note of issues.

---

‡ Frisch, Æleen. "Top Five Open Source Packages for System Administrators, Part 4." O'Reilly ONLamp.com, December 5, 2002; *http://www.onlamp.com/pub/a/onlamp/2002/12/05/essentialsysadmin.html* (accessed August 25, 2008).

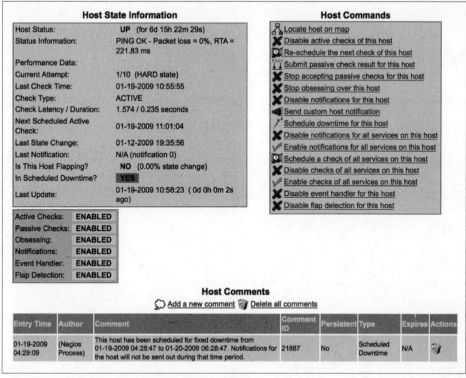

Figure 7-4. *Detailed device status displayed in Nagios*

Nagios normally installs scripts on the system to be monitored, allowing the central server to execute scripts via a "plug-in" framework that reports status back to the Nagios server. These scripts check the status of each monitored element within a set of "warning" and "critical" boundaries set for the element. For example, to monitor system memory, a Nagios plug-in allows the administrator to set both a warning and a critical alert, passed as parameters to the script when it starts. Here's syntax to start a plug-in that checks memory, returning a warning if free physical memory is below 10% of available memory and raising a critical alert if it's below 5%:

```
check_mem -w 10 -c 5
```

Most plug-ins are executed from the Nagios server via NRPE (remote procedure execution) or SSH. For cases where a system cannot be actively polled for its status, Nagios can accommodate a passive check, which allows a script on the monitored system to send its status directly to the Nagios server. In addition, on some of the systems you'll need to monitor, you will be unable to install any plug-in. For those cases, Nagios can run *Expect* scripts on the monitored system, connecting via SSH from the Nagios server itself.

The next section will illustrate how you can use Nagios to automate system and network monitoring for Blanco Wireless.

System Monitoring for Blanco Wireless

Blanco Wireless has configured targeted monitoring for its account management system. To monitor the system, Blanco is leveraging the following event sources:

- NetFlow collection at the data center and DMZ gateways
- Syslog collection from servers
- NIDS
- Database event logs from the Oracle 10*g* databases

Using Nagios, Blanco can automate system monitoring to ensure high availability for security monitoring (see Figure 7-5).

> Nagios setup and configuration is detailed on the Nagios website at *http://www.nagios.org/*. Plug-ins and scripts are listed at *http://www.NagiosExchange.org/* and *http://www.NagiosPlugins.org/*.

Monitor NetFlow Collection

The NetFlow collectors for Blanco are running OSU flow-tools for collecting and querying NetFlow records. To ensure continuous flow collection from critical sources (the DC and DMZ gateway routers sending flows to the collectors), Nagios plug-ins are configured to observe the following:

- Collectors are continuously receiving flows from both data center and DMZ routers.
- Collectors are in good health, so they're able to receive and store flows properly.
- Collection processes are running and functioning properly.

For Nagios to monitor the collectors, Blanco has deployed the NRPE daemon to run directly on the collectors. Blanco has configured the plug-ins to monitor system health and collector processes, and to check that data is still coming from the routers configured to send flows for collection.

Monitor Collector Health

To effectively monitor collector health, Blanco has configured the following series of Nagios plug-ins.

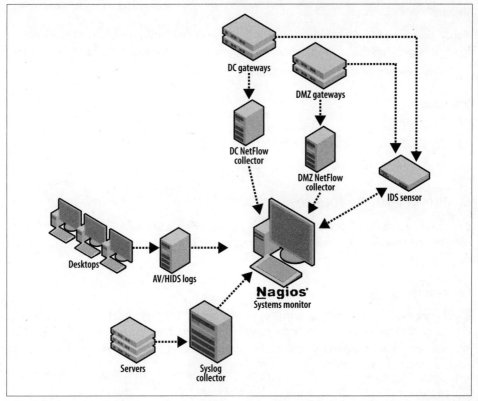

Figure 7-5. Automating system monitoring using Nagios to script checks for system health and continuous event flow

Disk space

Check to be sure there's adequate disk space by running the *check_disk* plug-in to watch the collection directory (*/apps/netflow/data*), warning if less than 10% is available and sending a critical alert if less than 5% is available:

```
check_disk -w 10 -c 5 -p /apps/netflow/data
```

Permissions

Ensure that the directory storing flows remains writable for incoming flows:

```
check_diskrw /apps/netflow/data
```

Load

Evaluate whether the system load is excessive. Warn if the load exceeds 5, 10, or 15, and raise a critical alert if it exceeds 20, 25, or 30:

```
check_load -w 15,10,5 -c 30,25,20
```

Memory

Verify that a reasonable amount of physical memory is still available on the system. Warn if there's less than 5% free memory, and raise a critical alert if there's less than 1%:

```
check_mem -w 5 -c 1
```

Swap space

Ensure that there's a reasonable amount of swap space on the box, warning if there's less than 90%, and raising a critical alert when it dips below 80%:

```
check_swap -w 90%% -c 80%%
```

Monitor Collection Processes

To make sure the software is continuously collecting and storing flows, watch the file system and processes to make sure they're doing their job. To accomplish this, watch the following.

Continuous flows

Configure the Nagios *check_latestfile* plug-in to watch the */apps/netflow/data* collection directory. Set the script to warn if the most recent file is more than 30 minutes old. This script does not accept parameters via the command line, so you must edit the script to set the required parameters.

Processes

Ensure that the correct number of collection and relay processes is running. First, make sure the `flow-capture` process is running, and that it raises a critical alert if there isn't at least one, or if there is more than five running:

```
check_procs -c 1:5 -C flow-capture
```

The parameters described here specify only an upper limit because the syntax requires us to do so. If you're running `flow-fanout`, add another `check_procs` to watch that process.

Monitor Flows from Gateway Routers

To ensure continuous flow collection, verify that each router is sending NetFlow to the collector as expected. Blanco could have scripted a configuration check on each router from which NetFlow is expected. Instead, it chose to watch the network traffic coming into the collector to ensure that the traffic is received from each expected router. There are no Nagios plug-ins to accomplish this, so Blanco has developed a custom script to watch network traffic via `iptables`. The script will read accumulated traffic received in an interval, drop the results into a file, and periodically push the file to the Nagios server via its NSCA framework.

Because Blanco is sending DMZ flows to one collector and DC flows to another, the configurations for monitoring will be identical. Here, Blanco has built an `iptables` rule script, using an "accept" rule for each router expected to send NetFlow. It's easy to see the two routers and the port where they're sending flows—UDP/2055, in the `iptables` configuration:

```
-A INPUT -s dc-gw-1 -p udp -m udp --dport 2055 -j ACCEPT
-A INPUT -s dc-gw-2 -p udp -m udp --dport 2055 -j ACCEPT
```

To determine whether traffic is coming from these gateways on the expected ports (per the `iptables` configuration), look at the accumulated packets from each rule on the line next to each router. Compare that to the values from the last check to determine whether more packets have arrived. Use the `-nvL` options on the `iptables` command and observe the accumulated packets for each gateway.

```
root@nfc ~]# iptables -nvL INPUT
Chain INPUT (policy ACCEPT 125K packets, 180M bytes)
pkts bytes target  prot opt  in out   source   destination
21986  32M ACCEPT udp  --   * *     dc-gw-1 0.0.0.0/0   udp dpt:2055
50059  72M ACCEPT udp  --   * *     dc-gw-2 0.0.0.0/0   udp dpt:2055
```

As described earlier in "Monitor collector network configuration," the script will zero the counters after each check to make comparison easier.

Monitor Event Log Collection

The event log collectors for Blanco are running `syslog-ng`. These collectors are receiving syslog from Unix servers, Windows servers, and the Apache web servers. Blanco must monitor to ensure that the event logs are in good health, and that event logs are being collected and stored. Blanco has configured monitoring for the following:

- Collectors are continuously receiving events from all expected servers.
- Collectors are in good health, able to receive and store events properly.
- Collection processes are running and functioning properly.

Using the NRPE plug-ins, Nagios will execute commands on the syslog collector and process the results on the central server.

Monitor collector health

Blanco will use the same techniques for monitoring collector health that it used for monitoring the NetFlow collector. This will involve watching load, memory, and disk to ensure that the system is functioning normally and can receive and store event logs. Configuration for checking load, memory, and swap will remain exactly the same, but we'll need to monitor the specific file system directories for syslog collection on this system.

Verify disk space

Check to verify that there's adequate disk space by running the *check_disk* plug-in and watching the collection directory (*/apps/logs*). Warn if there's less than 20% available, and send a critical alert if there's less than 10%:

```
check_disk -w 20 -c 10 -p /apps/logs
```

Ensure permissions

Ensure that the directory storing logs remains writable so that the events can be stored as they arrive:

```
check_diskrw /apps/logs
```

Monitor collection processes

Make sure the `syslog-ng` process is running, raising a critical alert if there isn't exactly one process running:

```
check_procs -c 1:1 -C syslog-ng
```

Maintain continuous logs

Configure the Nagios *check_latestfile* plug-in to watch the */apps/logs* collection directory. Set the script to warn if the most recent file is more than 30 minutes old.

Monitor collection from servers

When storing logs to the file system, `syslog-ng` collates the logs from all sources into a single file during collection. This makes it difficult to discern whether a recently written file contains events from every source. To monitor for events from each of Blanco's monitored servers, Blanco used the same approach taken with NetFlow monitoring: using `iptables` to watch for traffic volume.

The `iptables` configuration file will look similar to the one used to watch for NetFlow:

```
-A INPUT -s webserver-1 -p udp -m udp --dport 514 -j ACCEPT
-A INPUT -s webserver-2 -p udp -m udp --dport 514 -j ACCEPT
-A INPUT -s appserver-1 -p udp -m udp --dport 514 -j ACCEPT
-A INPUT -s appserver-2 -p udp -m udp --dport 514 -j ACCEPT
-A INPUT -s dbserver -p udp -m udp --dport 514 -j ACCEPT
```

A custom script regularly checks the accumulated data from each server via the `iptables` command, subsequently zeroing the counters in preparation for the next check.

Monitor NIDS

To ensure that Blanco receives a continuous stream of NIDS alerts, Nagios monitors NIDS device health, traffic feeds, sensor processes, and alerts from the NIDS. Because

Blanco is using the Cisco NIDS, it's not possible to run scripts directly on the sensors. All Nagios monitoring is therefore done using *Expect* scripts on the Nagios server, connecting to the sensors via SSH.

 The sensor must explicitly permit connections from the Nagios server for this to work. This is configured via an access list on the sensor.

Monitor device health

Blanco monitors the health of its sensors using SNMP and *Expect* scripts executed via SSH. To monitor the CPU, Blanco uses a built-in Nagios plug-in called *check_snmp*, which queries the sensor via SNMP, sending a warning if CPU usage is above 75%. The -H parameter specifies the sensor name (ids-1), and the -o parameter requires the SNMP object identifier corresponding to a check for the CPU value of the sensor:

```
check_snmp -H ids-1 -o "1.3.6.1.4.1.9.9.109.1.1.1.1.8.1" -w 75
```

To monitor available memory and disk space, Blanco executes an *Expect* script via SSH. The script connects to the sensor and parses the output of the show version command:

```
ids-1# show version
Application Partition:

Cisco Intrusion Prevention System, Version 6.1(1)E2

-- output clipped for brevity --

Using 1901985792 out of 4100345856 bytes of available memory (46% usage)
system is using 17.7M out of 29.0M bytes of available disk space (61% usage)
boot is using 40.6M out of 69.5M bytes of available disk space (62% usage)

-- output clipped for brevity --
```

The script parses the output, raising a critical alert to Nagios if memory or disk space is consumed beyond 90%. In the preceding output, all values are safely below this threshold.

Monitor traffic feeds

Because Blanco's sensors are receiving feeds directly from gateway routers, scripts are used to periodically verify that SPANs are properly configured. This confirms that the routers are properly enabled to mirror traffic to the sensor. Using *Expect*, Blanco scripted a regular comparison of the show monitor session all command with a stored baseline. This is best accomplished by storing an MD5 hash of the command output and subsequently comparing it to the new value upon each connect. The script raises a Nagios alert if the hashes don't match.

Blanco also monitors the percentage of missed packets. If the value is higher than 10%, it can indicate that the network has grown beyond the sensor's capacity to monitor traffic. Using the `show interface` command, the script parses the percentage of missed packets from the output:

```
ids-1# show interface
Interface Statistics
    Total Packets Received = 109049288548
    Total Bytes Received = 67536504907892
    Missed Packet Percentage = 2
    Current Bypass Mode = Auto_off
-- output clipped for brevity --
```

Note the value `Missed Packet Percentage = 2`. Because this value is less than 10, the script will not raise an alert to Nagios (recall that the script should alert only if the percentage missed is greater than 10%).

Check sensor processes

Most critically, Blanco wants to ensure that the `AnalysisEngine` and `MainApp` processes are running on its CS-IPS 6.1 sensor. If they're not running, the script raises a critical alert to Nagios. Using the `show version` command, the result is parsed to find an indication that these processes are running:

```
ids-1# show version
Application Partition:

Cisco Intrusion Prevention System, Version 6.1(1)E2

-- output clipped for brevity --

MainApp         M-2008_APR_24_19_16  (Release) 2008-04-24T19:49:05-0500   Running
AnalysisEngine  ME-2008_JUN_05_18_26 (Release) 2008-06-05T18:55:02-0500   Running
CLI             M-2008_APR_24_19_16  (Release) 2008-04-24T19:49:05-0500
-- output clipped for brevity --
```

The preceding output shows the `Running` keyword on the line with each of the two critical processes: `MainApp` and `AnalysisEngine`. If the `Running` keyword is not present, the script raises a critical alert in Nagios.

Monitor alert generation

Lastly, Blanco wants to monitor the sensors to ensure that they are still generating alerts. To check for recent alerts, the script checks the alert destination—the Security Information Manager (SIM), where alerts are reviewed by the monitoring staff. Blanco's SIM uses an Oracle database to store the alerts for processing, so the company uses a script to query the pertinent table looking for alerts generated within the past five minutes. If no alerts have been logged within the past five minutes, the script raises a critical alert to Nagios via the NSCA framework.

Monitor Oracle Logging

Because Oracle is configured to send events via syslog to the log collector, there's no need to directly monitor the databases. Rather, this information is logged via syslog directly to the event collectors.

Monitor Antivirus/HIDS Logging

Antivirus and host intrusion detection system (HIDS) logs are collected to their respective servers using the native facilities of the antivirus and HIDS software. Monitoring collection on those servers is identical to the techniques used for monitoring the syslog collection server.

Conclusion

To this point, you've developed the policies upon which you will base your security monitoring, and you've mapped your network and infrastructure. Using network metadata as a backdrop for monitoring, you've selected monitoring targets, chosen event sources, and fed them into your monitoring systems. This chapter aimed to professionalize your monitoring, preventing gaps that could allow an intrusion to succeed without notice. With these finishing touches in place, you've enabled monitoring for your systems with the confidence that events can be collected reliably.

## CHAPTER 8

Conclusion: Keeping It Real

For the past two years, I've been teaching my teenagers to drive. As my patience stretched, I began to wonder whether I could simplify things by writing down the steps for them to employ. Once I had documented the steps, my younger kids could eventually use them—maybe I could even sell the publishing rights! The steps would look something like this:

- Verify that all tires are properly inflated to within 35–37 PSI.
- Check for traffic on the street—do not proceed if there is a vehicle in motion within 750 feet.
- Open driver door.
- Be seated in the driver's seat.
- Adjust seat so that your torso is no more than 18 inches from the wheel and your feet can easily work the foot pedals.
- Adjust rear-view mirror so that the rear window is centered in your view.
- Place your hands on the steering wheel at the 10:00 and 2:00 positions.
- Verify that you know the location of headlights, windshield wipers, brake, and accelerator.
- Place key in ignition and start car.

You get the idea: this is tedious. Experienced drivers don't follow every step. Sure, on some occasions I plan more carefully, such as when leaving for a long journey. Most of the time, however, I skip most of these steps, such as when heading off to work. Some steps are executed subconsciously—I've done them for so long that I don't even think about them—whereas others I perform only occasionally.

Here's the point: the authors have a confession to make. We rarely follow the details of our own advice. Something always goes wrong, and we find ourselves speeding through the setup so that we can meet a deadline. We're almost never able to define policies or take time to choose the right event sources. Usually, we have two weeks to come up with a funding estimate, so we take an educated guess at our requirements, write up some brief monitoring playbooks, and begin ordering hardware.

In this final chapter, we'll give examples where monitoring ideals haven't always aligned with practical experience, including the consequences of those expediencies. We'll share the results of two case studies, including how the organizations deployed targeted monitoring. We'll conclude by stripping down the advice of this book to bare-minimum tasks for each step, leaving you with a checklist to start your own targeted monitoring.

What Can Go Wrong

We don't always follow our own advice. This section gives examples of teams that failed to implement a step of our monitoring approach, including the consequences that followed. Some of these examples are our very own, whereas others are the anecdotes of fellow incident response professionals. In every case, we've changed the names to avoid disclosing confidential details, and to avoid embarrassing any individuals.

Create Policy

Here are two stories that illustrate the importance of the first and most basic requirement: build and clarify policies before you begin monitoring.

Ryan monitors the risky venture

Ansalya Networks acquired technology that allowed mobile phone users to access the services of their desktop VoIP phones over the mobile carrier's network. Ansalya rapidly integrated the technology and piloted the product for customers, deploying a proxy server to provide access from the carrier's servers to Ansalya's VoIP infrastructure, carried via the public Internet (see Figure 8-1). Because the product team could not properly secure the proxy without architectural changes and long delays, Ansalya's chief security officer tasked Ryan, Ansalya's monitoring lead, to address the company's security concerns by monitoring the pilot systems. Because the pilot was deployed before policies could be discussed, no rules were documented to discern security incidents from the vast number of generated security events in this environment. This lack of documented policies left Ryan with few options, so he focused the team's efforts on the following available event sources:

- Standard, high-fidelity signatures on the existing perimeter NIDS
- NetFlow records highlighting Internet access originating from the proxy servers

As alerts were generated, the monitoring team analyzed and escalated incidents to the pilot support staff, but never received replies to any of their messages. Occasionally, traffic was interesting enough to investigate further—NIDS alerts of attacks against the proxy and NetFlow records showing suspicious traffic from the proxy. The pilot support staff, however, received the alerts but never took remedial action.

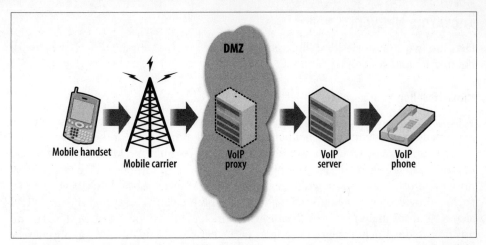

Figure 8-1. A VoIP proxy which provided a gateway between the mobile carrier's network and the VoIP server, but presented risk to Ansalya's network

Result: The pilot support staff never mitigated issues escalated by Ryan's team. In the end, the pilot was concluded without knowledge of any known incidents, and Ansalya continued to pilot solutions without mitigating security risks. The lack of documented security policy prevented Ryan from discerning which activity could indicate security problems.

Pam discovers network abuse by an extranet partner

In establishing extranet network connectivity to a contract manufacturer, Special Electric (SE) unwisely provided direct Internet access through its corporate Internet connection. This connection was quickly arranged and deemed critical to leverage the contract manufacturer's systems for a crucial product launch. While the security team was monitoring the extranet environment for SE, Pam discovered peer-to-peer file sharing and traffic obfuscation via Tor.[*]

Pam traced the access via SE's Internet connection to the new contract manufacturer, documenting hundreds of connections from two hosts at the partner's site. Pam knew that this access was an abuse of the partner's interconnection to SE, and raised the issue with the managers who had arranged the connection.

Result: Because policies had not been established to limit the partner's access, Pam's notifications to management regarding network abuse fell on deaf ears.

---

[*] See *http://www.torproject.org/* for more information.

Know Your Network

Here are two true stories that illustrate the importance of documenting your network boundaries and systems.

Michael monitors an acquisition

When Denata Financials acquired a small brokerage named MM, the acquisition was permitted to conduct its own incident response and monitoring for the first two years. MM had outsourced security monitoring to a service partner, and Michael was directed to retire that arrangement, integrating MM's security monitoring with Denata's enterprise monitoring. As he studied the existing setup, Michael learned that MM's service partner provided no context to alerts—it was simply escalating every high-fidelity NIDS alert to security analysts at MM. Because the work had been outsourced, MM had made no effort to document essential segments of the network so that it could apply context to its security monitoring. When Michael integrated MM into Denata's enterprise monitoring, this deficiency prevented context-based alerting. To remedy this, Michael documented the most important network segments—data centers, labs, and desktop networks—created variables in the NIDS to highlight them, and immediately improved the escalation path and fidelity of the security monitoring.

Result: Michael vastly improved MM's security monitoring, demonstrating the superior security provided by documenting and leveraging network context to security monitoring at Denata.

Helen adds context to the NIDS

Helen was getting frustrated. The NIDS team was escalating every "high-fidelity" security alert to her. She analyzed scores of alerts every day, but as she gathered incident details, she always seemed to uncover a mundane reality: another lab-infected system attacking a desktop PC. Helen patiently traced the alert details to find the path of attack, inferring information about the source and destination based on their network positions. Once she realized how much time she was wasting, she set out to fix the problem for good. Helen developed a project to identify all network segments in an Internet Protocol Address Management (IPAM) registration tool. Once complete, she leveraged the IPAM information repository by configuring the NIDS to incorporate network context into each alert.

Result: Pam's work to document network boundaries saved her team valuable minutes on each alert, and allowed them to prioritize their monitoring reports.

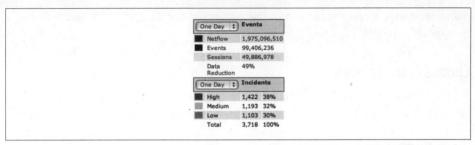

One Day	Events	
Netflow	1,975,096,510	
Events	99,406,236	
Sessions	49,886,978	
Data Reduction	49%	

One Day	Incidents	
High	1,422	38%
Medium	1,193	32%
Low	1,103	30%
Total	3,718	100%

Figure 8-2. A SIM, showing the vast number of alerts which made it impossible for Pam's team to focus their monitoring

In 2004, Cisco IT had a reasonably strong IPAM solution, but it lacked the ability to programmatically retrieve information about addresses, subnets, and descriptions. The data contained within IPAM was locked up and not configured into Cisco's NIDS. When NIDS alerts fired, they contained only the IP address and DNS name of the hosts involved. Once the Cisco NIDS product permitted configurations to accommodate hundreds of variables, the Cisco computer security incident response team (CSIRT) added network context from this central repository into the alerts. CSIRT then leveraged this configuration to tune hundreds of alerts, creating monitoring playbooks, and launched their first global monitoring team.

Choose Targets for Security Monitoring

Many efforts at security monitoring fail because they don't focus on critical risks. They "boil the ocean," forgetting to narrow monitoring to specific targets.

Pam and the failed pilot

The alerts were arranged by color—the most severe alerts colored red. Still, the team observed nearly 60 high-severity alerts per hour. Pam's team had deployed a Security Information Manager (SIM), which was supposed to provide correlation, de-duplication, and contextualization, aiming to reduce the number of alerts. Staring at the hundreds of "critical" alerts the team received each day, Pam realized this wasn't going to work. With nearly 100 NIDSs deployed, hundreds of servers sending logs, and billions of NetFlow reports from gateways all over the globe, the new SIM bogged down; there was simply no way to prioritize and keep up with the alerts as they appeared (see Figure 8-2).

Result: Pam's SIM project failed because the team did not select targets for monitoring, overwhelming them with "critical" alerts. However, the team later took on a well-defined project with clear policies and distinct network boundaries. The team selected three servers and an application against which to align security monitoring. With the same SIM, they found they were able to make productive use of the events, and alerts trickled in at a manageable rate of three to four per hour.

Choose Event Sources

In this section, we'll highlight what went wrong when an employee tried to conduct security monitoring without the necessary event sources.

Donald monitors high-risk employees

Donald's team received advance warning of an impending layoff. Because some of the employees held privileged accounts on critical infrastructure, he was advised to conduct monitoring of these employees to prevent "abuse of privileges" and "trusted insider" attacks. Donald began by reviewing the security policies surrounding employee logins, and found it easy to draw up plans for policy-based monitoring using logs from critical servers. He created a list of critical servers based on the rated priorities in the company's infrastructure registration system. He then focused his efforts on a few critical servers supported by the fated employees. As he began assembling a plan to monitor the employees, he discovered that NIDS and NetFlow feeds were working perfectly, but none of the servers were configured to log events for security review. Knowing that a request to enable logging on the servers would raise suspicion by the very employees he needed to monitor, Donald found himself without options.

Result: Donald failed to detect abuse of privileges by these employees. Lacking time to deploy appropriate event feeds, his team members found themselves sifting vast NIDS and NetFlow records looking for signs of abuse, but discovered nothing.

Feed and Tune

Here are two stories illustrating what can go wrong when event sources are not properly deployed.

Janet and the career-limiting false positive

Once the new NIDSs were deployed on the Toronto data center gateways, Janet began analyzing the events they generated. She had let the sensors run for a few days to ensure that they were functioning properly, but was eager to see new activity. She was alarmed by the sudden appearance of alerts indicating exploitation of RPC race condition vulnerabilities against the Windows domain controllers. As she further analyzed the traffic, she traced the source to other domain controllers. She had seen this activity before as compromised machines on the Internet attacked the organization's internal systems, but the firewalls always dropped the traffic. Confident that this indicated malicious, damaging attacks, she immediately engaged the Windows administrators, opening an urgent case with the network operations center. Two Windows admins joined the call, groggy due to the late hour at company headquarters in London. Janet related the problem to the admins, who looked for indications that something was wrong on the servers. Convinced that something was wrong but lacking a full explanation, Janet insisted that the servers be backed up and rebuilt, requiring more than 20 hours of work by the London Windows admins. Once the servers were brought back online, the alerts reappeared the following week near the same date and time. This time, when the admin joined the call, he was more skeptical. He noted that the timing was fishy, since it coincided with system maintenance of the domain controllers. Upon further research, he demonstrated that because the Windows servers exchange directory updates at regular intervals, it's common to see rapid DCOM connections, which can easily be mistaken for exploitation of the RPC vulnerability.

Result: Janet was reassigned to another team. As a result of this misunderstanding, the NIDS team realized that due to the massive number of protocols and traffic passing through the data center gateways, they would require several months to tune their NIDSs before they could reliably raise alerts for monitoring.

Dwight overwhelms the event collectors

Dwight had spent seven months convincing system administrators to send their event logs to his new log collectors. He had deployed a syslog server and spent several months preparing to monitor for signs that employees were sharing accounts on critical systems. Now that he was collecting the needed events, he found it a simple task to forward the events to the SIM, and configure it to store and relay the logs. When he was finished, he waited a few days and then logged in to the SIM to look for indications of account sharing—calling out simultaneous instances of user login from more than one IP at a time. He searched through the data, but found no initial indications of such policy violations.

Three weeks later, Dwight was called in to investigate an employee suspected of hacking a colleague's account to download sensitive files. He searched through the collected logs to trace the access, but it appeared that events for that date were missing. Upon further analysis, he found that the data on his new collector was retained for only three hours. Dwight had failed to account for the vast storage needed to support such "noisy" collection; his log collector was discarding data more than three hours old to allow newly collected events to be stored within the 500 GB allocated limit. In lieu of data supporting the investigation, he found the event collector clogged with messages about NTP sync and debugging messages from dozens of in-house applications.

Result: Dwight was unable to offer data in support of the investigation, and it was closed for lack of evidence. Had he been careful to tune his event feeds to capture only what was needed to support security monitoring and investigations, his team would have been able to support this investigation.

Maintain Dependable Event Sources

Here are two stories to illustrate what went wrong when security monitoring tools were not properly maintained.

Lyle and the broken NetFlow collectors

A lab had been compromised, and Lyle's analysis of the exploit made it clear that a determined attacker had compromised the lab, most likely from a remote connection. The team tried to analyze the events on the local machine, but found that the attacker had erased them. The NIDS identified the compromise, indicating a source originating from another development lab at a remote location. Lyle's effort now centered on finding the attacker, and he knew the best method for tracking down the attacker was to analyze NetFlow records from the lab over the days since the attack. He logged in to the NetFlow collector, querying records corresponding to the lab's Internet connection. Lyle squinted at the screen—no NetFlow records had been logged for three weeks. He didn't understand what had happened, but engaged the network engineering team to check the configurations on the routers connecting the lab to the internal network. They had never heard of Lyle's NetFlow collection servers, but had recently configured the routers to send all NetFlow to their own collectors for traffic analysis and accounting. Unfortunately, the network team's NetFlow collectors hadn't retained the data, and Lyle's investigation hit a dead end.

Result: Lyle's investigation failed. Though NetFlow had been collected, this gap in records prevented him from tracing the activity back to a clear attacker.

Marian and the threatening note

Marian was called into her director's office. Facebook, a popular social networking site, had just contacted her regarding a threatening note posted to an employee's profile. The note made reference to their company, Star Labs; Facebook's records proved that the connections originated from Star Labs' IP address space. Marian quickly traced the connection to the company's Pittsburg campus. Intersecting the IP location with the time of the incident, she was able to isolate the traffic to a wireless network in Building 22. Since it was a wireless network, however, the addresses were assigned dynamically—an address is reused several times throughout the day. She was relieved to find that the events had been captured from the DHCP servers to Star Labs' collection servers, but found that recent changes to the configuration of the servers' NFS mounts had prevented the events from being written properly.

Result: Marian's investigation hit a dead end because there was no way to isolate the source of the incident and correlate it with a real user.

Case Studies

As we were completing this book, we wanted to test our methodology against real experiences throughout the security community. As members of the Forum for Incident Response and Security Teams (FIRST), Cisco has established a trusted relationship with fellow incident response teams. Through FIRST, we found two other security teams interested in sharing some perspective regarding their security monitoring. This highlights how their security monitoring aligns with the methodology presented in this book. Here are case studies from two respected security teams: KPN-CERT and Northrop Grumman.

KPN-CERT

KPN is a Dutch telecommunications company that operates fixed-line and mobile telephony, Internet, wireless television, ICT, retail, and IPTV services. The company, which employs nearly 30,000 people, has an active computer security incident response team called the Computer Emergency Response team (KPN-CERT). This team provides security monitoring and response for KPN's company network as well as the networks over which KPN offers its services, including Internet services.

Like all companies in the Netherlands, KPN is governed by Dutch and European Union laws. These regulations limit the depth of KPN's security monitoring, and require retention of some event records. Because KPN is a telecommunications company, the customer data it stores is further regulated, and the security team must actively monitor for security breaches.

 KPN has several divisions, with policies and response processes applied differently to each. The information represented in this section is specifically for monitoring XS4ALL, an Internet service provider (ISP) owned by KPN.

Policies

KPN's culture empowers employees, allowing them to do their jobs as they see fit. The security team, therefore, tries not to limit their access any more than necessary. To develop policies, KPN-CERT analyzed its network traffic to characterize threats to its environment; the security officers then developed policies based on the legitimate traffic generated by its employees and customers. Here are their five primary policies, mainly directed at employees:

- *Security*, which creates a framework for all other policies. This covers the role of InfoSec, how information is to be classified, and the duties of employees.

- *Data Sharing*, which governs how data is to be handled and protected.

- *Logging*, which governs what events should be logged, how they are to be recorded, and secure methods of access.
- *Office Network*, which directs acceptable use of computers and the network. This policy prescribes which computers are allowed to connect to KPN's network, and explicitly bans some network activities, including the use of peer-to-peer applications. This policy also requires that every device register its MAC address as a condition for using the KPN network, but will be updated to require 802.1x authentication in 2009.
- *Third Party*, which governs how KPN-CERT interacts with external organizations, and declares their right to audit activity and services provided by those organizations.
- *Security*, which covers the role of InfoSec, how information is to be classified, and the duties of employees.

Network

KPN-CERT applies different types of monitoring based on the type of network being monitored, including wireless, desktop, server, and so forth.

Monitoring targets

KPN-CERT applies monitoring where security controls are weakest. This philosophy directs its policies and selection of targets for security monitoring. Such prioritized monitoring allows KPN-CERT to quickly react to new threats. This prioritized threat monitoring was employed when an IRC trojan emerged on EFnet, causing security administrators to ponder whether an IRC server binary within their own network was trojaned during the incident. The CERT team provided monitoring for the hot threat, leveraging their knowledge of the network segments to apply targeted monitoring against the likely IRC servers running within KPN. Such knowledge allows CERT to prioritize based on risk, even those that rapidly escalate as this one did.

Event sources

KPN-CERT collects NIDS, NetFlow, and syslog data for security monitoring, making heaviest use of NIDS data. KPN traffic volumes require that the NIDS support multi-gigabit throughput, requiring deployment of NIDS gear appropriate to the task. The team also makes use of network intrusion prevention systems (NIPSs), to automatically block certain "known evils" and recreational traffic. The NIPS rules are based on CERT's own security policies highlighted earlier. Traffic that isn't automatically blocked is inspected via the NIDS for security monitoring and forensics. For example, when CERT identifies SSH access over a nonstandard port (something other than port 22), security analysts monitor and analyze the NIDS alerts.

NetFlow is collected regionally, sampling NetFlow v5 from all choke points. Using Arbor Peakflow the CERT team watches for anomalies in traffic to alert them of suspicious behavior. NetFlow is further used as a short-term audit history for network traffic, which is analyzed via Argus. NetFlow monitoring was instrumental in discovering IPv6 experimentation on the office network, as Peakflow highlighted a spike in IPv6 traffic. This allowed the security team to identify the source of the traffic and restrict it before the traffic disrupted the network.

Syslog is collected to a central server from routers, switches, firewalls, and Unix servers. CERT uses syslog from switches to find security problems such as DHCP snooping and rogue DHCP servers. Firewall logs are monitored to ensure proper functioning, and to watch for signs of intrusion attempts. Unix servers, which account for the largest proportion of servers on the network, are monitored by CERT for standard security problems, such as repeated authentication failures.

The CERT team does not make use of a SIM, as it has not demonstrated value for their monitoring. Security analysts require powerful flexibility and human analysis to pick out anomalous patterns. In lieu of a SIM, they observe the event sources in real time, with some limited auto-alerting for known bad security events.

Maintenance

KPN-CERT conducts limited monitoring of its security event feeds via human analysis, built-in tools, and custom scripts. The team's careful observation is often useful in highlighting genuine security incidents. For example, when an email virus disrupted the KPN network, CERT analysts were observing the NIDS. The alerts were indicating the problem, but the NIDS was missing much of the data and wasn't capturing trigger packets. Based on the analysts' experience, this problem indicated that a configuration change had been implemented on the routers feeding the NIDS. This misconfiguration limited CERT's ability to investigate the impacted users, as well as its ability to trace the activity to its source. After investigating the NIDS configuration, the CERT analysts discovered that an employee had enabled a new link on the office network, changing the traffic path and causing their NIDS to miss half the traffic. To prevent this problem in the future, CERT changed access permissions on the routers to limit access.

 Though NIDS traffic was impacted by this incident, NetFlow was not. This highlights the additional value in using multiple sources of security event data.

The system used for monitoring anomalous activity via NetFlow also monitors itself, raising an alert when activity exceeds or falls below defined thresholds. A recent alert from this system showed that activity had stopped completely. CERT's analysis uncovered a routing problem—routing had been reassigned through a different interface, but was quickly repaired.

Syslog feeds are monitored via Perl scripts, which watch for substantive variation in the number of events logged to their central collectors. Allowance is made for peak periods, when employees are arriving or departing work.

An approach to protect customer data

KPN-CERT recognizes the value of its customer data, and balances its responsibility to monitor for security breaches against a culture that promotes creativity in its workforce.

Northrop Grumman

One of the largest defense contractors in the world, Northrop Grumman employs 120,000 people worldwide. Its large InfoSec organization includes teams to address advanced threat analysis, intelligence, information assurance, monitoring, and incident response. Due to state-sponsored espionage aimed at defense contractors, Northrop Grumman's security teams address threats beyond those of most enterprises, while typical organizations focus on protecting against opportunistic attackers.[†]

Policies

Like most companies, Northrop Grumman provides acceptable use policies to guide employee behavior, including directives for use of email and attachments. Northrop Grumman's monitoring is not primarily directed by employee policies, but rather by threats and the value of protected data.

Network topology, metadata, and monitoring targets

Northrop Grumman leverages its documented network topology to prioritize monitoring, but in a unique way. Most organizations delineate server networks from desktop and lab networks, but Northrop Grumman prioritizes based on Internet exposure and business criticality. This information is intersected with a dynamic threat landscape using CERT's OCTAVE[‡] risk assessment methodology. OCTAVE highlights critical, sensitive areas, allowing Northrop Grumman to label the network segments for priority monitoring.

Event sources

Northrop Grumman uses a SIM to gather security events from most sources, allowing the security analysts to correlate and report security events against known threats. The SIM is fed by NIDS and NIPS data, along with firewall and proxy logs. Like most

---

[†] McNab, C. 2007. "Classifying Internet-based Attackers," in *Network Security Assessment*. Sebastopol, CA: O'Reilly Media, Inc.

[‡] See *http://www.cert.org/octave/* for more information.

enterprises, Northrop Grumman has found perimeter monitoring less valuable as it has become more porous; correspondingly, threats have driven deeper into the infrastructure. Northrop Grumman's CSIRT finds itself monitoring end hosts more frequently, especially as more virtual machines (VMs) are deployed into the data center. (A compromised VM could have access to all VMs on the same physical host without traversing routers or network monitoring tools.)

Northrop Grumman collects and analyzes any data that can reflect a change to the infrastructure:

- NetFlow and syslog have proven useful for detecting changes and alerting.
- Windows event logs are collected but not gathered into the SIM for automatic correlation and analysis.
- Full packet capture is collected at network choke points. Experts analyze this traffic, searching for behavior patterns and problems. Data indicators spotted via packet capture sometimes end up as primary indicators in the SIM.

Two additional event sources are used to augment Northrop Grumman's real-time detection capabilities, leveraged during incident response and investigations:

- Vulnerability scans, used to correlate host data with real-time alerts and discover fresh threats. Scans include all servers, network devices, applications, desktops, and databases.
- Windows domain controller logs and host intrusion prevention system (HIPS) logs.

Maintenance

System administrators at Northrop Grumman are responsible for monitoring all systems, including security monitoring tools. Their support addresses the overall throughput and health of such systems. To supplement the system administrators' support, one network engineer is assigned to observe events from the NIDS and NIPS.

Availability metrics from event sources are analyzed and reported via a daily status summary, which shows:

- Utilization
- Throughput
- General system health (uptime, etc.)
- Event volumes

Selected event types are trended and correlated with announced vulnerabilities to ensure that Northrop Grumman stays on top of hot threats. This allows Northrop Grumman to prioritize patch rollouts and awareness campaigns within the organization.

Though Northrop Grumman monitors security event sources, maintaining adequate storage for all event sources is challenging, especially for packet captures. During a recent multistage attack, the NIDS sensors raised unique alerts, leading security analysts to quickly trigger full packet capture to support their investigation. Due to the nature of the attack—a coordinated intrusion against multiple company sites—the incident was not immediately recognized. While the traffic was being analyzed, the packet capture devices rolled their storage, overwriting data from the beginning of the attack. In the end, the analysts were able to initiate a response, but they lacked the depth they needed for a full investigation.

A dynamic-threat-oriented security team

Northrop Grumman places value in dynamic threat analysis, and orients a large proportion of its monitoring toward responding to such threats. Much of its approach aligns with the targeted monitoring principles we've encouraged in this book, but you can clearly see how they are tilted toward sophisticated threats.

Real Stories of the CSIRT

To illustrate the monitoring steps we've recommended in this book, we collected stories from security monitoring teams in peer organizations. These stories illustrate incident response and some of the limitations of enterprise security monitoring.

Because we were asked to keep some stories anonymous, we've added small embellishments to prevent identification of affected organizations as necessary. Similarities with actual events, individuals, or corporations are neither intentional nor implied.

Stolen Intellectual Property

A customer alerted Mike, a security investigator for Wirespeed, that source code belonging to his company had been posted on the Internet. Following the leads provided, he visited a web address that confirmed the information. Mike noted that the source code was visible due to a misconfiguration of the site's Apache web server, allowing unauthenticated directory traversal. Mike perused the code, immediately recognizing it as Wirespeed's order processing software. He even found some embedded system credentials, database accounts, and passwords within the open directories. Mike traced the web server's IP address to a home ISP connection, and was surprised when it correlated to the home IP address of a Wirespeed employee.

Because Wirespeed managed the Internet connections of its employees, he was able to immediately disable the employee's network connection and investigate further. With the website now disabled, he turned his attention to the search engines now caching the source code. Using his extensive industry contacts, Mike quickly secured agreement from Google, Yahoo!, and MSN to delete the information. Thankfully, there were no indications that the code had been discovered and reposted by others.

Investigating how the source code was leaked, Mike found that the employee had "borrowed" the source code to start his own company, forgetting to remove identifying and sensitive information. Mike directed the application support team to change their database passwords, added network access controls to prevent external connections to the impacted database, and directed the employee and his boss to human resources for review of the employee's policy violations.

A post-mortem review of the monitoring systems uncovered no alerts logged for this incident. Mike concluded that the event was missed because the employee's ISP connection was not in the scope of the company's network monitoring. Wirespeed's network access controls allowed all employees' home networks to access its internal network as part of their supported configuration. The incident report did not recommend any changes to the company's monitoring systems or access controls, but directed the awareness team to remind employees of their duty regarding the protection of Wirespeed's confidential information.

Targeted Attack Against Employees

Due to the sensitive nature of its data and the unique threats faced by its enterprise, Northrop Grumman maintains an active relationship with its user base. Users are employed as a first line of defense against social engineering attacks and suspicious activity. In October 2008, the company's CSIRT received a user report concerning a suspicious email attachment. CSIRT passed the report to George, who coordinates deep threat analysis for Northrop Grumman. George searched for correlation with complementary data sources, querying the SIM for NetFlow records and NIDS alerts during the same time period, and comparing the trapped binary against captures from the proxy server. George's analysis of proxy logs clearly indicated that more than 20 employees had received the same attachment within the past few hours.

Using a proprietary database, George found an immediate connection shared by all affected employees: their work for Northrop Grumman was all within the same program. As the investigation turned toward response and remediation of this targeted attack, George turned to CSIRT, whose analysis confirmed that none of the victim employees were compromised. The company's wide deployment of automated patching and host-based intrusion prevention tools to the desktops had prevented compromise.

To ensure that Northrop Grumman had addressed the problem, the InfoSec team built a micro-awareness campaign, quickly informing users of the specific risks posed by the trojan. InfoSec further conducted a risk assessment against the affected program, highlighting that the company was sufficiently protected from the threat. In its post-mortem assessment, Northrop Grumman found that strong collaboration and timely, in-depth threat analysis allowed for a rapid and effective response, containing the threat.

Bare Minimum Requirements

When my first child was born, our annual Christmas trek to Iowa required me to stuff our 1989 Ford Taurus with every item of clothing, toy, and article of portable baby furniture we owned. Three children later, we've discovered how little we truly need for a week at Grandma's. Likewise, you can often succeed with far less than your ideals, especially when you reduce your scope. In the spirit of efficiency, here are a few essentials to apply for success in targeted monitoring.

Policy

You can't escape policy—it's your security monitoring anchor. Still, it's hard to know where to begin. Here are the essential policies for most organizations, against which you can conduct productive security monitoring.

Policy 1: Allowed network activity

Be clear what network access is allowed and what isn't. This is especially true of the most sensitive and critical network segments. When analysts detect activity toward the Internet from data centers, they need clear, documented policies regarding what network activity is allowed so that they can conduct fruitful investigations.

Policy 2: Allowed access

Document who can and should access the organization's most critical, sensitive servers. Documenting who is allowed access creates a reference point against unauthorized access. It permits discovery and enforcement of access that is out of alignment with security policy.

Policy 3: Minimum access standards

Dictate the security standards expected of devices present on the network. This must include:

Identification and naming
  If the device doesn't tie activity back to individuals, investigations will hit dead ends.

Logging
  If the device isn't required to maintain logging or unique logins, it's not possible to effectively trace activity.

Authentication
  If there's no standard for access control, misconfigurations and weaknesses may permit security incidents.

Know the Network

Without basic knowledge of the organization's network segments, security analysts lack the most fundamental means of prioritizing and contextualizing security alerts. Greater detail is helpful, but in a pinch, at least set up an IPAM solution and document the most basic demarcations.

Step 1: Set up an IPAM solution

Organizations need a means of documenting their hierarchy of IP addresses. For most networks, it's impractical to represent a hierarchy of addresses in anything but a database. Rather than trying to see how many rows Excel 2007 will support, spend time setting up an IPAM solution. IPplan is a free and open source solution that runs on LAMP (a Linux server with Apache, MySQL, and PHP).

Step 2: Document basic IP demarcations

In the IPAM solution, document all network address space owned by the organization, grouping and identifying the following networks:

DMZ
> Document the space assigned to Internet-accessible machines, as you can expect them to see a lot more attacks.

Data center
> Data centers are home to the most critical infrastructure. At least document the subnets corresponding to the data center. It will overlap (or fully contain) the DMZ address space, but it's good to know where it is.

Labs
> Document the address space used by labs (both DMZ and internal) on the network, as they will generate events that are more unusual (hopefully) than those seen on the rest of the network.

Partners
> If there are extranet connections—places where partners are connected directly to the organization's network—segment and document them.

Remote access
> Many organizations allow remote access via a virtual private network (VPN) of some kind (software or hardware). Document those network subnets here.

Desktop
> Lastly, the "rest of" the network is probably available for end users as the "desktop" networks; document the address ranges of those subnets.

Figure 8-3 depicts the network ranges and their relationships that you should document in the IPAM system.

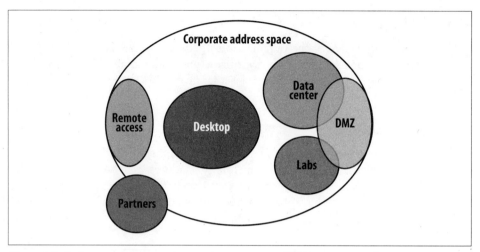

Figure 8-3. Basic network demarcations to document in an IPAM system

Select Targets for Effective Monitoring

Target monitoring toward areas of risk and sensitivity:

Risky systems

Systems that present clear risk—such as those called out by a formal risk assessment—are excellent targets for security monitoring. This is especially helpful where the risk cannot be sufficiently mitigated with controls such as network ACLs or account restrictions.

Systems with sensitive data

Wherever sensitive data is stored, such as the Social Security numbers stored by Blanco Wireless, it's vital to conduct security monitoring to prevent data loss and liability. Be aware of government regulations, which may specify and detail the type of monitoring that is required.

Choose Event Sources

Choose event sources that will allow effective monitoring of the selected targets. This requires records to detect activity on the network around the targets, and on the servers themselves. We believe the most essential event sources are those which provide the best alert-to-message ratio. In other words, event sources that produce a lot of un-actionable messages should not take first priority. The best event sources for targeted security monitoring are often NIDS alerts, network flows, and server logs.

NIDS alerts

Alerts from a NIDS can be tuned to the organization's specific environment, and can detect specific patterns of activity that will highlight policy violations for action.

Network flows

Cisco records network flows very efficiently with NetFlow, and similar event types can be captured on other vendors' hardware, including Juniper and Huawei. Network flows capture just a few important attributes of IP packets, allowing efficient storage and analysis of network traffic.

Server logs

Collect the events generated by servers via syslog. This is native on Unix servers, and can be captured on Windows systems via third-party tools such as Snare. Collect the following events: authentication, config changes, and daemon start/stop events. You should collect these events from every server that is material to your targeted monitoring.

Feed and Tune

Here are some simple guidelines for deploying equipment to collect and analyze NIDS alerts, network flows, and server logs.

Set up a Security Information Manager (SIM)

Not everyone believes a SIM is necessary for security monitoring, but it's a simple solution for aggregating the event sources articulated in this section. A SIM will receive traffic from each event source, highlighting and correlating related security events.

Deploy the NIDS

Deploy the NIDS to network choke points in promiscuous mode (so that it can see all the traffic). Choke points are normally at the Internet connection and data center gateways, and may be found at branch offices and lab gateways in some organizations.

1. Configure the NIDS to send alerts to the SIM (or the SIM to pull alerts from the NIDS).
2. Tune the NIDS, beginning with alerts that fire the most.
3. Configure the NIDS to use information about basic network demarcations of the organization, adding the data to the NIDS alerts.
4. Retire unwanted or irrelevant NIDS signatures.

Point NetFlow at the SIM

Though we recommend intermediate NetFlow collection via the open source OSU flow-tools, the simplest solution is to point NetFlow at the SIM and to configure it to notify you of traffic patterns forbidden by policies. Once it is deployed, configure the choke point routers to send their network flows to the SIM.

Configure server logs

Configure targeted servers to log authentication, services that are starting/stopping, and configuration changes to the SIM.

Maintain Dependable Event Sources

To ensure that security events are reliably and continuously captured, monitor the SIM to make sure events are arriving from each expected event source regularly. For each event source, query for a recent event and alert support staff if a recent event has not been posted from each source.

Monitoring Setup Checklist

Finally, here's a checklist to guide the application of the steps presented in this book:

1. Document top threats. This includes the agents that can harm the organization, and the expected methods or circumstances employed to bring harm.
2. Establish policies. Base policies on threats, regulations, and standards to which the organization subscribes (such as ISO).
3. Place policies on a central website and communicate them clearly to staff.
4. Determine which policies and threats should be monitored.
5. Conduct a Business Impact Analysis (BIA) to determine the organization's most critical infrastructure.
6. Conduct a risk assessment against the critical infrastructure highlighted in the BIA.
7. Based on risk assessment and top threats, determine which targets (applications, networks, etc.) to monitor.
8. Choose event sources to support security monitoring.
9. Determine size requirements for monitoring equipment, based on factors such as necessary throughput, event retention times, price, and enterprise fit.
10. Deploy and tune monitoring equipment.
11. Negotiate service level agreements (SLAs) with IT staff to support security event sources.
12. Deploy configuration templates for devices that are sending security events to keep events flowing reliably.
13. Choose and deploy a SIM.
14. Configure security event sources to feed into the selected SIM.
15. Develop monitoring, escalation, and remediation procedures for security monitoring.

---

16. Acquire and train monitoring staff.
17. Choose and deploy a system to monitor security event sources.
18. Begin executing monitoring procedures.

Conclusion

Each year, network security monitoring gains more capabilities for finding and mitigating security risks. With a focus on actionable monitoring (which you can achieve only if monitoring is prioritized and aligned with policies), organizations can meet their goals without compromising security.

We hope you've benefited from this book, and that we'll see you at a security conference soon!

Detailed OSU flow-tools Collector Setup

This appendix gives detailed information on setting up and running a NetFlow collector based on OSU flow-tools, followed by some simple commands to enable NetFlow generation from a Cisco IOS router.

OSU flow-tools is a set of open source NetFlow collection utilities, which you can reference at *http://www.splintered.net/sw/flow-tools/*. Before you begin, ensure that your hardware meets the installation requirements, which are as simple as the following:

- One server (or virtual server instance) running the *nix operating system
- An appropriate amount of disk space (250 GB to 500 GB is a good starting point, though we've run some low-traffic environments on as little as 100 GB)

Set Up the Server

To prepare your server for NetFlow collection, follow these steps:

1. Download the latest package of flow-tools utilities (in this case, the version is 0.66) from *ftp://ftp.eng.oar.net/pub/flow-tools/flow-tools-0.66.tar.gz*. Place the file in the */tmp* directory of your server.

2. Extract the files in */tmp* with the following command:

   ```
   tar -xzvf flow-tools-0.66.tar.gz
   ```

3. This creates a *flow-tools-0.66* directory. Run the *install-sh* shell script in that directory as root. It will install flow-tools to */usr/local/netflow*, containing all the flow-tools binaries.

4. Create a `netflow` user to run the collection software.

5. su to the netflow user and start the flow-capture process, which prepares the system to receive forwarded flows. There are several options in the startup command which can be found on the flow-capture manpage. Of course, you must determine the correct settings for your own environment, but here is an example to get started:

```
/usr/local/netflow/bin/flow-capture -w /var/local/flows/data -E90G -V5 -A1134
0/0/9999 -S5 -p /var/run/netflow/flow-capture.pid -N-1 -n288
```

The preceding line of code will:

- Capture flows to the */var/local/flows/data* directory (make sure the netflow user can write here!).
- Begin rolling over once there is 90 GB of flow data (useful, for example, if you have a 95 GB drive).
- Collect and store NetFlow in version 5 format.
- Tag flows with your AS number—for example, AS1134.
- Listen and capture on UDP 9999. Note: you may have to poke a hole in your firewall if you are collecting from routers in the DMZ, but this collector is inside the firewall.
- Log a stats message every five minutes.
- Specify the process ID *flow-capture.pid* in location */var/run/netflow/*.
- Set the nesting level to *YYYY-MM-DD/flow-file* (see man flow-capture for options).
- Create a flow file 288 times per day (every five minutes).

You need to ensure that flow-capture starts when the system reboots. To do so, simply add the following *init* script to */etc/init.d/*:

```
---------------------------------BEGIN init script----------------------------
#! /bin/bash
#
# file to stop and start netflow

prog="flow_capture"

start() {
echo -n $"Starting $prog: "
su - netflow -c "/usr/local/netflow/bin/flow-capture -w /var/local/flows/data -
E90G -V5 -A 0/0/9999 -S5 -p /var/run/netflow/flow-capture.pid -N-1 -n288"
RETVAL=$?
echo
return $RETVAL
}

stop() {
echo -n $"Stopping $prog: "
kill -9 'ps -ef|grep flow-capture|grep -v grep|awk '{print $2}'`
kill -9 'ps -ef|grep flow-fanout|grep -v grep|awk '{print $2}'`
RETVAL=$?
echo
return $RETVAL
}
```

```
restart() {
stop
start
}

case "$1" in
start)
start
;;
stop)
stop
;;
restart)
restart
;;
reload)
reload
;;
*)
echo $"Usage: $0 {start|stop|restart}"
exit 1
esac
--------------------------------END init script--------------------------------
```

Configuring NetFlow Export from the Router

The following is a simple configuration stanza to enable NetFlow generation and export from a Cisco IOS 12.x router. Refer to your router documentation for software and platform-specific commands:

```
Router1(config)#ip route-cache flow
Router1(config)#ip flow-export source Loopback 0
Router1(config)#ip flow-export destination 10.1.1.1 9999
Router1(config)#interface FastEthernet0/0
Router1(config-if)#ip route-cache flow
```

SLA Template

In this appendix, you will find a sample service level agreement (SLA) for supporting security event feeds from network devices. This sample SLA is arranged between the network support team (NetEng) and the team to whom security monitoring is assigned (InfoSec). Following the practice of this book, the scope belongs to our fictitious company, Blanco Wireless.

Service Level Agreement: Information Security and Network Engineering

Overview

This is a service level agreement (SLA) between Information Security (InfoSec) and Network Engineering (NetEng). The purpose of this document is to clarify support responsibilities and expectations. Specifically, it outlines:

- Services provided by NetEng to support network security event recording for monitoring and incident response
- General levels of response, availability, and maintenance associated with these services
- Responsibilities of NetEng as a provider of these services
- Responsibilities of InfoSec as the client and requester of these services
- Processes for requesting and communicating status of services

This SLA shall remain valid until terminated. Approval and termination indications are noted by signatures in "8.1: Approvals."

Service Description

This service includes configuration of network devices to support security monitoring. It specifically requires:

- NetFlow configuration to InfoSec NetFlow collectors
- Logging configuration to log appropriate syslog messages to InfoSec syslog collectors
- SPAN configuration on routers to mirror traffic to network intrusion detection systems (NIDSs)

Scope

The scope of this agreement includes the following devices where registered in Blanco's device management system, and operating within the bounds of Blanco's global network:

- All NetEng-supported distribution layer aggregation routers (choke points) including, but not limited to, the perimeters of the DMZ, production, extranet, and data center networks
- All InfoSec-supported NIDSs

Roles and Responsibilities

The NetEng team will support the process in cooperation with InfoSec.

NetEng responsibilities

NetEng will maintain the following configuration on every Blanco choke point router:

- Log NetFlow v5 to port 2055 of the InfoSec-designated NetFlow collection server.
- Log auth and daemon messages to the InfoSec-designated syslog collection server.
- Configure one SPAN to mirror both Rx and Tx traffic to the NIDS. For routers in HSRP, RSPAN must be configured to mirror all traffic.

This configuration will be maintained during normal operations of all network devices. NetEng will coordinate configuration changes and downtime with InfoSec via Blanco's change management process.

InfoSec responsibilities

InfoSec will maintain collection of security events in support of incident response, monitoring, and investigations on Blanco's network. InfoSec will also:

- Provide access to NetFlow and network device log messages stored on collection servers.
- Monitor for security events on network infrastructure.
- Provide incident response and investigations during security incidents involving network infrastructure.

Service Operations

This section details how service is requested, hours of operation, expected response times, and escalation paths.

Requesting service

Service requests and change management will use Blanco's in-house tools to log and route information.

- InfoSec will request service by logging cases to NetEng via the Blanco Service Request System (BSR). Urgent requests will be escalated via Global Operations.
- NetEng will communicate all outages and configuration changes by adding the group "InfoSec" to the approval group on all change requests.

Hours of operation

Both InfoSec and NetEng will maintain 24/7 operations and support for the services noted in this SLA.

Response times

NetEng agrees to support the security event feeds as a P2 service, which allows for up to four hours of downtime to resolve problems.

Escalations

Should either party require urgent attention to a problem, Global Operations will conduct priority adjustments and coordination of response. Assistance with resolution of ongoing but nonurgent problems will be handled by engaging the management of each respective organization.

Maintenance and service changes

Routers supporting security event feeds will maintain 24/7 operations. There will be no regularly scheduled maintenance, but necessary service outages will be requested and communicated via the change management system.

Security event collectors supported by InfoSec will maintain 24/7 operations with scheduled downtime on Sundays from 1:00 a.m. to 2:30 a.m. PST.

Agreement Dates and Changes

This document has been placed into effect January 20, 2009 and will remain in perpetuity. This document will be reviewed for changes and new approvals every two years or when director-level management changes are made to either the NetEng or InfoSec organization, whichever comes first.

Supporting Policies and Templates

This document is in support of the following Blanco Wireless policies:

- Device Logging Policy
- Network Security Incident Response Policy
- Network Security Monitoring Policy

This document requires that the following templates be applied to all devices within the scope of this SLA. These templates will support the configuration required by this document:

- NetFlow Logging Template for Cisco IOS 12 Routers
- Event Logging Template for Cisco IOS 12 Routers

Approvals, Terminations, and Reviews

This document must be electronically signed by a director in both the NetEng and InfoSec organizations.

Approvals

This section should note the approver, title, and effective date.

Approver	Title	Date
John McCain	Director, Network Engineering	1/20/09
Barack Obama	Director, Information Security	1/20/09

Terminations

This section should note the terminating director's name, title, and effective date. This section is left blank until this agreement is terminated.

Terminating director	Title	Date

Reviewers

This section should list the contributing editors and those whose review affected material changes to the document.

Reviewer	Title	Date
Jason Bourne	Network Engineer	12/15/08
Michael Steele	Security Engineer	12/09/08

Calculating Availability

 Much of the information that follows is based on the concepts presented in the book *High Availability Network Fundamentals*, by Chris Oggerino (Cisco Press). At the time of this writing, the book is unfortunately out of print. If you can get your hands on a copy, it is worth your while.

This appendix provides richer detail to help you evaluate the components of system availability, as an extension of what was presented in Chapter 6. You can calculate the availability of a single component with the following equation:

$$\text{Availability} = \frac{\text{MTBF}}{\text{MTBF} + \text{MTTR}}$$

So, the availability of a component whose Mean Time Between Failures (MTBF) is 175,000 hours and Mean Time To Repair (MTTR) is 30 minutes would be:

$$\text{Availability} = \frac{175000 \text{ hrs}}{175000 + 0.5 \text{ hrs}}$$

Availability = 0.99999714

Availability = 0.99999714 x 525600 minutes

Availability = 525598.497 minutes

Downtime = 525600 - 525598.497 minutes

Downtime = ~1.51 minutes

In other words, according to the manufacturer's testing results, the component is expected to have only 1.51 minutes of downtime per year.

Most systems are composed of more than one component, of course. Multicomponent systems are arranged in a serial or a parallel fashion. For a serial component-based system, each component is a single point of failure, and so each component depends

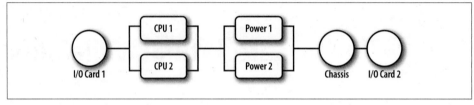

Figure C-1. Block diagram of a simple redundant system (Source: Chris Oggerino, High Availability Network Fundamentals, Cisco Press)

on the other for system availability. In contrast, a parallel component system has redundant components built such that the failure of a single component will not cause the entire system to fail. You can calculate the availability of serial redundant components by multiplying together the availability numbers for each single component:

$$\text{SerialAvailability} = \prod_{i=1}^{n} \text{ComponentAvailability}_{(i)}$$

Here's how to calculate the availability of a serial multicomponent system, consisting of a processor, bus, and I/O card:

SerialAvailability = (processor)*(bus)*(I/O)

SerialAvailability = (.999999881)*(.999993)*(.999991)

SerialAvailability = (0.9999838)

This represents 99.998% availability, which is also called "four 9s and an 8." That was a simplified example. Now, let's look at a redundant system availability calculation (see Figure C-1).

Figure C-1 shows a diagram of a simple redundant system with two CPUs, two power supplies, and two I/O cards. You can calculate availability on such a system in the same way you would calculate serial availability. The difference here is that each redundant system is calculated as the difference of 1 minus the product of each redundant and serial component. Note this key qualifier: a single redundant component (i.e., two power supplies) is 1 minus the product of the individual component's availability. The following formula should help clear this up:

$$ParallelAvailability = 1 - \left\{ \prod_{i=1}^{n} (1 - Availability_{(i)}) \right\}$$

$$ParallelAvailability = 1 - \left\{ 1 - CPU1)*(1 - CPU2) \right\}$$

$$ParallelAvailability = 1 - \left\{ 1 - .99995)*(1 - 99995) \right\}$$

$$ParallelAvailability = 0.9999999975$$

Now that you understand serial versus parallel systems, you can begin to calculate more complex scenarios, such as what's shown in the following calculation. Assume that you know your I/O card availability is .99995, your CPU availability is .99996, your power supply availability is .99994, and your chassis availability is .999998. The availability calculation would be as follows:

$$\left[1 - \left\{ 0.0000000025 \right\} \right] * \left[1 - \left\{ 0.0000000016 \right\} \right] * \left[1 - \left\{ 0.0000000036 \right\} \right] * \left[.999998 \right]$$

0.9999999975   *   0.9999999984   *   0.9999999964 *   .999998

0.999997992300015   x   525600 minutes = 525598.94475288809 minutes of uptime

The preceding calculation shows that, based purely on hardware MTBF numbers, this scenario should have only 1.05 minutes of downtime per year; in other words, it is a "five 9s" system.

You can obtain the MTBF component of the equation from your hardware manufacturer, which, if it is a network vendor, most likely uses the Telcordia Parts Count Method, which is described in document TR-332 from *http://www.telcordia.com/*. Cisco lists MTBF information in its product data sheets, as do Juniper and others.

Index

A

access controls
   enumeration for security monitoring, 81
   policies, minimum for security monitoring, 196
access_log files (Apache), 132
account access, detection of, 23
ACLs (access control lists)
   blocking connection from offending IP address, 102
   creating for botnet virus IRC command and control server, 49
   limiting negative impacts of ACL logging on systems, 91
   logs, push method of event collection, 88
   network ACL logs, 98
administrative privileges, monitoring for Oracle database, 166
administrator user IDs, 80
aggregate bandwidth, 108
alert level, 89
alerts
   CS-IPS alert generated by web server using BitTorrent, 95
   monitoring from NIDS on Blanco wireless (example), 178
   monitoring NIDS alerts, 157
   network context for NIDS alerts, 184
   overwhelming numbers of, resulting from not choosing monitoring targets, 185
   security alert for configuration change, 20
   security alert sources for Blanco wireless network, 143

tuning of NIDS alerts, 102
AngryMintStorm/32 virus, 48
anomaly monitoring, 12, 16
   Arbor Peakflow, 54
   KPN-CERT case study, 191
   NetFlow OSU flow-tools solutions for, 142
   NIDS capabilities for, 102
antivirus logs
   Blanco wireless network (example), 146
   monitoring on Blanco wireless (example), 179
   querying to find reported and unresolved viruses, 137
   syslog collection from, 136
   Windows security application events (example), 131
antivirus software, failure of, 4
Apache Web Server
   access_log files, 132
   configuration for logging to syslog (example), 145
application acceleration, 115
application events, security (see security application events)
application logging, 132
   Blanco wireless network (example), 145
application logs, 96
application service providers (ASPs), 67
Arbor Peakflow, 16
   anomaly monitoring by KPN-CERT, 191
asymmetric routing, 115
auditing
   maintaining Oracle audit settings on objects, 165

We'd like to hear your suggestions for improving our indexes. Send email to *index@oreilly.com*.

hardware and software failure scenarios, 104
Health Insurance Portability and
        Accountability Act of 1996 (HIPAA),
        19
    monitoring HIPAA applications for
        unauthorized activity, 22
health monitoring
    collector health on Blanco wireless
        (example), 172
    event log collectors, 175
    for health of monitoring system, 154
    for network flow collector, 157
    NIDS sensors, Blanco wireless (example),
        177
    system health of event log collectors, 161
HIDS (host intrusion detection system) logs,
        136
    Blanco wireless network (example), 146
    monitoring on Blanco wireless (example),
        179
Horizon Blue Cross Blue Shield, theft of data
        from, 6
host intrusion prevention systems (HIPs), 89
host IPS logs, monitoring of, 81
host logs, 94
host variables for NIDS, 120
hostnames for monitoring targets, 80
hosts, scanning for on network segment, 161
HP OpenView Network Node Manager
        (NNM), 168
Huawei, 199

I

IBM Tivoli Monitoring, 168
ifconfig command, 155
incident response and investigation, event
        sources for, 85
Information Security Management Systems
        (ISMSs), 23
information technology security assessment
        (ITSA), 77
insider threats, 6
intellectual property, theft of, 194
internal networks, 36
Internet connection (direct), from production
        servers, 26
Internet Relay Chat (IRC), 27
intrusion detection (see NIDS)

Intrusion Detection Systems Consortium
        (IDSC), 88
IP address assignment, Blanco wireless network
        (example), 57
IP address information, 34
    server IP addresses, 80
    using for network variables in NIDS
        configuration, 118
IP network type classification, 34
    external networks, 35
    internal networks, 36
IP packets, analysis by NIDS, 102
IPAM (IP address management) data, 37–40
    Cisco Network Registrar storing IP
        addresses, 37
    documenting basic network demarcations,
        197
    example of, 38
    listing of IPAM solutions, 40
    using to add context to NIDS, 184
    using to provide context for NIDS alert, 38
iptables
    configuration rule for flows from Blanco
        wireless routers (example), 175
    creating rules for NetFlow collector, 158
    event log collectors, monitoring network
        traffic for, 163
    flushing the counters using zero counters
        option, 159
    running with -VL INPUT, 158
    watching for traffic volume in server
        collection monitoring, 176
IRC command and control server IP address
        (virus), 49
ISO 1799 monitoring, 23
ISP gateway routers, NetFlow collection at, 44
ITSA (information technology security
        assessment), 77

J

jumbo frames, 115
Juniper, 199

K

Kerberos error codes, Windows domain
        controllers, 130
KPN-CERT case study, 189
    event sources, 190

monitoring targets, 190
policies, 189
protection of customer data, 192

L

lab (networks), 36
Lancope StealthWatch, 54
legal requests
    event sources for, 86
    example request, 86
legal requirements for monitoring, 65
    regulatory compliance, 65
load balancing, NIDS sensor in data center
        network, 113
load, monitoring for a system, 154
log retention, 164
logging, 121
    (see also application logging; system
    logging)
    application logs, 96
    archiving monitoring and secondary events,
        76
    Blanco network configuration (example),
        99
    configuring server logs, 200
    database logs, 98
    establishing policy for event source
        monitoring, 150
    event logging configuration, impact on
        system performance, 91
    event sources for security monitoring, ERP
        system, 79
    host logs, critical details captured with
        correct logging configuration, 94
    host logs, using canary event to monitor
        sources, 167
    level of, event volume and, 90
    minimum for security monitoring, 196
    monitoring event log collectors, 161–164
    network ACL logs, 98
    server logs collected via syslog, 199
    volume of messages and, 8
LogLogic syslog collectors, 137

M

malware
    detection by antivirus products, failure of,
        5

distribution by targeted websites, 74
prevalence and advanced capabilities of, 5
use by organized crime, 6
Marshall's discount clothing store, insecure
        wireless network, 25
media, physical, 116
memory
    monitoring availability for NIDS, 177
    monitoring for monitoring devices, 154
    monitoring for NetFlow collectors, 174
metadata
    Northrop Grumman case study, 192
    Oracle audit settings on a table, 165
    pertaining to IP communications between
        systems, 40
Microsoft SMS, 168
monitoring, 86, 164
    (see also security monitoring)
    automated system monitoring, 167–172
        how to monitor the monitors, 169
        monitoring with Nagios, 170
        traditional network monitoring and
            management systems, 168
    databases, 164
        MySQL servers, 166
        Oracle capture of audit information,
            164
        Oracle logging, 179
    security monitoring system, 153–164
        event log collectors, 161–164
        network flow collection, 157–161
        NIDS, 155
        system health, 154
    system monitoring for Blanco wireless
        (example), 172–179
MRTG (Multi Router Traffic Grapher), 55,
        147
    monitoring traffic volume with, 156
MTBF (mean time between failures), 104
MTTR (mean time to repair), 105
Multi Router Traffic Grapher (MRTG), 55
MySQL database, monitoring servers, 166

N

Nagios, system monitoring with, 170
    Blanco wireless network (example), 172–
        179
NAS (network attachment storage), 78

production servers, direct Internet connection from, 26
proprietary information for companies, 68
proxy server logs, 96
pull method (event collection), 88
push method (event collection), 88

Q

Qualys scan for risk assessment, 73

R

Red Hat Network (RHN), using to push configuration files to managed servers, 152
regular expressions
    matching to find credit card numbers traversing network, 23
    matching U.S. Social Security number, 145
regulatory compliance, 86
regulatory compliance policies, 19–24, 65
    COBIT configuration control monitoring, 19–21
    contractual obligations, 67
    Gramm-Leach Blilely Act (example), 66
    HIPAA applications monitoring, 22
    ISO 1799 monitoring, 23
    Payment Card Industry Data Security Standard (PCI DSS), 23, 66
    SOX monitoring for financial apps and databases, 22
    standards for critical infrastructure protection, 67
remote access networks, 36
resources for further information, xii
revenue impact analysis for security monitoring, 64
risk assessment methodology (OCTAVE), 192
risk assessments, 71
risk profiles, 70
risk, security monitoring to minimize, 9
rootkitted machines, 137
routers
    Cisco router ACL log, 98
    COBIT configuration monitoring on, 19
    ISP gateway and DMZ backbone, NetFlow collection at, 44
    monitoring flows from gateway routers, 174

NetFlow configuration for Cisco router, 45
    traffic feeds from, monitoring for NetFlow collection, 157
    traffic graph by MRTG showing dramatic drop in traffic, 147
routing topology, 56
    asymmetric routing, 115
    Blanco wireless network (example), 58
RPC race condition vulnerabilities of Windows domain controllers, 187

S

SAP R/3 monitoring, 78
Sapphire (worm), 1
Sarbanes-Oxley Act of 2002 (SOX), 19
    monitoring for financial apps and databases, 22
SCADA (Supervisory Control and Data Acquisition) systems, 70
SDBot virus, 3
secondary events, importance of, 76
security application events, 126
    Windows systems, 131
Security Device Event Exchange (SDEE), 88
Security Information Manager (see SIM)
security monitoring, 164
    (see also monitoring)
    challenges to, 7
    event sources for, 86
    minimum requirements for, 196
        choosing event sources, 198
        feeding and tuning event sources, 199
        maintaining dependable event sources, 200
        policies, 196
        selecting monitoring targets, 198
    open source versus commercial products for, 10
    outsourcing, 8
    reasosn for, 5
    setup checklist, 200
security monitoring teams, stories from, 194
    stolen intellectual property, 194
    targeted attack against employees, 195
self-defeating network, characteristics of, 33
sensitivity of data, 67
    systems accessing classified information, 69

About the Authors

Chris Fry, a security investigator for Cisco Systems Computer Security Incident Response Team (CSIRT), joined Cisco in 1997 as an IT analyst specializing in production services support. Fry spent four years as a network engineer within Cisco IT, gaining enterprise network knowledge and a unique insight into monitoring production networks. In 2007, he presented "Inside the Perimiter: 6 Steps to Improve Your Security Monitoring" at the annual conference for the Forum for Incident Response and Security Teams (FIRST) in Seville, Spain, and at the Cisco Networkers conventions in Brisbane, Australia, and Anaheim, California. Fry received a B.A. in corporate financial analysis and an M.S. in information and communication sciences from Ball State University. He lives in Cary, North Carolina, with his wife, Laurie, and their daughter and two sons.

Martin Nystrom is a member of technical staff (MTS) for the Computer Security Incident Response Team (CSIRT) at Cisco Systems. He leads the global security monitoring team and provides guidance for incident response and security initiatives. Prior to joining Cisco's CSIRT, he was responsible for designing and consulting on secure architectures for IT projects. Nystrom worked as an IT architect and a Java programmer for 12 years; during this time, he built his experience in the pharmaceutical and computer industries. He received a bachelor's degree from Iowa State University in 1990, a master's degree from North Carolina State University in 2003, and his CISSP certification in 2004. Nystrom is the author of O'Reilly's *SQL Injection Defenses*, is a frequent conference speaker, and was honored on the Java One Rock Star Wall of Fame. He enjoys speaking at FIRST and Cisco Networkers conferences and providing security guidance to customers via Cisco's Executive Briefing program. Most of Nystrom's papers and presos can be found at *http://xianshield.org*.

Colophon

The image on the cover of *Security Monitoring* is a man using a telescope. While the telescope is primarily used for the viewing of distant objects, a host of earlier, cruder telescopes were used simply for the purposes of magnification.

Euclid wrote about the reflection and refraction of light, and Aristophanes later showed that a globe filled with water could enlarge objects. Yet the invention of a proper telescope was delayed in part because its effects were thought to be so astonishing that the instrument and its creator were deemed evil. In the 13th century, Roger Bacon documented the effects of magnification and wrote about the use of lenses to study the sky: "The Sun, Moon, and Stars may be made to descend hither in appearance...which persons unacquainted with such things would refuse to believe." Subsequent to his observations, Bacon was labeled a magician and imprisoned.

The use of the lens for magnification only became acceptable with the invention and general usage of eyeglasses. Then, in the late 16th and early 17th centuries, eyeglass maker Hans Lippershey of Holland reportedly noticed a church tower jump to the front doorway of his shop when he stared at the tower through two differently shaped lenses at once. Lippershey then succeeded in making the telescope known more widely, and it was he who piqued Galileo Galilei's interest in the instrument sometimes dubbed the "far looker."

Galileo and Lippershey each independently thought he could profit from the distribution of telescopes, and both men also foresaw the military advantages of the instrument. Galileo famously went a step further with his use of the telescope and sought out sun spots, moons of Jupiter, and new "lands" in the sky above. Although Galileo was eventually persecuted for saying that the sun was at the center of the solar system, his and Lippershey's military application of smaller telescopes later became useful to strategists during the U.S. Civil War, when military personnel often used telescopes designed like the one on the cover of this book to spy on their enemies.

The cover image is from the *Dover Pictorial Archive*. The cover font is Adobe ITC Garamond. The text font is Linotype Birka; the heading font is Adobe Myriad Condensed; and the code font is LucasFont's TheSansMonoCondensed.